British Democracy at the Crossroads

British Democracy at the Crossroads

Voting and Party Competition in the 1980s

Patrick Dunleavy
and
Christopher T. Husbands

London School of Economics and Political Science

London
GEORGE ALLEN & UNWIN
Boston   Sydney

**George Allen & Unwin (Publishers) Ltd,
40 Museum Street, London WC1A 1LU, UK**

George Allen & Unwin (Publishers) Ltd,
Park Lane, Hemel Hempstead, Herts HP2 4TE, UK

Allen & Unwin, Inc.,
Fifty Cross Street, Winchester, Mass. 01890, USA

George Allen & Unwin Australia Pty Ltd,
8 Napier Street, North Sydney, NSW 2060, Australia

First published in 1985.

British Library Cataloguing in Publication Data

Dunleavy, Patrick
    British democracy at the crossroads: voting
    and party competition in the 1980s.
1. Elections – Great Britain
I. Title   II. Husbands, Christopher T.
324.6'3'0941   JN956
ISBN 0–04–324010–0

Library of Congress Cataloging in Publication Data

Dunleavy, Patrick.
    British democracy at the crossroads.
Bibliography: p.
Includes index.
1. Elections – Great Britain. 2. Voting – Great Britain.
3. Political parties – Great Britain. 4. Great Britain –
Politics and government – 1979–   .
I. Husbands, Christopher T.   II. Title.
JN956.D86 1985   324.941   84–24264
ISBN 0–04–324010–0 (alk. paper)
ISBN 0–04–324011–9 (pbk.: alk. paper)

Set in 10 on 11½ point Plantin by Computape (Pickering) Ltd,
North Yorkshire
and printed in Great Britain by Mackays of Chatham

Contents

Preface and Acknowledgements

This book uses the general election of June 1983 as a starting-point for a wide-ranging review of the operations of the electoral system and of party competition in modern Britain. Most existing work in this area has been organized heavily around a specific type of data – such as survey evidence or aggregate data on constituency characteristics. We have tried to draw upon a much wider range of information, looking at a number of different sources. The chief of these was our own survey of British electors that was carried out within two weeks of the general election. However, we also collected and analysed aggregate data on constituencies, time-series data on party popularity and its corollaries, and a mass of more qualitative data – such as newspaper coverage of the campaign, other media reports, observation of some of the relevant political actors, and so on.

Of course, preparation of a work such as this creates numerous debts of thanks for a whole variety of services and assistances rendered. Our primary debt is to the International Centre for Economics and Related Disciplines at the London School of Economics and Political Science, especially to the Centre's Director, Professor Tony Atkinson, for making available at short notice and from a tight budget the funds that allowed us to conduct our survey. We are also grateful to Professor Donald MacRae for supplementing this grant from LSE's Research Fund. John Barter, Managing Director at NOP Market Research Limited, and Nick Moon, Group Head of the Social Research Unit at NOP, capably oversaw the fieldwork for the survey and were most helpful in drafting the questionnaire. We are also grateful to NOP for granting us the use of some of their unpublished polls and to Social Surveys (Gallup Poll) Limited for allowing the transcription and computer-analysis of some of their data.

A project such as ours requires large-scale and efficient computer support and we are grateful to LSE's Computer Unit for vital assistance during a difficult period when the Unit was switching its operation and its users on to new and occasionally temperamental computer hardware. In particular, we owe a heavy debt to Robert Clark; without his services in solving the many technical problems of data management that were encountered, this book could not have been written. Also helpful with computer problems were Anne McGlone and Jeremy Skelton. We thank our research assistant, Dina Cohen, for speedily preparing a large amount of the quantitative data used in our analyses. Dilia Montes of LSE's Economic Documentation and Research Centre assembled some of the data used for the time-series analyses in Chapter 7. David Blake advised on some econometric problems encountered in these analyses.

The design and cartographic expertise of the Drawing Office in the LSE Department of Geography produced all the figures in the book. We thank the Office's Supervisor, Jane Pugh.

We are grateful to the national offices of the Labour Party, the Conservative Party, the Liberal Party and the Social Democratic Party for confirming, correcting (where necessary) and supplementing our own information on specific points, especially our listing of women candidates in the 1983 general election. Marian FitzGerald was similarly helpful in identifying ethnic-minority candidates.

Numerous personal contacts in political life and in the mass media helped us on points of detail and with their ideas; to all of these not here thanked by name we are very grateful. Participants at the Annual Conference of the Political Studies Association in April 1984 helped us to define our ideas more clearly by commenting on two research papers from the project. Above all, numerous LSE colleagues from various disciplines provided us with a flow of ideas, suggestions and criticisms; to all of these, teaching staff, students and researchers, we record our appreciation. We do not believe that this book could have been produced in any better academic context.

Both authors were heavily involved in drawing up the questionnaire, in the data analysis and in writing all the chapters, but initial drafting of Chapters 1, 2, 4, 5 and 6 was carried out by Dunleavy, while initial drafting of Chapters 3, 7 and 8 was done by Husbands. Husbands prepared all the computer programs not written by members of LSE's Computer Unit and was responsible for data preparation and supervision of the survey contract.

Lastly, much of the burden of sustaining the project to its conclusion rested on our families. To Sheila, Rosemary and Christopher, and to Pam, Thomas and Jessie, goes much of the credit for stimulating any good ideas that we have had, and our heartfelt apologies that it took so much longer than we had anticipated.

PD/CTH
*London School of Economics
and Political Science*
August 1984

List of Tables

List of Figures

British Democracy at the Crossroads

Introduction

Those who feel the pulse of liberal democracies often pronounce the patient to be in crisis. Observers of British politics have been no exception to this practice. In the 1970s critics on the right detected what they saw as the congenital vices of social democracy – adversary politics, excessive corporatism, an overloaded centre and a more general 'crisis of governability' (Finer, 1975; A. King, 1975; Rose, 1976; Brittan, 1977). For some American observers Britain in the late 1970s demonstrated the inherent contradictions of 'collectivism'; it was 'the future that failed' (Gwyn, 1980). Since the election of the Thatcher government in 1979 these siren voices have fallen strangely silent. Even the evils of 'over-polarization' in political life seem no longer to trouble them. Instead, it is on the left and amongst the liberal-minded that anxieties have multiplied. Marxists especially have been quick to detect signs of a creeping authoritarianism in public life, evident in the Conservative challenge to civil liberties, local government autonomy and the basic fabric of the welfare state (Gamble, 1979, 1983; Miliband, 1982, pp. 146–60), a development greatly magnified in significance by the mood of popular chauvinism created during the Falklands war (A. Barnett, 1982; Hall, 1982; Hobsbawm, 1983; Nairn, 1983).

Given the perceived stability and longevity of the current British political system, it is not hard to see why gloom merchants of both left and right have tended to be discounted. Yet we believe that British politics has now reached a turning-point of considerable significance, a crossroads in the development of our public life. By the mid- or late-1980s one of a number of basic changes in the operation of party competition will have occurred. We could have moved into a one-party-controlled 'democratic' state in which a third successive Conservative government is installed on the basis of perhaps two-fifths of the popular vote, simply because a fairly evenly divided opposition can have no hope of competing effectively under the current electoral arrangements. This outcome would be avoided if Conservative support collapses for some reason, if the Labour Party stages a dramatic recovery of its fortunes or if the SDP–Liberal Alliance succeeds decisively in displacing Labour as the main opposition.[1] We are, then, in a period of decision – unique in the context of postwar British politics – whose resolution in one direction or another will have profound consequences in the years ahead for the development of the economy, for the fabric of social life and for the legitimacy of democratic government.

To make sense of the choices ahead we need to know how they will be made; here the story necessarily becomes complex. The new path that the political system will take cannot be seen simply as the product of voters' decisions. Voters' ballots do of course play a part in the switch from one avenue of development to another. However, as we set out to show in this volume, there is no simple sense in which voters decide. Citizens choose within options that are predefined for them by the process of party competition, by the action of other key social institutions (such as the mass media, business or the labour movement) and by the reactions of their fellow voters. To make sense of this process we need to have some simplifying theories or models that can reduce the complexity of political life to manageable proportions; we need to understand how these models can be applied to, or make sense of, the recent history of party competition; we need to analyse how changes of mass alignments and attitudes take place; and lastly, we need to consider how patterns of voting are translated into political representation. Each of these concerns is covered in one or more of the following chapters.

Before considering in more detail our organization of material, it is worth pausing briefly to indicate how this enterprise differs from previous work. First, our objective has been to break out of the sterile compartmentalization of professional political science, which dictates that electoral studies or psephology should be practised in isolation from a detailed understanding of the context in which voting occurs. We are sceptical of the tradition inaugurated by Butler and Stokes (1969; 2nd edn, 1974) and continued by other writers (e.g., Miller, 1977, 1978; Himmelweit *et al.*, 1981; Särlvik and Crewe, 1983), in which large research monographs on citizen attitudes are produced with only a minimal specification of the events that gave rise to their decisions. Meanwhile, in other books the dynamic of party competition *is* analysed but in a descriptive historical fashion that is significantly divorced from the analysis of survey material (e.g., Butler and Kavanagh, 1975, 1980). We believe that electoral analysis can be used in an effective, non-empiricist way only by deploying it in the service of a general understanding of political developments. Equally, we believe that a history of ideas, events or personalities that incorporates no account of the dynamics of mass changes in alignments can only scrape the surface of explanation. By bringing both components together in this volume we hope to inform both, while using modern political theory to select out the phenomena of critical significance for analysis.

Secondly, we have set out to build up a distinctively radical perspective on the interconnected themes of party competition and electoral behaviour. The features differentiating our approach are simply stated. We believe that previous accounts of voting behaviour have operated with oversimplified and anachronistic models of the British social structure. A more dynamic and differentiated approach to structural features can shed a great deal of light on the social origins of macro-political changes, such as the trend towards class dealignment in political life. We reject the newer orthodoxy that ascribes such trends to changes in citizens' issue attitudes. In our view many people form their detailed opinions in order to fit a pre-existing alignment. In deciding their views, citizens are heavily dependent on the political parties, the mass media and other institutions. Only quite a small part of what is normally construed as 'public opinion' can be unambiguously seen as the product of citizens' autonomous preferences or evaluations. Lastly, we argue that parties do not compete solely or even primarily in terms of 'presenting a case' to voters.

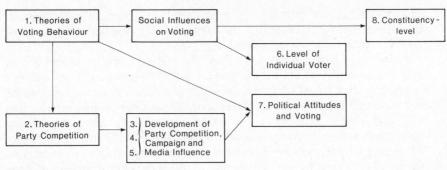

Figure I.1   The plan of the book

Among the most important influences on the parties' fortunes are their efforts to deploy power for electoral advantage, both the state power controlled by the incumbent administration and the party power that accrues in some degree to any potential government.

The Structure of the Book

There are a number of possible pathways through the book and people with different interests may want to follow the lines of interconnections shown in Figure I.1. The three parts of the book essentially progress through a consideration of theories of voting behaviour and party competition in Part I, to an analysis of the process of party competition between 1979 and 1983 and a mapping of the various attitudinal corollaries of the 1983 result in Part II. Part III presents a detailed account of the major social background and issue influences on electoral behaviour and then selectively explores some of the implications of differential party success across spatial areas for the resulting pattern of political representation.

Chapter 1 gives a full account of orthodox theories of contemporary British voting behaviour and sets out the 'structural' component of our own radical model. Chapter 2 presents a description of theories of party competition and includes our own critique of their deficiencies. In both chapters we concentrate on basic models that underlie the richer and more differentiated views of a wide range of individual authors. Some of the writers whom we identify with each school of thought may wish to distance themselves from our 'constructed' core models. However, we feel that it is important to concentrate attention on a deliberately simplified set of approaches if we are to have any success in applying these models to 'real life' British politics.

In Part II Chapter 3 looks at the development of party competition under the first Thatcher government, a period when party fortunes varied dramatically in response to worsening economic crisis, divisions in the Labour Party, the advent of the Social Democratic Party (SDP), and the loss of life, military successes and media manipulation during the Falklands war. Chapter 4 focuses specifically on the election campaign of May and June 1983. Chapter 5 explores the political meaning of the 1983 result by looking at party loyalties, the images that voters formed of the parties and the part played by the mass media in influencing voters' views.

In Part III Chapter 6 moves on from the analysis of party competition to begin an in-depth look at voting behaviour in the 1983 election. The focus here is on the ways in which people's social positions influence their voting behaviour. Chapter 7 examines the relationships between voting behaviour in 1983 and voters' attitudes on the central issues of the campaign, looking particularly at the relative salience and influence of different attitudes. Chapter 8 focuses upon aggregate voting behaviour at the constituency level, examining the social-structural factors that account for the geographical patterning of the vote and looking at their implications for future party success and failure.

Finally, Chapter 9 is a short Conclusion and Afterword that summarizes our interpretation of our findings and their significance for the future of British politics and also includes comments upon the major developments in party competition since June 1983.

PART I

Theories and Models

1 Explaining Voting Behaviour

Electoral studies from the 1950s until the early 1970s were carried out almost from a single perspective. This political science orthodoxy, the party identification model, was first challenged by an economic or public-choice theory of voting and, at the end of the 1970s, by the emergence of a radical-structural explanation. Two major empirical changes in the 1960s and 1970s evoked these challenges. The first was the declining association between occupational or social class position and political loyalty, a process known as *class dealignment*. The second was the weakening relationship between support for a political party and agreement with its policy positions, a process known as *partisan dealignment*. Neither phenomenon could be easily explained by the mainstream approach to electoral studies. The economic model sees partisan dealignment and the associated growth of third-party support as the crucial trend that requires explanation, whereas the radical view argues that understanding class dealignment is the critical problem. For each of these approaches we discuss the model's core propositions, the relationship between voters and political leaders, and the explanations given of class dealignment and partisan dealignment.

1.1 The party identification approach

1.1.1 *The core model*

The party identification (PI) approach is best expressed in the classic work by

Butler and Stokes (1969; 2nd edn, 1974). They argue that voters find deciding between competing parties' policy proposals too complicated a task to undertake in any deeply considered manner. On the other hand, most people want to vote (because of moral and social pressures to fulfil civic duties) and do feel some mild degree of psychological tension in being unable to decide what to do. They therefore short-circuit making a closely rationalized decision by voting in line with the commonly held views that they encounter in their dealings with other people. This influence starts with socialization. People tend to form their political views quite early, especially in their teens, under the dominant influences of their parents and their family's social environment. In a heavily class-structured society, the schooling of children and the sort of people who become their friends also exert a strong influence. These socialization influences tended to be cumulative in their impact up to the 1960s, reinforcing and solidifying a pattern of Labour and Conservative alignments on broadly 'working-class' versus 'middle-class' lines.

People's personal relations in their everyday lives may also provide cues that they can follow in deciding between political parties. Thousands of chance conversations and exchanges about current news and political developments, which occur in work-places and families and between neighbours, as well as other social contacts, interact with the more generalized information provided by the mass media to provide most people's political consciousness. Citizens tend to screen out from the formalized political communication provided by the mass media those kinds of messages that fit the priorities and preconceptions which their upbringing and current social life provide. Occupational class positions are thus a good guide to how people vote, not because class is an 'issue' or a 'problem' that is consciously perceived by voters, but because knowing someone's occupational class is the best summary index that we have of the kind of contexts in which he or she passes his or her daily life. Of course, as with socialization influences, the tendency for people to imitate a 'class' pattern is strictly a matter of probabilities. Many voters encounter divergent political cues in their personal relations. People may find that influences from their upbringing and those of their current social position conflict, especially if they are upwardly (or downwardly) mobile in occupational terms from one class context to another; work-place influences may also differ considerably from those acting in a home and neighbourhood context.

How do voters think about political choices without making closely rationalized decisions? Most voters develop long-run, emotive or habitual 'identifications' with one party, usually quite soon after they enter the electorate and certainly by the time they are middle-aged. This low-level but none the less real attachment in turn produces the habit of interpreting political events from a partisan perspective. A variable but always relatively modest minority of voters either form no party identification at all (around 8 per cent in 1979; Särlvik and Crewe, 1983, p. 294) or agree to 'feeling closer' to one party at one time but will change their minds by the time of the next election (around 15 to 25 per cent in the 1970s). Most people construe the political world in terms of feeling close to or hostile to one of the two 'major' parties.

1.1.2   Voters and political leaders

The PI approach rests on a general pluralist 'realism' which assumes that most people place politics on the fringe of their interests, seeing it as 'a remote, alien, and unrewarding activity' (Dahl, 1961, p. 279). However, it also argues that a voting choice, such as deciding between monetarist policy or an 'alternative economic strategy', is complex chiefly because voters have simultaneously to make empirical judgements, clarify their values and decide how they rank different outcomes:

> The process of voting is ... not simply a voyage of discovery, although one may make some discoveries about one's preferences. It is instead a mixing of preference, analysis and moral judgement to arrive at a state of mind and will that did not before exist. It could not have been observed as a datum because it only now has come into existence. (Lindblom, 1977, p. 136)

Because of the involvement in voting of empirical judgement and moral evaluation, citizens are fairly dependent on political leaders. Most people most of the time have firm or settled preferences covering only relatively few high-order issues, not necessarily in a very detailed or precise way. Hence considerable scope exists for political leaders to swing uncertain voters towards a particular judgement of the likely consequences of their own versus their opponents' policies, or into firm moral evaluations that legitimize their own party's stance or impugn that of their rival.

One type of opinion leadership involves attitude crystallization via party campaigning. Parliamentary debating and party controversy in the year or so before a general election play a key part in hardening voters' views on those few issues which are already salient to them but on which they remain unsure how to choose between the parties. However, the main way in which opinion leadership occurs is in generalizing an initial commitment to one party across a broad range of issue attitudes. Once people have decided to support a party, they may adjust their wider empirical views and moral evaluations to fit the policy positions of their chosen party. Supporting a party overall, while disagreeing with many of its specific policies, can cause a certain degree of psychological tension. This anxiety can be reduced or managed by changing position on lesser issues until they are congruent with those of the chosen party. Party ideologies help to suggest similar solutions to problems across different issues.

All of this implies that voters are not always the sources of their own intentions. Citizens' attitudes are extensively shaped by the process of party competition itself. Of course, citizens know what they want on at least some issues, especially on those most important for them. Yet knowing what to want is not enough. (Nearly) everyone wants lower unemployment and lower inflation simultaneously. The problem is to know what policies might feasibly achieve this and to evaluate their costs and consequences not only for oneself but also for society as a whole. It is here that citizens tend to be quite heavily reliant on political leaders for information, criteria and cues.

1.1.3   Explanation of class dealignment

In the PI model 'class' is the dominant social feature influencing British political behaviour. By 'class' is meant, of course, occupational class, a summary index of people's chances in life which assumes that the best predictor of their education, income or life-style is knowledge of what kind of job they do. Using elaborate surveys of how occupations are perceived, different jobs are sorted into similar status or prestige rankings. These hierarchies of occupations are very extended and so, to be useful, they have to be reduced to a manageable number of occupational classes. How many classes are distinguished and where the boundary lines between them are drawn depend on the analyst. For example, the scale of occupational classes developed by the Institute of Practitioners in Advertising (and frequently deployed in opinion-poll reports of political affiliations) refers primarily to differences in buying power between occupational groups (Reid, 1977, pp. 46–7). All categorizations make a distinction of some kind between non-manual, white-collar occupations and those designated as manual, blue-collar ones. This 'middle class'/'working class' dichotomy is widely seen as the major feature of British social stratification. It is closely bound up with levels of educational attainment, patterns of consumption and life-style, and with apparently quite refined demarcations in prestige within work-places.

In 1963 Butler and Stokes found a stark contrast between non-manual and manual groups' support for the major parties. Non-manual people split four to one in favour of the Conservatives and manual workers two to one in favour of Labour. Because of the smaller size of the non-manual group, Conservative

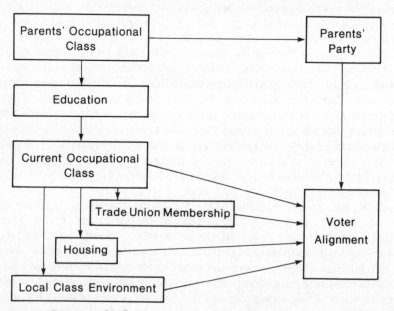

Figure 1.1   Patterns of influence on voter alignment in the party identification model

support was drawn almost half and half from the two classes, while Labour's support was overwhelmingly (80 per cent) derived from manual voters. PI accounts found this simple class polarization of political life seductive and extended it to incorporate many other aspects of social influences on voting. These 'class-inclusive' explanations eventually included three main components, as Figure 1.1 shows. First, parents' class positions influence their own voting patterns and hence children's earliest political socialization. Parental class plus children's education both indicate the 'class milieu' in which people have been brought up and so help to determine children's eventual occupational class positions. Secondly, voters' current occupational class directly influences their political behaviour. Thirdly, current class has a number of indirect effects on voting. People's job positions influence whether or not they join a trade union. Union membership is an important 'class corollary' because it provides a channel of personal interaction that reinforces some group loyalties with political implications. For example, unionized workers in a large factory with little direct work contact with managerial staffs are usually much more Labour-oriented than non-union staff in a small work-place who are closely involved with its middle-class owners or managers (Lockwood, 1966). Similarly, income inequalities between class positions influence whether people can afford to buy their homes and, if so, in what kind of neighbourhood. Housing in turn shapes families' home life, social contacts and the political micro-climate of local class environments. Finally, PI models suggest that, where one class predominates in a local area, everyone in that constituency tends to be pulled into greater conformity with the politics of the majority. In a non-manual suburb, white-collar people interact chiefly with each other, reinforcing their predominant Conservatism; but manual people interact more across the class division, thus weakening their propensity to support Labour.

In the 1950s and early 1960s 'class voting' meant that political alignments were class-influenced and transferred on the same basis between generations. Class influence was demonstrated partly by 'objective' associations between social backgrounds and voting but also by explanations of voting and references to the parties in terms recognized (by the analysts at least) as class-related – for example, identifying Labour as 'the party of the working man' (Butler and Stokes, 1969, pp. 80–94). Of course, 'class' or 'class inequality' (let alone 'class conflict') never appeared on a list of the manifest issues that voters saw as important. However, vague partisan images associating them with different classes seemed to influence how most voters chose between and saw the parties. In addition, 'subjective' class and voting were clearly associated. Manual workers who saw themselves as 'middle class' were much less likely to vote Labour than those who described themselves as 'working class', while non-manual people locating themselves in the 'working class' were less likely to vote Conservative.

Twenty years after Butler and Stokes's first survey the pattern of class alignment looks markedly different. The class balance of occupations has shifted considerably in favour of non-manual groups. The growth of third-party voting has greatly reduced Conservative predominance in the 'middle

Table 1.1   *Conservative and Labour voting across the manual/non-manual dichotomy in general elections from 1959 to 1974*

Percentages voting for:	1959	1964	1966	1970	Feb 1974	Oct 1974
			Election year			
Non-manual						
Conservative	69	62	60	64	53	51
Labour	22	22	26	25	22	25
CON Lead	+47	+40	+34	+39	+31	+26
Manual						
Conservative	34	28	25	33	24	24
Labour	62	64	69	58	57	57
CON Lead	−28	−36	−44	−25	−33	−33

Source: B. Särlvik and I. Crewe, *Decade of Dealignment* (CUP, 1983) p. 87.

class' and has decisively removed Labour's majority support amongst manual workers. However, although the Labour non-manual vote at 14 per cent is considerably down, the Conservatives' manual-worker vote at around 34 per cent looks remarkably stable, despite these changes.

There were in fact two distinct stages in the process of class dealignment. As Table 1.1 shows, from 1964 to 1974 the balance of Conservative and Labour support amongst manual workers remained little changed – although third-party support clearly grew markedly in 1974. At the same time the Conservative/Labour ratio amongst non-manual people fell from three-to-one in 1964 to two-to-one ten years later. The second phase of class dealignment took place in 1979, when Conservative support bounced back remarkably at Labour's expense and held steady at this level in 1983, despite a major Alliance challenge; Figure 1.2 depicts this second stage of class dealignment. The difference in the levels of Conservative support between junior non-manual people and skilled manual workers was 26 percentage-points in October 1974 but almost half this figure in 1979. The 1983 election saw the consolidation of Conservative gains among manual voters, as well as the defection of large numbers of non-manual Labour voters to the Alliance. The earlier trend for the Conservatives' dominance of non-manual grades to diminish continued only in the managerial group, where more Conservative than Labour voters defected to the Alliance.

The differences in occupational classes' voting have clearly diminished but this overall convergence may mask a number of more detailed effects. Franklin (1984) suggests that between 1964 and 1974 the link between current class and voting declined by about a half when assessed in a regression model resembling Figure 1.1. The indirect relationships between parents' class and voting also weakened dramatically. However, class corollaries such as trade union membership and housing tenure have both become *more* closely linked with patterns of party support (see also Rose, 1976, pp. 29–59; Franklin and Mughan, 1978). The perplexing persistence of 'class corollary' effects while

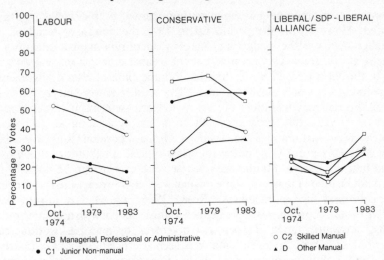

Figure 1.2   Vote by occupational class of head of household, October 1974 to
1983

'central class' effects have declined is also shown by the survival of a strong
'class environmental' effect in patterns of constituency voting (Miller, 1978).

In the 1950s and 1960s, before dealignment was widely recognized, PI
writers were preoccupied with 'working-class conservatism' – that is, the
allegedly greater propensity of manual workers to support a 'class deviant'
party. Some strange explanations were put forward. Sections of the British
working class were supposedly socialized into 'deferential' attitudes by the past
predominance of the aristocracy in public affairs (McKenzie and Silver, 1968).
Others thought that working-class people were forsaking Labour voting as
they became more affluent. Alternatively, a more complex process of embourgeoisement was under way, as the values of manual workers responded to
postwar changes and they adopted more privatized, home-centred, consumer-
oriented life-styles and moved away from involvement in the solidaristic social
life of work-place or local community that had previously sustained Labour
loyalties. Spread of home ownership, acquisition of consumer durables,
changes in child-rearing patterns towards more equal parental involvement
and even renting a telephone or owning a car were all linked with reductions in
Labour voting or with the growth of more qualified Labour support
(Goldthorpe *et al.*, 1968, pp. 73–82; Crewe, 1973; Rose, 1974, p. 504).

None of these explanations could account for the dynamic development of
class dealignment. The 'deferential worker' studies suggested that working-
class Conservatism would decline in line with the 'secularization' of British
political life. The other accounts predicted that working-class Conservatism
would grow, either directly in line with real incomes according to the affluence
model, or with a time-lag behind economic indicators according to the
embourgeoisement thesis. Yet none of these theories said anything about
changes in middle-class voting patterns. If anything, they assumed that

Conservative predominance amongst non-manual people would be consolidated. However, in the period up to 1974 the dominant trend of class dealignment was the weakening Conservatism of non-manual categories and the relatively stable Conservative/Labour balance amongst manual workers.

In the short term PI writers reacted to indications of class dealignment by redefining what they meant by class. Class corollaries were incorporated into multidimensional definitions of class no longer based simply on occupational positions. Attention broadened out from simply looking at people's job categories to examining instead their overall social position (Rose, 1974; 1976, pp. 29–59), especially including the 'class-typical' attributes of unionization and housing tenure. Middle-class people were expected to be home-owners and not be union members, while manual workers were expected to be council tenants and union members (Rose, 1976, pp. 34–41; Jessop, 1974, pp. 159–62). 'Core classes' were defined as those people with multiple 'middle-class' attributes (about 12 per cent of voters) or multiple 'working-class' attributes (around 7 per cent) and were seen as crucial locations of Conservative and Labour support respectively. Everyone else in the electorate is polarized primarily by the extent of his or her personal interaction with people from one or the other of the 'core classes'. Voters who depart from the analysts' 'ideal type' classes are more likely to be involved in networks of personal relations that do not consistently support a particular pattern of alignment. At the constituency level 'class environmental' influences also reflect how much voters interact in neighbourhood contexts with people in 'core classes' (Miller, 1978).

'Core class' explanations are problematic because they have never demonstrated that people outside the 'core classes' are politicized by virtue of their social contacts with those inside them. In addition, these models follow a basically circular pattern of reasoning. 'Core classes' are more closely associated with voting patterns than occupational class proper, but this is because 'core classes' have no other purpose or rationale than to correlate closely with political alignments. Such alignments cannot be the criteria used to constitute 'core classes' and simultaneously in any worthwhile sense be 'explained' by them.

Over the longer run PI writers eventually produced three serious explanations of trends in class dealignment. The first argues that occupational class is a weakening political force because social inequalities have progressively declined. The correlation between positions in the middle/working-class dichotomy and incomes received has declined sharply, with a large area of overlap between skilled manual wages and intermediate non-manual salaries. Absolute poverty has been drastically curtailed, if it has not yet disappeared, taking with it a distinctive sense of the shared position of manual workers (Seabrook, 1978, 1982). These trends have reduced non-manual employees' sense of relative advantage and manual workers' feeling of relative deprivation. Class inequalities matter less to most voters by comparison with a range of small-group bases for political alignment.

Secondly, PI writers point out that the postwar period was characterized by a rapid growth in absolute social mobility (Goldthorpe, Llewellyn and Payne,

Table 1.2 *Voting in the 1983 general election amongst non-manual and manual people in single-class and mixed-class households (in percentages)*

Respondent's class	Spouse's class	Labour	Conservative	Alliance	CON lead over LAB	N
Non-manual	Non-manual	9	56	35	+47	183
Non-manual	(Live alone)	24	50	26	+26	103
Non-manual	Manual	21	55	25	+34	101
Manual	Non-manual	29	34	38	+5	80
Manual	(Live alone)	44	31	24	−13	99
Manual	Manual	50	26	25	−24	157

1980). Recruitment for an enlarged number of non-manual job positions could not be confined to the children of a previously restricted 'middle class'. In the 1950s and 1960s a growing number of children from manual backgrounds moved through the educational system into 'middle-class' jobs. Decreasing Conservative hegemony in the non-manual classes reflects chiefly the presence of people from family backgrounds where Labour voting was the norm rather than the exception (Franklin, 1984).

Thirdly, PI writers argue that social mobility, the development of service industries and the growth of female employment have all helped to change the occupational mix within households. In the past, there was greater homogeneity in family environments – husbands and wives tended to do the same kind of jobs. Now husbands' and wives' jobs more frequently place them on different sides of the non-manual/manual division. Table 1.2 shows that mixed-class households are common and that people in such households have a lower propensity to vote for one party than is true of households where husbands and wives have similar-status jobs.[1] However, this effect is not strong and nor do people in mixed-class households have less distinctive voting patterns than those who are unmarried.

1.1.4 Explanation of partisan dealignment

PI writers see partisan dealignment – the weakening association between party support and endorsement of that party's issue positions – as a natural consequence of class dealignment, produced by many of the same background trends. Social inequalities have lessened, partly because of the growth of an extended network of 'welfare state' services and of transfer payments. Institutions previously involved in providing these benefits have decreased in salience. For example, the family unit has become less significant than it once was in organizing the care of children, the elderly and the sick. Trade unions and the labour movement have also seen many of their previous social welfare roles disappear, since state provision is more comprehensive and generous than a voluntary association can provide. Closely associated with such changes, political parties have become less important in the fabric of everyday social life. Local Labour parties were once an important channel by which housing allocations took place in inner-city areas (Rex and Moore, 1967; Hindess, 1971) but this role has been routinized by the development of council-housing waiting lists drawn up by local authorities using bureaucratic criteria (Lambert, Paris and Blackaby, 1978). The Conservative Party still plays a co-ordinating role in suburban and rural areas, providing a forum where local interests in education policy or urban planning can be balanced (Saunders, 1974). However, even its once-flourishing socio-cultural functions have withered away.

At the same time party memberships have fallen precipitately. This partly reflects the pull of more direct and immediate small-group affiliations. Single-issue interest groups have mushroomed while overarching, class-related institutions such as parties have declined (Johnson, 1973; Dowse and Hughes, 1977). Mass party organizations have also been marginalized in terms of political campaigning. While the central offices managing parties' media relations and national activities have expanded in terms of finance, organizational complexity and personnel, local branch activity and grass-roots membership efforts have seemed less important in influencing election outcomes (Pinto-Duschinsky, 1981). The process has been uneven in the major parties. Labour's individual membership has fallen rapidly, while many of those who are formally levy-paying union members seem to have let their loyalties go elsewhere. The Conservatives have held on to a nominal mass membership of around 1 million despite some substantial losses, but many party activities are less well-supported than they were.

The long-run implication of these gradual changes has been a progressive hollowing-out of the meaning of party identification. Fewer people are now party members or active sympathizers and hence the number of voters with well-packaged views supporting overall party platforms has fallen. In consequence, the reinforcement previously given to voters at large to define coherent positions consistent with a partisan identification has declined. People interpret political life largely in terms of general party images and affective attachments. However, the meaning of such attachments has changed, becoming more tolerant of lack of fit between supporting a party and dissent from its individual issue positions.

1.2 The issue voting approach

1.2.1 The core model

The issue voting (IV) model applies the assumptions of the rational choice model used by economists to explaining voting decisions, but with some important differences. The consumer operating in an economic market has a finely divisible stock of money to distribute over a wide variety of goods in order to express his or her preferences in a sophisticated and gradual way. Voters in a 'political market' have only one vote to 'spend' and must allocate it to one political party offering a whole package of policies, each of which must be bought simultaneously by a favourable vote. However, individual voters still act rationally when choosing how to vote, that is, they act so as to maximize the benefits of voting net of any costs (Downs, 1957; Barry, 1978; Mueller, 1979). Voters have a great deal of information about the political parties' positions on issues salient for them. After comparing them with their own preferred outcomes, they choose the party closest to their preferences. Voters know their own minds on relatively few issues but, since these are the same ones that count in deciding how to vote, their ability to make autonomous decisions remains unimpaired. It follows that party leaders cannot effectively change voters' preferences, and indeed they know that they cannot. The most they can hope to do is to alter the political information available to voters in a favourable way, so influencing their judgements of how their preferences can best be realized. Rational voters may not form stable views on some issues simply because it is not worthwhile being well informed about minor questions. Voters' attitudes on key policies are internally consistent, with clear rankings of issues.

Any rational choice model can be put forward in forms which are almost tautologous; for example, we may say that party images can count as 'an issue' and that the habitual or affective voter of party identification models is 'acting rationally'. However, if the model of issue voting is to be empirically useful, voters' interests and political issues must be defined more restrictively. The most common way of making the model meaningful is to suppose that citizens are basically self-interested rather than other-regarding and that 'issues' are limited to proposed changes in public policies. Hence IV writers argue that we should expect to see economic issues such as inflation, unemployment and growth in personal incomes at the top of most citizens' priorities. In postwar British politics these concerns have consistently dominated citizens' agendas.

IV writers still debate whether citizens make forward-looking judgements of their interests in one party winning an election or retrospective evaluations of the existing government's policies. A prospective assessment of the benefits and costs of competing party programmes may involve high information and uncertainty costs. Instead, therefore, voters might simply ask of the parties, especially the government: 'What have you done for me lately?' If the answer is 'not much', they then experiment by voting for an alternative party. If citizens frame their evaluations influenced by current perceptions and recent trends, governments may be able to manipulate the economy along a 'political business cycle' in order to create an appearance of good times in election years (Section 2.2.4).

In the IV model there is no room left for party identifications. Voters with clear interests removed from the mid-point of the political spectrum often find that their interests are best catered for by one party across several elections (Robertson, 1976, pp. 23–54). For them it may not be rational to go through an elaborate process of re-evaluating each party's programme at each election. Instead, they develop 'brand loyalties' to one party that simplify their decision and cut their information costs. However, as in economic markets, if a party ceases to deliver on benefits previously generated or if a very attractive alternative emerges, these political brand loyalties will be reconsidered (Himmelweit *et al.*, 1981).

1.2.2   Voters and political leaders

In IV models voters know what they want. Voting expresses clearly ordered and consistent preferences on salient issues or, alternatively, evaluations of how they have fared under incumbent government policies in comparison with the broad outlines of other parties' programmes. Voters always choose the party whose views are closest to their own. A more difficult task for them is to weight the various issues or retrospective evaluations that are to count in how they 'spend' their single vote. Since the vote choice is such a gross effect relative to the sophisticated preference rankings underlying it, the IV model argues that we need to look at how large groups of voters behave in order to analyse the association between alignments and issue preferences.

To combat the claim that people adjust their views on policy questions to fit in with a partisan choice made on other grounds, IV writers try to show that changes in issue attitudes occur *before* changes in voting behaviour. If attitudes alter before partisan alignments among those people who change their votes between elections, this strongly suggests that the direction of causation is from issues to party affiliation. Since full-scale over-time studies are very difficult to run, the main evidence for this claim comes from 'panel' studies that re-interview the same people as were surveyed at the previous election. Only one British study has followed the same voters over several elections; it unfortunately ended with a very small and socially biased sample (Himmelweit *et al.*, 1981; reviewed by Dunleavy, 1982).

In the IV model citizens' preferences on salient issues are exogenously fixed (Dunleavy and Ward, 1981). If we imagine for a moment that voters' preferences are placed along a single left–right political continuum, then a curve showing how many people adopt each position does not change its shape during party competition (Section 2.2.1). The parties can move to and fro *along* such a curve as they seek to obtain a position that appeals to the maximum number of voters. However, they cannot change the curve itself by persuading voters to want what they have not wanted before. They can in fact only accommodate voters' preferences, not restructure them.

1.2.3   Explanation of class dealignment

IV models make relatively little attempt to explain class dealignment as a trend separate from partisan dealignment. The declining association of occupational class and party loyalty simply reflects changes in the way people view issues and party policies. If issue attitudes are initially class-structured but at a later stage come to be influenced on different lines, then the class/party link is automatically weakened.

IV writers deny that any postwar social changes have been commensurate with the scale of class dealignment:

It is . . . difficult to think of any social cleavages or fundamental changes in the social structure in the last twenty years that could have affected *national* partisan alignments in any way comparable to the substitution of the religious cleavage by the class cleavage in the first three decades of this century. *Glacially slow changes in the British social structure have undoubtedly taken place.* The emergence of coloured immigrant communities, the growth of white-collar employment (and of white-collar 'trade unionism'), the movement of agricultural workers to the towns and their displacement by commuters and the retired rich, a further spread of secularization and a growing disparity of income between the organized and unorganized working class are all cases in point. . . . But in all these cases, shifts in party support have been small, often only temporary, and always localized; *no shift in the social structure has produced an enduring, nationwide realignment of party support since 1945.* (Crewe, 1976, p. 46, second emphasis added)

In the past the blocs of voters most likely to develop (conditional) brand loyalties were those with clear-cut occupationally based interests. However, there is no inherent reason to suppose that this situation is immutable. On the contrary, this pattern of attitudes was a product of a specific politics and a particular time period. In the postwar era new issues have grown up organized along quite different lines.

1.2.4 Explanation of partisan dealignment

Explaining partisan dealignment then is the central problem for the IV model and involves several connected trends. The first and most important is the growth of third-party voting. Starting in 1962, and recurring every ten years or so, there have been three major periods of rapid surge in Liberal and later Liberal/SDP support in Britain, all of them occurring under unpopular Conservative governments. All three upward 'blips' in third-party voting were initially associated with, and later fuelled by, some spectacular by-election victories. The 1981–2 surge is exceptional because it was connected with the carefully orchestrated defection of a large number of Labour MPs and notables to form the Social Democratic Party. None of these upward surges of support has yet translated into any major success in winning seats at general elections. In 1962–3 the Liberal surge died away before the 1964 election; in 1972–5 Liberal support peaked in 1973 but held on quite near its peak level during the two 1974 elections, only to crumble away quite dramatically thereafter, partly in the wake of scandals surrounding the previously popular Liberal leader Jeremy Thorpe. By the end of 1982 Liberal and Social Democratic support had fallen by half from its peak levels of the year before, chiefly because the successful Falklands war with Argentina restored the Conservative government's popularity. During Labour's two recent periods in office (1964–70 and 1974–9) support for third parties has tended to lapse back to much lower levels and to remain depressed at the end-of-term elections. This has been taken to indicate that under unpopular Conservative governments, many people want to register discontent but are unwilling to vote Labour, looking instead for some safer 'half-way house' to express their discontent. By contrast, under unpopular Labour administrations, third-party support is unattractive since

Table 1.3   *Percentages of the electorate who either did not vote or voted for a party other than the Conservative or Labour parties in general elections from 1951 to 1979*

	1951	1955	1959	1964	1966	1970	Feb 1974	Oct 1974	1979
Did not vote	18	23	21	23	24	28	21	27	24
Voted for other party	3	3	5	10	8	8	20	18	15
Not voting for a major party	21	26	27[1]	33	32	36	41	45	39

Source: Computed from Särlvik and Crewe (1983, p. 6).
Note:
[1] This percentage total contains a rounding error.

anti-government feeling can be most effectively expressed by a straight Conservative vote.

The growth of third-party voting has been linked with an alleged trend for turnout to fall, since both are seen as expressing disaffection from the two-party system in British politics (Crewe, 1974; Finer, 1980, pp. 60–5; Särlvik and Crewe, 1983, pp. 5–7). It thus becomes legitimate to cumulate the effects of both trends to show how many voters have not expressed positive support for one of the Conservative and Labour parties. Table 1.3 presents these data for the general elections from 1951 to 1979. However cyclical the patterns of third-party support may look, and however modest the decline in turnout may seem, combining the two has the happy result (for IV writers) of producing a dramatic and consistent fall in electoral endorsement of the two-party system.

A second aspect of partisan dealignment is declining support from voters at large or the major parties' own supporters for their 'basic principles' or 'articles of faith'. IV writers see a marked difference here between the Conservatives and Labour. Conservative governments in 1970–4 and 1979–82 generated high levels of public disillusion with their economic policies. However, most of the time Conservative attitudes predominate in public opinion on many secondary issues, some of which the party has been able to promote to major-issue status for at least one election (for example, 'law and order', immigration, opposition to trades unions and dislike of taxes in 1979; or defence/patriotism in 1983).

By contrast, Labour has faced growing public hostility to further nationalization, its links with the trade unions, trade union power and even the extension of social services. These antagonisms alone may not decide how large numbers of people vote but they do indicate very restricted public support for Labour's core ideals and philosophy (Crewe, Särlvik and Alt, 1977; Crewe, 1982b). On secondary issues such as 'law and order' or levels of taxation, Labour's disadvantage is even more plain. These questions are mentioned by only a minority of voters but Labour has none the less lost votes amongst people for whom they are salient, especially in 1979 – when they more than offset public perceptions of the party as doing better than the Conservatives on prices and unemployment and as having a better leader (Särlvik and Crewe, 1983, pp. 7–29 and 159–66).

A third component of partisan dealignment is increased electoral volatility. Naturally, if third-party voting grows, the rate of vote turnover between parties also increases; the 1970s and 1980s have seen more than 20 per cent of the electorate voting differently from one election to the next. In addition, however, IV writers detect bigger swings of opinion in inter-election periods, more by-election surprises, more fluctuation in opinion poll scores and more fluidity within the campaign period itself (Crewe, 1974). Some of these claims made in the early 1970s now seem more dubious. Mid-term swings against governments, leaving aside third-party surges, have not become much more marked than they were already under the 1964–70 Labour government. Opinion poll ratings have still stabilized for some lengthy time periods, as in the aftermath of the Falklands war.

Three central reasons have been cited to explain why partisan dealignment has taken place. First, the Conservative–Labour two-party system created in the interwar period simply began to age. New issues emerged and these did not fit easily into the conventional left–right spectrum: for example, whether Britain should join (and later leave) the Common Market; whether governments should control inflation using incomes policies; and whether devolved Parliaments should be established in Scotland and Wales. On all three issues the Conservative and Labour parties have either changed their minds or been troubled by serious internal dissent. Other issues – such as policy on Northern Ireland, the management of race relations or attitudes towards a civilian nuclear energy programme – have never been incorporated into the framework of two-party competition, thus effectively denying voters any real choice in these matters. The cumulative effect of these apparent 'anomalies' in the framework of party competition has been to open up a substantial body of voters to change, to wean them away from habitual or affective loyalties to one of the major parties and to make them more aware of the need to reconsider their alignments in a flexible way.

Secondly, both the major parties have moved away from the 'Butskellite' consensus on the welfare state and the mixed economy, which seemed such a dominant feature of British politics in the 1950s and 1960s. In a series of unsteady lurches, the Labour Party has moved markedly to the left, beginning in the early 1970s with the adoption of a radical programme for government intervention in the economy. This relapsed into a kind of 'phoney war' under the minority Wilson and Callaghan governments of the 1970s. However, there was a new vigorous leftward impetus after 1979, focusing on the party constitution, the 'Alternative Economic Strategy', opposition to nuclear weapons and withdrawal from the Common Market. The Conservative Party has shifted markedly to the right, starting in 1968–70 with the 'Selsdon man' era and continuing in the early 1970s with policies such as the Industrial Relations Act. Despite a lull in 1974, since Thatcher's accession to the leadership in 1975 the party has swung towards market liberal or new-right principles, particularly by adopting monetarism as a central tool of economic management, cutting government deficits and curtailing welfare state services.

IV writers see both these shifts by the major parties as unpopular with most voters, who still occupy a 'middle-ground' position. The new-style Conservatism seems abrasive and uncaring, even if public opinion will go along (slowly) with some of the envisaged changes. However, the new Labour commitments are much more serious, because they are intrinsically more novel and more disliked than Conservative policy shifts and because Labour's party loyalists are fewer and its capacity to attract new voters is much weaker. Conservative support has gradually decayed, notwithstanding its apparent resurgence in 1979 (Ross, 1983). There has also been a veritable 'haemorrhaging' of Labour votes, chiefly amongst manual workers, previously the core of its support.

Lastly, the IV model relates partisan dealignment to the increased volume and quality of political information available to voters, especially via television news and current affairs coverage. Free political information is disseminated by four television channels, four national BBC radio services and growing commercial and local radio networks, all covered by rules of public service broadcasting that require impartiality in the treatment of the major parties, as opposed to the traditionally partisan national press. In addition, the broadcast media focus pre-eminently on individual topics or issues rather than on the discussion of coherent party ideologies. The combination of impartiality rules and single-issue analysis tends to fragment public opinion and it changes the way in which people gain and use political information. Both effects produce a long-run decline in adherence to the major parties' ideological views of the world.

1.3   The radical approach

Initially focusing mainly on the influence of social structure upon alignments (Dunleavy, 1979, 1980b), the radical model is extended (in this volume) to analyse the role of dominant ideological influences and of party competition itself in structuring voters' views (Chapters 2 and 4).

1.3.1   The core model

Other approaches to explaining voting behaviour stress the need to explain individual voting behaviour, even though they cannot feasibly do more than give probabilistic accounts of the behaviour of large numbers of voters. The radical model explicitly rejects individualistic assumptions, arguing that the analysis of voting behaviour must deal strictly with aggregate social phenomena, focusing on shifts of party support in a mass electorate. These changes cannot be reduced to individual accounts of why particular voters acted as they did; even if we had a plausible explanation for every single voter, the aggregate phenomenon still has its own collective properties and identity.

In the radical model people's political alignments reflect a small number of influences, as depicted in Figure 1.3. The first is their position in a complex structure of social inequalities and conflicts of interest. People will not necessarily (and perhaps not often) articulate the influence of their social location in structuring their votes – the phenomenon may be objectively apparent to an analyst without being explicitly recognized by voters as in-

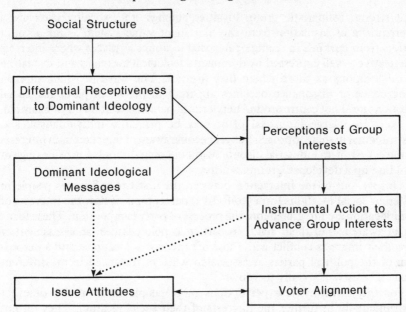

Figure 1.3 Patterns of influence on voter alignment in the radical model

volved in their decisions. Certainly we should not expect to find any one-for-one correspondence between social-structural influences on alignments and voters' attitudes, any more than occupational-class influences on voting have been reflected in explicit references to the existence of class struggles or the like. Social-structural influences are simply not manifest 'issues' or 'problems' in this naive sense. Social locations are extremely complex constructs. No single index can encapsulate all the elements that define the social structure. As we shall see in Chapter 6, a wide variety of production influences (such as social class, economic activity status, sectoral location, unionization and gender) and consumption influences are important determinants of alignments.

Secondly, the way in which people vote is conditioned by a set of dominant ideological messages formulated by institutions of central social significance. Chief amongst these are the mass media, which play a central and highly specialized function in disseminating political information. Collectively, media messages exert an overwhelming hegemony in the field of formal political communication, defining what are to count as acceptable or legitimate political views and constituting a body of political cognitions or 'facts' around which political consciousness is formed. The mass media may also be a substantial influence in creating an overtly biased stream of messages favouring one party in a competitive process.

There is an important interaction effect involved in the reception of dominant ideological messages. Some social locations tend to insulate their incumbents from mass media influence, while other ('open') social locations foster it. This distinction has been made before by Parkin (1971), who argued that strong, solidaristic group loyalties amongst the working class are a prerequisite of insulation from the 'dominant value system'. Our account differs from Parkin's in seeing open social locations as places where interests are relatively well expressed by dominant ideological messages and insulating social locations as those where they are not. The ways in which interest congruence or dissonance becomes apparent to people in particular social locations need not centre around networks of personal relations. For example, workers in a large industrial plant may be primarily individualistic and instrumental in their approach but yet become aware of their common interests in the course of an industrial dispute, without going through any prior stage of building up a developed group identity.

Thirdly, out of the interaction between the first two influences people in different social locations form (collective) perceptions of how the interests of their location are integrated into the process of party competition. These focus on an awareness of their 'stake' in particular policy issues, an assessment of how their interests conflict with those of other social locations, and a perception of the political parties as associated with, or distanced from, different social interests, especially their own.

Fourthly, within these perceptions most people most of the time act instrumentally to further the interests of their social location. They do not undertake an analysis of their individual household situation but rather act to promote the collective interests of their social location, as these have been defined in their society.

Finally, in this account attitudes are formed simultaneously with alignments and as a result of many of the same influences. They do not constitute important causal factors in structuring the way in which people vote, however closely voting and attitudes may be associated. Even if shifts in issue attitudes predate shifts in alignments, these leads and lags demonstrate only that a change in people's overall political orientation shows itself first in more finely graduated responses to issue questions, and only later becomes evident as a switch in the relatively crude indicator provided by actual voting behaviour.

1.3.2 Voters and political leaders

In the radical view voters are heavily dependent upon parties, political leaders, the mass media and other organizations, which collectively define the political agenda, no doubt with some reference to citizens' concerns but not directly determined by them. These institutions have considerable discretionary ability to shape the identification of 'policy problems' and the recognition of 'feasible solutions', especially where many agenda-setting institutions have similar values, personnel, sources of information, and so on.

Political leaders have an extended ability to create and reshape 'public opinion', particularly if they can engage other agenda-setting organizations in similar activity. This potential shows up clearly in switches of mass attitudes following changes of tack by political élites, especially where the conventional wisdom of the mass media and party leaders moves in step (see, for example, Chapter 7 on attitudes to the Common Market). It will not be manifest in the

Table 1.4   *The growth of public sector employment from 1961 to 1982*

Year	Public services		Public corporations		Total state employment	
	Number (000s)	*% of employees*	*Number (000s)*	*% of employees*	*Number (000s)*	*% of employees*
1961	3,169	14	2,200	10	5,369	24
1966	3,661	16	1,974	9	5,635	24
1971	4,212	19	2,001	9	6,213	28
1976	5,027	22	1,951	8	6,978	31
1982	5,277	23	1,759	8	7,036	31

Sources: Central Statistical Office (1976, pp. 119–27; 1983, pp. 78–83).

same form or to the same extent in political alignments *per se*, because voting behaviour is not grounded in issue attitudes but in more durable features of the interaction between social structures and dominant ideological messages.

1.3.3   Explanation of class dealignment

For the radical model class dealignment is the dominant electoral trend requiring explanation. When an existing line of political cleavage begins to be less important in structuring alignments, we should expect to find that some new fault line has emerged which has cut across the previous cleavage, fragmenting earlier lines of differentiation. Far from having changed at a 'glacially slow' rate, as IV writers would have us believe, postwar British society has seen some very rapid socio-economic trends, whose timing and importance are commensurate with the observed patterns of class dealignment.

The most important shift has been the growth of the state, which has had three key effects. First, in the sphere of production, Table 1.4 shows that the numbers of public service workers have increased, especially in health care and local government. In addition, although the workforce totals in many nationalized industries have declined, extensions of state ownership have kept personnel numbers in the public corporation sector roughly stable until very recently. In the 1940s and 1950s these trends were offset by the run-down in the armed forces and overseas colonial administration. However, substantial growth in overall public sector employment occurred between 1960 and 1976.

The growth of state employment was politically influential because of its effect on a pattern of production sector influences on voting which already existed. The attitudes of unionized manual workers employed in large corporations and plants were very different from those of non-union workers in the market sector of small firms. However, before the growth of state employment these differences were taken chiefly to express varying levels of (occupational) awareness and class consciousness rather than a distinctive production sector effect. Public service growth and nationalization radically changed previous patterns of union membership and industrial action. Most public sector employees join unions, even (and perhaps especially) in the non-manual grades. As the public services expanded and the rate of unionization there increased, so the social base of union membership changed. By the 1970s non-manual and manual public sector workers constituted a majority of TUC-affiliated memberships. Public sector workers, like manual workers in large private firms, have used their unions successfully to preserve their relative wage position, with industrial militancy increasing especially in the period between 1968 and 1975. These developments have made clearer than ever before the divergences of interest between unionized and non-union employees across all classes.

Public sector growth also created an entirely new fault line around which people could define the interests of their social location. The public services are widely seen as areas of low productivity growth, compared with the faster rates of improvement in large-scale private industry (Baumol, 1971; O'Connor, 1973). Similarly, some declining nationalized industries have had undistinguished records of productivity improvement compared with faster-growing industrial areas. Yet, if unionized public sector workers can maintain their relative wage position despite lower productivity growth, and especially if their point of comparison is the corporate sector of large private firms, then the real labour costs of producing a given level of public services (or low productivity public corporation outputs) will tend to rise over time. Thus, unless public sector employment falls for some other reason, the tax costs of state activity increase. Hence a potential conflict of interest is established between public sector employees advancing their wage levels (and interested in expanding services) and private sector employees anxious to minimize their tax burdens.

Both conflicts of interest, between organized and unorganized labour and between public and private sector employees, are increasingly expressed in mass media coverage and the pattern of competition between the Conservative and Labour parties. Labour is identified with the trade union movement and advocacy of expanded state intervention. The Conservative Party has become progressively more critical of organized labour and of all forms of state intervention, especially under Thatcher. Because the public–private employment cleavage cuts across the occupational class divide and because unionization is also determined chiefly by sector, these new cleavages fragment the previous class–party linkage.

The second structural change underlying class dealignment has been the polarization of consumption patterns between a commercial, commodity mode and a public service mode. In some areas, such as education and health care until very recently, publicly organized consumption has been the dominant form of provision. In other areas, commercial firms have operated virtually without competing public agency involvement. In neither situation should we expect to see strong consumption influences on political alignment. If 95 per cent of people consume a good or service in one way, then there is little incentive for any political party to appeal to the minority 5 per cent, since the potential votes to be gained are small (Rae and Taylor, 1970). However, where the electorate is much more evenly divided between those involved in private and public sector consumption, as in housing and transport, then the situation

Table 1.5   *The development of consumption patterns in housing and transport from 1949 to 1982*

Housing tenure[1]

Percentages of households:

Year	Renting from landlord	Renting from council	Home-owners
1950	53	18	29
1960	31	27	42
1965	26	28	46
1971	19	31	50
1976	15	32	53
1982	12	29	59

Transport position

Percentage of households with access to:

	No car	One car	Two or more cars
1949[2]	93	7	NA
1961	84	16	NA
1966	55	39	6
1971	48	44	8
1976	44	46	10
1982	38	44	16

Sources: Housing: Central Statistical Office (1972, p. 75; 1977, p. 88; 1984b, p. 88).
Transport: Halsey (1972, p. 551); Central Statistical Office (1977, p. 365; 1984b, p. 39).
Notes:
[1] The figures are for Great Britain, except those for 1950, which are for the United Kingdom.
[2] The figures for 1949 are based on the percentage of persons with access to cars.

is transformed. Table 1.5 shows that the predominance of private rented housing in 1945 disappeared completely by the end of the 1970s, with consumption locations polarizing between home ownership and local authority rental. In transport, growing car use has progressively displaced public transport; by the 1970s a minority of households were dependent on collective forms of transport (even if a majority of household members still did not have personal use of a car) (Hillman, 1973).

Paying for housing and transport absorbs over half average household incomes, and so there is no reason to suppose that these interests are not important to people. Again, the two major parties have clearly lined up on opposite sides of the conflicts of interests involved. Throughout the postwar period the Conservatives have been committed to a 'property-owning democracy', keen to encourage private housebuilding, firm in their defence of mortgage interest tax reliefs and opposed to general council housing subsidies. By contrast, Labour has been committed to building council housing and maintaining subsidies to tenants. In transport, two-party differentiation was a later phenomenon. Originally most public transport (except the railways) covered operating costs, so that subsidies were small. Both parties until the mid-1960s favoured growth in car use and heavy road-building programmes.

Table 1.6   *The growth of the state-dependent population on supplementary benefit in the United Kingdom from 1961 to 1982 (in thousands)*

Year	Pensioners	Numbers of recipients: Unemployed	Others	Total
1961	1,323	142	437	1,902
1971	1,979	407	628	3,104
1976	1,743	684	623	3,050
1982	1,836	1,798	798	4,432

Sources: Central Statistical Office (1979, p. 138; 1984a, p. 61).

However, in the late 1960s urban public transport systems ran into deficit and opposition to urban motorways grew sharply. Big-city Labour parties changed their local transport policies to increase bus and mass transit subsidies and halted construction of urban motorways (Grant, 1977). The Conservatives still insist that market criteria should determine public transport operations and give priority to motorists' interests. With this background we might expect housing and transport locations to become more important influences on political alignments. As the Conservative Party in the 1980s presses ahead with plans to encourage private provision in health care and education, so patterns of sectoral differentiation in voting might come into existence in these areas as well.

A third shift in the social base with political implications is the increasing number of people living on state pensions, drawing unemployment pay or reliant on supplementary benefit; Table 1.6 shows the increase since 1961 in the last of these categories. Both parties have been careful to appeal to pensioners, but they have adopted a very different attitude to the remaining categories of state-dependent people. Labour advocates extending and improving state benefits, while the Conservatives are critical of 'scroungers' and anxious to maintain a gap between state welfare levels and wages at the bottom end of the labour market. The Conservatives have tried in a muted sort of way to extract political advantage from a widespread populist suspicion of the state-dependent population.

In all three public–private sector conflicts Labour is associated with the public sector side of the cleavage and the Conservatives with the private side. However, the implications of this pattern are different across production and consumption cleavages, as Figure 1.4 shows. In employment terms, around 30 per cent of the employed population in all occupational classes work for state agencies. However, in consumption terms, most non-manual people are involved in private, individualized consumption. Hence cleavages between those involved in collective and individualized consumption primarily affect only manual workers. In both cases, non-manual private sector groups should provide the strongest levels of Conservative support, while manual workers in the public sector provide the core of Labour support. Over the postwar period, however, the increasing importance of sectoral cleavages implies that Labour has lost support amongst a large group of private sector manual workers and

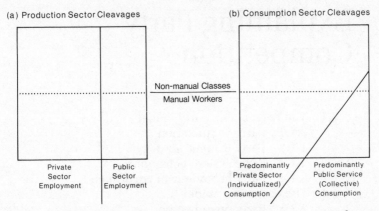

(a) Production Sector Cleavages

(b) Consumption Sector Cleavages

Non-manual Classes

Manual Workers

Private Sector Employment

Public Sector Employment

Predominantly Private Sector (Individualized) Consumption

Predominantly Public Service (Collective) Consumption

Figure 1.4 The patterning of production and consumption sector cleavages

gained support only amongst the much smaller public sector non-manual group.

A dynamic hypothesis on these lines illuminates three crucial components of trends in class dealignment. First, more cross-pressuring of people by different social location influences could have helped produce increased third-party voting. Secondly, the growth of non-manual Labour voting until 1974 probably took place chiefly amongst non-manual public sector people (Dunleavy, 1980b). Thirdly, the major decline in Labour's working-class vote in 1979 followed directly from the Conservatives' 'new right' shift after 1975 towards a populist commitment to 'roll back the frontiers of the state' and reduce taxation levels.

1.3.4 Explanation of partisan dealignment

For the radical view, partisan dealignment is largely a by-product of changes in the social basis of political life. The growth of sectoral cleavages cross-cutting occupational class not only makes third-party voting more likely but also implies a blurring of issue attitudes, especially those where class and sectoral interests diverge. In particular, where people's social interests become more complex, their insulation from exposure to dominant ideological messages is reduced. Changes in the pattern of sectoral locations may not directly change people's attitudes. However, they do mean that the grounding of political views in everyday life experiences becomes less clear and secure, making voters more inclined to accept external political communications as being valid or appropriate. These chiefly originate from the mass media. Yet they may also be structured by business, government agencies and by party sources (especially where there is major imbalance in parties' access to the mass media).

2 Explaining Party Competition

How political parties behave in order to attract support has been a question central to liberal democratic theory ever since Schumpeter's famous re-formulation of democracy as a political system where two or more (party) élites must periodically compete for mass electoral endorsement in order to gain temporary control of governmental power. We concentrate on four key accounts integrally related to the models of voting behaviour discussed in Chapter 1:

View of voting behaviour	*View of party competition*
Party identification approach	Responsible party model
Issue voting approach	{ Economic model { Adversary politics model
Radical approach	Radical model

We discuss how each account explains party organization, party leaders' strategies, party system behaviour and party behaviour in government.

2.1   The responsible party model

The political science orthodoxy of the 1950s and 1960s was a strong defence of the Conservative/Labour two-party system as giving citizens a clear choice between rival approaches to public policy-making. Either party could assume governmental power alone, without the muddying intermediary of majority coalition-building and hence could be held directly responsible at the polls for its performance. The model continues to form the major justification of plurality-rule elections, which insulate the major parties from third-party competition.

2.1.1   Party organization

The early accounts of party organization stressed that political parties are run by small insider groups, a caucus (Ostrogorski, 1964) or a 'bourgeois' leadership élite (Michels, 1962), even in socialist parties with an overt commitment to intra-party democracy. This tradition of analysis was powerfully restated by McKenzie (1955; 2nd edn, 1963), who argued that the Conservative and Labour parties had converged over time in their methods of operation. McKenzie wrote initially at a time when the Conservative Party's leader still emerged from secret 'consultations' amongst Conservative 'notables', while Labour had an elaborate machinery of party democracy embedded in its constitution. Despite these overt differences, McKenzie argued that both party leaders fixed strategy and policy in collaboration with a small leadership élite drawn from Parliament and party-affiliated interests. The mass membership arms of each party functioned chiefly as sounding boards to give early warning of changes in public opinion. Party debates could help to sort out feasible and infeasible policy ideas but mass party institutions were very sporadically involved in new initiatives.

Changes since this period have altered the parties' organization considerably. The Conservatives introduced election of their leader by MPs in 1965 and ten years later required leaders to be re-elected. Their view of party democracy stresses the linkage that runs from local memberships to the selection of a candidate at constituency level. Some candidates are elected as MPs and gain a voice in the leadership selection process and in setting parliamentary strategy. The party leader has sole control over the composition of the Cabinet or Shadow Cabinet and runs the party bureaucracy at a national level. The leader is unequivocally responsible for party strategy, and if he or she loses the support of a majority of MPs (as Heath did in 1975), all of the leader's powers pass into other hands. Local party organizations have a more continuous role to play in selecting candidates for local authority elections, sending representatives (not delegates) to the party's consultative Annual Conference and selecting people to serve on regional and national bodies that advise the leadership on detailed party policy and membership views.

Labour's organization shows similar major change. The federal structure of the party, with two separate avenues for membership (via the trade unions and via local constituency parties), remains intact. Local constituency parties select parliamentary candidates and since 1981 have been able to reselect or deselect sitting MPs. Successful candidates join the Parliamentary Labour Party (PLP), which sets its own policy, elects the top fifteen positions in Labour Shadow Cabinets and casts 30 per cent of the votes in the electoral college set up in 1981 to choose Labour's leader and deputy leader. Previously the PLP elected the party leader on its own. Local parties carry out all the functions of Conservative constituency associations. In addition, however, they cast 30 per cent of the votes in the electoral college for leadership elections, a dramatic increase in their influence. They also send mandated delegates to the Annual Conference but in this forum their voting power is dwarfed by that of the fifty-nine Labour-affiliated unions, who account for 90 per cent of Conference votes. Membership of the party via the trade union avenue remains more complex. Each union has its own more or less democratic set of procedures for subscription-paying Labour members to have a say in its policy stance, especially as it relates to voting at the Annual Conference and in the electoral college, where the unions collectively cast 40 per cent of the votes. Each union casts a bloc vote, however, with all of its membership being counted up behind the policy favoured by the majority opinion. The power to define this 'majority opinion' rests variously with members, branch activists, full-time union officials, Conference delegations or national executives, depending on the union involved. There is almost always some role for members, via election of officers or delegations and via the different systems of consultation operated. However, few would deny that effective power to shape the details of how union votes are cast rests principally with their Conference delegations or national executives (Minkin, 1980).

Third parties have contributed their own push towards change. The Liberals altered their constitution to introduce a system for choosing the party leader that combined membership balloting and MPs voting, which was the method that produced David Steel as leader in 1976. The SDP at its formation in 1981 heavily publicized its direct election of the party leader by grass-roots members. However, another requirement that leadership candidates be nominated by an eighth of SDP MPs meant that in the summer of 1983 David Owen assumed the leadership without *any* election because all of the party's other five MPs nominated him. The SDP's restricted membership of about 58,000 makes it effectively a cadre party, so that its internal organization can stress procedures that are much less feasible with larger numbers and smaller membership fees. For example, the Transport and General Workers' Union (TGWU) in 1983 charged its 1 million members who pay the political levy only 50p per year; a postal ballot to decide to which potential leaders or policies the union's bloc vote should go would effectively expend its annual contribution to the Labour Party.

Despite this rapid pace of change, the responsible party model still suggests that in all the parties a small group around the party leader, chiefly the Cabinet or Shadow Cabinet plus variously selected leader cronies, key interest-group backers or other party notables, effectively shapes their national programmes. The Conservatives allocate a marginally greater role to peers. Labour's federal structure means that leaders of the largest affiliated unions are normally incorporated into the leadership via the National Executive Committee (NEC), which runs the extra-parliamentary party. The unions have twelve reserved NEC seats; there are another eighteen members, almost all (like the union representatives too) elected by Conference, and so the union votes can be decisive on closely contested issues. The Liberals and the SDP (since June 1983) have a different problem, that of a 'dwarf' leadership. Because their available parliamentary talent is so restricted, greater influence accrues to national-level 'notables' (chiefly ex-MPs or peers), their small party bureaucracies and leading figures in local government.

The involvement of party members or activists in setting national party policy is restricted and episodic. In the Conservative Party the normal situation is one of undisputed leadership hegemony. This changes only in exceptional circumstances, such as particularly severe electoral reversals, leading to enough serious dissent within the parliamentary party and amongst members to allow back-bench MPs to deselect the party leader. In the Labour Party McKenzie argued that the 'normal' situation was for a secure parliamentary leader with backing from the big union leaderships to wrap up Conference policy-making. Clearly the constitutional changes of 1979–81 have altered this pattern somewhat, especially by introducing the electoral college with its bigger role for constituency parties. However, the conduct of party affairs since the 1982 Conference looks remarkably similar to Labour's earlier style of operating, except that the leadership is in better touch with membership views than in the 1970s. Moreover, for all the Liberal and SDP talk of grass-roots membership involvement, these parties' overall standing in the polls depends so critically on their leaderships' performance that party leaders are quite decisive in setting a policy line.

In normal circumstances party leaders have only manageable problems in persuading their MPs, party activists or memberships to follow their lead, since they share similar ideological convictions and want to win elections. Leaders may have a more sophisticated understanding of electoral feasibility, while members and activists might go out on a limb more for their less popular policy commitments. However, this difference is a matter of shading and degree rather than the unbridgeable chasm portrayed by Michels. Leaders' freedom of action is also protected by organizational inertia, which makes it hard for rank-and-file movements to shift an established party policy. Even in the Labour Party short-run campaigns cannot succeed without winning over the affiliated unions, which in practice means bloc-vote support from some of the big five unions (the TGWU, the Amalgamated Union of Engineering Workers, the General, Municipal, Boilermakers and Allied Trades Union, the National Union of Public Employees, and the Union of Shop, Distributive and Allied Workers). A movement responding to long-term changes in a party's membership base may have more influence in all parties. However, in 'normal' circumstances, the responsible party model expects long-run changes to be reflected in shifts within the party's leadership that reduce conflict to manageable levels.

The most interesting exception here is the left/right fission within the Labour Party in the 1970s. The declining Labour vote by 1979 reduced

Labour MPs to those in relatively safe seats. The PLP moved to the right because longer-serving MPs came preponderantly from a particular political generation in the Labour movement. Most new party members (and the fewer new MPs) were well to the left of the PLP norm, however, so that the bulk of Labour's MPs became increasingly divorced from the activists running a majority of the constituencies. The swing to the left also affected the Labour-affiliated unions, creating an unprecedented gulf between the PLP and both wings of the extra-parliamentary party, especially between the 1979 defeat and the exodus of thirty-two MPs to join the SDP in 1981. So great was the gap in perceptions and outlook involved that both Callaghan from the winter of 1978 onward, and Michael Foot for most of his term as party leader, were unable to put together a stable coalition inside the NEC.

Party leaders are additionally insulated from losing control of party policy-making by external factors, such as the constitutional role of leaders as Premiers in appointing and reshuffling their Cabinets. At end-of-term elections, the governing party's manifesto is effectively written by the Cabinet or Prime Minister, since a defence of the government's record is crucial to re-election chances. Even in opposition party leaders derive power from being potential Premiers. The doctrine of parliamentary privilege also affords Cabinets, parliamentary parties and individual MPs considerable protection against being told directly what to do by an outside party caucus. Finally, the mass media and public opinion consistently focus on party leaders' performance. Party disunity is taken as damaging evidence of weak leadership and lack of commitment to party policy.

2.1.2   Party leaders' strategy

Leaderships usually control party organizations but their ability to change party policy is none the less heavily constrained. Because voters' long-run party images are so important in securing a stable level of political support, party leaders can make only incremental changes in party ideology and in the way in which they depict past policy commitments or their record in government. Attempts to transform party policy are rare and traumatic, as in 1959 when Hugh Gaitskell unsuccessfully urged the Labour Party to change 'Clause IV' of its constitution, which commits the party to public ownership of the means of production. Most major policy shifts are implicit, hollowing out existing commitments via 'quiet revolutions' rather than explicitly repudiating past ideas or achievements.

Leaders' main efforts go into trying to persuade voters that the party's programme, changed incrementally to accommodate new developments, is feasible. Detailed party position statements are worked out and presented in the Commons and via the mass media, especially in pre-election manifestos. 'The major parties feel they must have an answer and a policy for anything that is even remotely in the public sphere of interest' (Finer, 1980, p. 171). Manifestos also reformulate each party's priorities and demonstrate to voters that its programmes express morally, socially and economically desirable values. Lastly, the 'manifesto doctrine', which both major parties support, claims that every commitment made in the party manifesto will be carried into effect during a five-year parliamentary term with a secure majority.

The formal election campaign is a critical period for leadership strategies to be evaluated by voters under particularly intense media scrutiny. Campaign activities may influence relatively few voters, but their choices are decisive in an evenly matched race. Class and partisan dealignment have contributed to increased shifting during the campaign itself and hence have further enhanced the importance of leadership roles.

2.1.3 Party system behaviour

The responsible party model argues that competing parties will remain quite distinct in their appeal, especially in a two-party system. Leaders take care not to let their party's image converge with their rivals', for this would put at risk much of the voter loyalty and identification with the party built up slowly over previous campaigns and periods in office. Parties in decline are under greater pressure than those whose vote is growing to change their commitments and approach. However, such a shift is a delicate operation, requiring skill in adding on new voters without losing the support of existing identifiers. It can be achieved most easily by new leadership or a new gloss on pre-existing policies, rather than by radical surgery to remodel what the party stands for. The mass media and public opinion tend to penalize inconsistency. Party memberships, recruitment of activists and internal morale can all fluctuate dramatically if attempts are made to change the party's basic image. Party leaders normally have strong ideological attachments to the party's current stance, built up over years of service to its ideals, institutions and purposes.

The responsible party model stresses that an outcome where party positions remain distinct is normatively desirable. Clearly marked out alternatives between which voters can decide, 'a choice, not an echo' (Page, 1978, p. v), are vital because the most insidious danger to liberal democracy is that of élite collusion to keep key issues out of party competition. Distinct party appeals provide the best guarantee available that competition is real, as well as clarifying the responsibility of the incumbent governing party for policy performance. Finally, 'conviction' politicians of both left and right stress the important educative role that political parties can play in persuading citizens to think through their values and attitudes, in mobilizing people out of apathy and into participation, in giving expression to deep beliefs and major societal concerns. None of these functions can be served by a system of 'me too' politics, where the rival parties are differentiated only in terms of personalities or advertising strategies.

2.1.4 Party behaviour in government

The crystallization of partisan positions reaches a peak at election time because opposition parties invest more heavily in formulating new programmes and because all parties reaffirm a clear partisan image during the run-up and the campaign. Hence a new administration imports many manifesto commitments that form its legislative programme and provide some guidance on executive action for at least its first two years in power. A new government usually pushes ahead on its convictions, despite evidence of unpopularity or opposition that may arise.

On the other hand, the passage of time reduces some of this partisan distinctiveness. Some commitments are implemented and prove non-controversial, others die a slow death in Whitehall files or become obsolete because of shifts in the policy environment. Many governments experience a mid-term popularity slump (e.g., Miller and Mackie, 1973), although this is not always to be explained as a simple cyclical phenomenon (Husbands, 1985). Local authority elections provide an annual index of this change, with effects in many local party organizations as the party of government loses council seats or control over local authorities. Similarly, by-elections provide a running measure of popularity, with cumulative effects upon media assessment of the government's performance and incremental effects upon the composition of the Commons.

Hence governments tend to embark on a 'U-turn' towards the middle of their terms of office, moving away from an overtly partisan or manifesto style of government. Instead, they adopt more pragmatic strategies designed to demonstrate competence in office and to stabilize the economy, although they may in some cases return to their more partisan approach in order to rebuild electoral support before the next election (Hibbs, 1977; Tufte, 1978, p. 102). We should expect new Labour governments to try to expand the economy and to increase social services but to swing back into a more constrained approach after a couple of years, perhaps returning to expansion as a general election approaches. Since Conservative commitments are the opposite of Labour's, their U-turns tend to be away from restrictive economic policies or attempts to cut back welfare state services, towards a more relaxed fiscal and monetary stance and acceptance of the status quo in social policy, a stance that may be maintained as a general election approaches. Where a government regains office, its re-election campaign, the effort of producing a new manifesto and changes of personnel in the new Cabinet help to reactivate a more partisan approach to some issues of policy-making, perhaps for a shorter period than with a new government.

2.2   The economic model

The economic model of party competition (like the issue voting approach in Chapter 1) assumes that people are rational actors who maximize their benefits net of costs; however, it applies this idea to the interaction of both voters' and parties' interests at elections. Party competition is seen as a 'political market' where leaders compete to 'sell' policies to voters. In its pure form the economic model does not have great applicability to recent changes in the British political system. However, it is an important account for two reasons. First, it provides a key analysis of party behaviour in government in terms of a political business cycle. Secondly, it forms the basis for the much more directly applicable adversary politics model, discussed in the next section.

2.2.1   Party organization

Economic models make simplifying assumptions about the world, without setting too much store by their 'realism'. From the assumptions a series of deductive steps yield predictions that are tested empirically. If they survive attempts to refute them, the whole model extending back to the initial assumptions is taken as having some measure of validity. That the assumptions are known to be disputable on details or in substance is not very relevant for this method (Friedman, 1953). If the model survives, then the world runs in a fashion 'as if' the assumptions were correct.

Transposed into political analysis, these procedures mean that economic models assume that political parties are run solely by their leaderships. Political leaders are 'pure office-seekers', that is, they want above all else to win the next election and hold government office. Hence leaders want to maximize support for their party. Other groups in party organizations, such as party activists and MPs, are uninvolved or unimportant. MPs also have to stand for election and so they have a similar incentive to maximize party support levels (although there is obviously considerable variation between members in marginal and safe seats). Party activists may be success-oriented for a number of reasons. Perhaps they are interested in enjoying the fruits of party patronage, rather than in indulging in ideological debate, and hence they want their party to gain office – at least locally, where most party patronage is dispensed. Or activists may have stronger ideological convictions but be prepared to defer to leaders as long as they are successful at election time. Or activists may prefer to have 'their' party in government even if it is not living up to expectations, rather than have the opposing party running the country; hence they avoid electorally damaging splits, even if they strongly oppose aspects of their leadership's strategy. Lastly, activists may have strong ideological convictions but no real influence over party policy, because of the leadership's political predominance and control of the party organization.

2.2.2   Party leaders' strategy

Since leaders are vote maximizers, and voters' preferences cannot be changed by shifts in the party campaigning, the options available to party leaders are drastically reduced. Their task is to assess the distribution of voters' preferences on existing and potential issues and the relative importance of these. Party policy should then be adjusted to fit as closely as possible with the preference of the majority on each of the salient issues. Some minority issues that are very salient for small groups may also be included, provided that for the majority these are minor questions unlikely to affect their vote. Leaders take firm stands on issues where a large majority exists – for example, all parties are in favour of 'law and order'. However, where the division of opinion is more even and passions on the minority side of the issue run deep, political leaders make their positions sufficiently ambiguous to limit possible political damage, but attempting to avoid the appearance of indecisiveness. Party

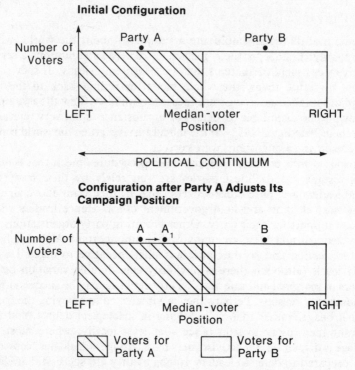

Figure 2.1   The basic logic of convergence in a two-party system

strategists also exploit opportunities for saying different things to different audiences, varying their message across different regions or in appeals to different interest groups.

2.2.3   Party system behaviour

The central empirical prediction of economic models is hedged around with various qualifications in the now mushrooming technical literature on the subject. One of the most important of these is that each voter has one best policy preference and that, as we move away from this optimum point to right or left, his or her level of satisfaction continuously declines – a situation known as 'single-peaked preferences'. However, if we simplify, the core proposition of the economic model becomes: in a two-party system, where vote-maximizing leaders seek the support of rational voters, the parties' policy positions tend to converge on the position of the 'median voter' in the society. For the sake of simplicity we can think of voters as arrayed along a single left–right political continuum, called by Downs the 'ideological scale' (Downs, 1957). On such a scale, the median voter is the person in the middle, who has as many voters on his or her right as on his or her left. To see how this convergence mechanism operates look at Figure 2.1, which assumes that voters are distributed evenly along a left–right continuum. The parties start off quite far removed from each other. Voters to the left of party *A* support it, while party *B* mops up those to the right of its position. Voters between *A* and *B* divide, casting their ballots for the party nearest to them. If both parties remain as shown, then the election would be a draw. Assume party *A* realizes the situation and shifts position towards the centre. This decision pushes the boundary between voters choosing *A* or *B* towards the right-hand end of the continuum so that party *A* has majority support and wins the election. Party *B* can respond to defeat only by itself moving towards the median-voter position. Over several elections the parties shift progressively towards the median voter, becoming minimally differentiated from each other.

If voters are not evenly distributed along the left–right continuum but instead cluster near the centre of the political dimension, with the political 'extremes' relatively unpopulated positions, then the incentives for party convergence are greatly strengthened, as Figure 2.2 shows. Even if those on left and right fringes feel so remote from both parties that they abstain, parties can still increase their total vote by cultivating the centre.

Convergence on the median voter in a two-party system is a long-run equilibrium solution. Once there, neither party leadership can improve its chances of being elected by moving away. Not only is this outcome empirically likely but also it is normatively desirable. The responsible party model allows voters a choice only between the lesser of two potential evils rather than a government that must carry out positively preferred policies. By contrast, party convergence ensures that whichever party wins the election carries out policies that are positively valued by the largest possible number of voters. In certain special circumstances convergence on the median-voter position may be a welfare-maximizing outcome, where no change of party position can make even one voter better off without making a larger number worse off.

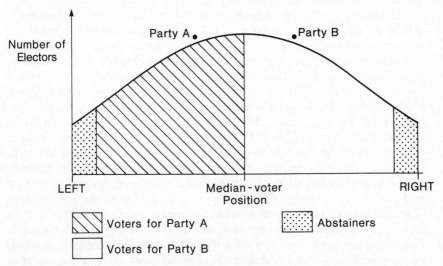

Figure 2.2 Voter curve showing centrist clustering of voter preferences

The issue voting approach to voting plus the economic model of party competition confront some acute logical problems. First, if voters act rationally in choosing between the two parties, they must also act rationally in deciding whether to vote or not. People will go and vote only if the benefits they receive from one party's victory, discounted by the probability that their vote will be decisive in determining the overall result, outweigh the costs of voting. Although most people may obtain quite large benefits as a result of one party's victory, none the less this does not guarantee a high turnout since each voter's influence on the outcome is negligible. Hence rational voters should free-ride, letting other people bear the costs of voting, even though these may be very small (for example, keeping informed about politics, or going to the polling station). If everyone thinks in this way, clearly few people will vote. Yet about three-quarters of the electorate vote in British general elections, a phenomenon that issue voting and economic models cannot really explain. Secondly, this difficulty is intensified where median-voter convergence takes place; for, as the parties move closer together, so it matters less and less which of them wins.

2.2.4   Party behaviour in government

The economic model applied best in the 1959–70 period when studies of party manifesto commitments suggested considerable convergence (Charlot, 1975; Robertson, 1976, pp. 93–124) and many voters found it hard to see much difference between the parties. Even in October 1974 this trend remained, despite the confrontational quality of the February general election and efforts by Labour's left wing to shift its manifesto into a more radical form. By 1979, however, although Labour's manifesto moved back to pragmatism, ignoring the radical ideas proposed but not implemented in 1974, the Conservatives' move to the right under Thatcher meant that the two parties diverged markedly, a trend obviously continued in 1983.

One element of the economic model has proved much more widely applicable, however, namely its account of how parties behave in government. All new administrations, of whatever complexion, use the first part of their term of office to engineer any unpopular but necessary changes in the economy, such as correcting the balance of payments (in the fixed currency era before 1971) or 'squeezing inflation out of the economic system' since then (Frey, 1978; Mosley, 1984, pp. 87–161). Governments try to ensure that the economy is growing again, that unemployment is falling and that living standards are increasing, in the run-up period to the next general election, while inflation (or the balance of payments) is still under relatively tight control. If citizens place most of their emphasis on current conditions when deciding how to vote and do not especially want to punish the government for past periods of austerity, this strategy may maximize re-election chances. Whereas, failing to take action to remedy economic problems early in its term may be costly if the government runs into the election period with economic indices out of control or with an austerity programme still being implemented. Hence governments tend to deflate the economy soon after gaining power in order to acquire space for a controlled reflation when they come up for

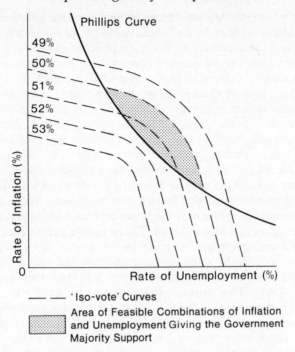

Figure 2.3 A government's management of inflation and unemployment when trying to be re-elected

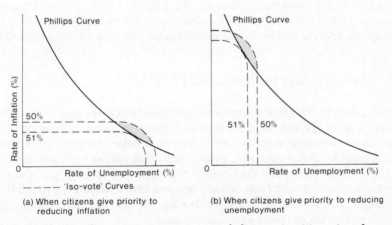

Figure 2.4 The effect on 'Iso-vote' curves of changes in citizens' preferences

re-election. Early deflation can also be attributed to the spendthrift policies of the previous administration.

Managing the economy to maximize re-election chances is not a simple operation. First, there is a tension between maintaining low inflation and keeping down unemployment, a relationship expressed by the Phillips curve.

Reflating the economy reduces unemployment but fuels inflationary pressure because of increased demand for products and labour. Deflating the economy usually reduces the inflation rate, but at a significant cost in terms of job losses as high interest rates or measures to protect the currency put marginal firms and operations out of business. In deciding what combination of inflation and unemployment rates to choose, the government needs to discover how most voters evaluate various economic outcomes. We can analytically draw on to a graph a series of 'iso-vote' curves, that is, lines showing those combinations of inflation and unemployment rates that will produce a given level of electoral support for the incumbent government party – such as 49, 50, 51, 52 or 53 per cent. For the sake of simplicity we assume a two-party system and that a government needs 50 per cent or more of the vote to regain office. Delicate policy management is needed to move the economy along the Phillips curve to a point inside or at least touching the 50 per cent 'iso-vote' curve, the situation depicted in Figure 2.3. Nor is this all. The electorate's preferences as between inflation and unemployment may not be stable over time. Voters may be tremendously concerned about rising prices when inflation is high and relatively unconcerned about job losses, as was true during most of the 1970s (Husbands, 1985). This situation is depicted in Figure 2.4(a). However, if effective action is taken on inflation at a cost in terms of unemployment, voters' preferences may switch quite sharply into placing primary emphasis on job protection, as shown in Figure 2.4(b). Clearly changes in the shape of the 'iso-vote' curves may mean that the government is shooting at a moving target in economic management terms. Its very success in moving towards the previous optimum may be instrumental in shifting public opinion towards a radically different optimum point on the Phillips curve. We explore the empirical evidence for this model in more depth in Chapter 7, where data on the public's relative aversions to unemployment and inflation are presented.

2.3 The adversary politics model

The adversary politics model closely resembles the economic model in putting forward a rational choice account of politics and in being based upon an issue voting theory of electoral behaviour. However, it makes two assumptions that are different from the economic model: first, that parties are controlled by activists, and secondly, that the electoral system protects existing parties from competition from new entrants to party competition. Their effect is to produce completely different predictions, explaining why parties may remain unresponsive to citizens' views over a long period.

2.3.1 Party organization

The adversary politics model assumes that leaders are primarily office-seekers rather than ideologically committed people. However, office-seeking entails both gaining the leadership of a major party and ensuring that the party is elected as the government. Leaders therefore want to be party leaders first, and to gain government power second – an important point if leaderships require the support of their party's activists in order to retain their office.

Assume that party activists are pure ideologues, that is, they join the party initially, and remain members thereafter, because they want to see something close to their personal views being publicly espoused by a major party. Activists may then be almost completely immune to the electoral consequences of advocating particular desired policies. Even if this seems a bit far-fetched, we can safely assume that activists are much less vote-conscious than party leaders in the policies which they want to see the party adopt, and much more concerned to see it adhere to a correct political line in terms of their values. The same diluted view could also be plausibly applied to interest groups funding the party and functioning as party backers, although their concern about electoral viability is typically greater. Similarly, rank-and-file MPs are usually more concerned about maximizing votes than are activists, but they are less concerned than the party leadership. All one needs in order to complete the switch from the economic model is the assumptions that political parties are internally democratic in some form and that the views of activists (or financial backers or MPs) fundamentally determine who becomes party leader and how long he or she stays in office.

2.3.2   Party leaders' strategy

If political parties are internally democratic and leaders' first priority is to retain their position, they must shape overall party strategy by reference to the distribution of activist opinions and the standing of alternative leaders within their party. Only where their internal position is secure are they able to alter party policy – always within the strict limits set by activists' tolerance of change or of ambiguity – in order to compete against the rival party for voters' support.

To see the implications of this for party competition, consider a two-party system where there is no overlap of the parties' activists in ideological terms, as represented in Figure 2.5. We assume for the sake of simplicity that the parties compete along a single left–right political continuum and that activists in both parties are also placed along this spectrum, as in the bottom section of Figure 2.5. Leadership selection (and reselection) involves rival figures in each party in a competitive struggle for majority support amongst activists. The basic logic of party convergence set out in the economic model implies that the candidate whose ideological appeal most nearly conforms to the views of the *median party activist* will win. Since each party's activists are drawn exclusively from one half of the overall ideological spectrum, however, convergence on the median-activist positions in both parties implies that neither offers the electorate a choice that is close to the position of the *median voter*. Activists (and the mass media) expect their party leaders to say to the electorate the same things as they say inside the party. As a result, the position that leaders adopt within the party becomes that on which they campaign for voters' support.

Of course, a great deal of party leaders' time and energies may go into trying to escape the constraints that activists impose upon them. Leaders may try to

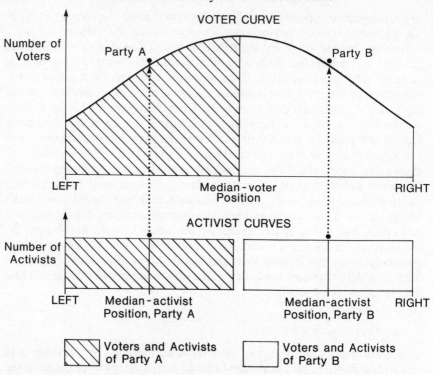

Figure 2.5 Party competition in the adversary politics model

'educate' their party activists in 'political realities', highlighting the different distribution of activists' and voters' opinions and trying to persuade activists to accommodate majority voter preferences on some issues. Similarly, they may adopt the median activist's views when competing for the leadership but gradually try to shift their ground once elected, relying on organizational inertia to protect them from any adverse repercussions. Especially during a general election, when internal party opposition is usually inhibited, leaders have some discretionary scope for manoeuvre. However, the adversary politics model stresses that activists' tolerance of deviations from median-activist policies will not be great. This leaves party leaders to concentrate on maintaining party unity by presenting median-activist policies to the electorate in the best possible light, for example, by emphasizing popular aspects of party policy but trying not to draw attention to unpopular elements. We might expect to see a regular cycle of intra-party conflict. Just after an election party leaders try to enlarge their area of discretionary policy-making or presentation – especially if the party lost. In the run-up to an ensuing election, party unity requires that there be a period when internal debate is suppressed and a more uniform adherence to the 'party line' is imposed. Hence, only in the last few weeks, when the formal campaign is under way, do the constraints on party leaders ease, allowing them to make strenuous last-ditch efforts to present the party's policies in a more popular form.

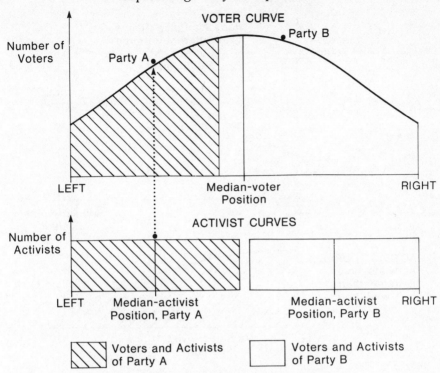

Figure 2.6 Party competition with one internally democratic party (A) and one leadership-dominated party (B)

If this sort of situation is to be a long-standing feature of a two-party system, both party leaderships must be similarly constrained. If one party *A* is internally democratic and its opponent *B* is not, then *A*'s leaders are locked into median-activist policies, while their rivals (protected from being displaced or even threatened by internal disagreement) are free to shape their policies in order to create an electoral majority, as Figure 2.6 shows. If the less constrained party leadership of party *B* is confident that party *A* is constrained by its activists' views, it may concentrate on simply gaining a safe margin of victory amongst voters rather than on moving fully to the median-voter position and the maximum possible number of votes. A landslide defeat for party *A* (the internally democratic party) could precipitate major changes in its policies or procedures but, if party *A* loses less dramatically, the favourable situation for party *B* is more likely to continue.

If party activists are drawn exclusively from different sides of the political spectrum, it is not really very important how their views are distributed inside each party. Figure 2.5 showed this distribution as a rectangle, with the party's median activist lying exactly in the middle of that part of the voters' ideological spectrum from which the party recruits activists and members. Even if we were to draw the distribution of activists in party *A* as sloping upwards to the left (see activist curve 1 in Figure 2.7), so that the party was attracting

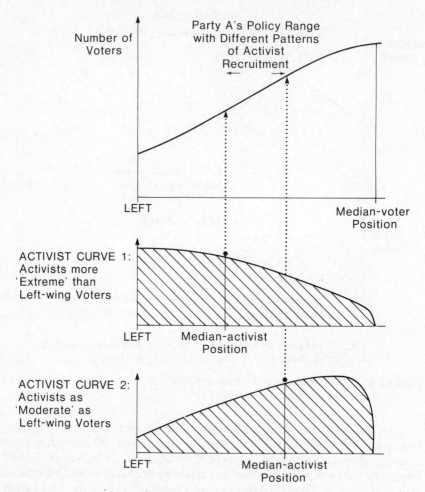

Figure 2.7 The impact of differing distributions of party activists on its possible campaign positions

activists especially amongst people with 'extreme' views, or as sloping upwards to the right (activist curve 2 in Figure 2.7), so that the party was attracting them especially amongst 'moderate' people, it might not make much difference to party policy. Figure 2.7 demonstrates this. Recruiting more 'extreme' activists shifts the party further away from the median-voter position, but not by much when compared with the rectangle-shaped distribution of party activist opinion shown in Figures 2.5 and 2.6. Similarly, recruiting more 'moderate' activists is very unlikely ever to shift the party's policy much closer to the median-voter position. Two-party divergence follows primarily from the fact that each party recruits activists across only half of the total political spectrum along which voters' opinions are distributed.

Only if there were greatly overlapping recruitment of party activists around

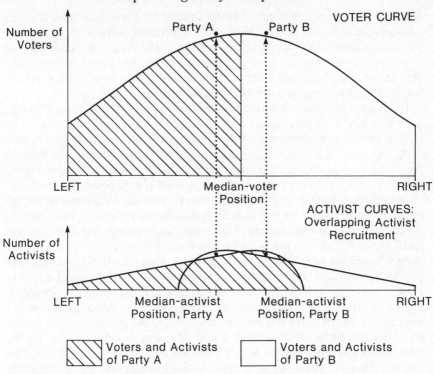

Figure 2.8 Party competition with overlapping activist recruitment

the median-voter position could the precise distribution of activist views greatly influence the parties' overall positions. This situation is depicted in Figure 2.8. A party leadership might now hope that, by recruiting sufficient numbers of activists 'from the wrong side of the tracks' (that is, amongst voters on the *other* side of the median-voter position), it could balance the opinions of its existing activist support and so move towards the median-voter position. On the other hand, why should anyone go to the trouble of joining a political party that is further removed from his or her views than is its rival? This might be rational in some circumstances. For example, where one party dominates local politics in an area, people with opposing views might disguise their objections in order to gain access to local political patronage or to have an effective say in running local affairs. However, it is unlikely that such behaviour happens on any large scale.

2.3.3 Party system behaviour

In a two-party system where both leaderships must adhere to median-activist policies, the parties may be over-polarized and locked into rival policy platforms, neither of which approximates majority voter preferences. Instead, a large group of centrists (perhaps a majority of voters) find themselves forced to choose between over-differentiated alternatives. Although voters at either pole of the political spectrum are better catered for than under median-voter convergence (because one political party is offering policies closer to their personal preferences), the adversary politics model argues that this effect is swamped by the negative consequences for the 'middle mass' of voters who face an unappetizing choice between the lesser of two evils and are permanently denied more graduated intermediate options.

If this situation is to endure for any length of time, however, it is not enough to assume that both party leaderships are more or less equally constrained by their activists (or alternatively by their financial backers or their back-bench MPs; the logic of Figure 2.5 applies equally well). In addition, the existing parties must be protected from losing votes to new political parties entering the fray. Without barriers to new parties, a new party C with policy commitments close to those of the median voter could win sizeable support from the 'middle mass' of opinion, when a situation such as that shown in Figure 2.5 emerges. In Britain the plurality-rule system of elections clearly affords the Conservatives and Labour just such a method of protection. A first-past-the-post electoral system based on local constituencies erects a high 'threshold' for any new entrant to surmount before being able to compete effectively. Winning 5, 10 or 15 per cent of the votes fairly uniformly from across the country as a whole is unlikely to win many seats because the party can almost never come first in a local area. If the base of party support is geographically restricted (as it is with the nationalist parties in Scotland or Wales), the same threshold applies but the total number of votes needed to win a limited number of seats is fewer. The 'winner takes all' character of British elections means that a small minority party with many votes but few seats has negligible impact on public policy-making and cannot offer its supporters concrete evidence of the efficacy of their votes. One interpretation of the ten-year cycle of 'blips' in third-party support (Section 1.2.4) suggests that 'surges' occur when enough voters are persuaded that a third party can have an impact. The sharp fall-offs reflect the disillusion that sets in when the electoral system excludes the third party from winning seats proportional to its vote.

In addition, the older established parties are protected by the constituency's role as the fundamental unit of the electoral system. Because Conservative and Labour support are still class-specific and spatially concentrated, both parties have many 'safe' seats that are relatively immune even to quite large shifts of public opinion (see Chapter 8). New parties whose support is not patterned in this way have no 'safe' seats at all. Their seats/votes ratios are consequently much worse, even allowing for their problems with a lower vote base under a plurality-rule system.

The adversary politics model predicts that the party system will be unstable in a number of ways. Party policies may change rapidly and erratically, because they respond not to leaders' perceptions of what voters want but to what activists (or MPs or financial backers) want. Since activists are a much smaller group of people, their attitudes can change much more suddenly and completely than will be true of voters as a whole – for example, because parties recruit different sorts of people as members or because activists embrace new social philosophies. The trend since the 1960s away from mass party member-

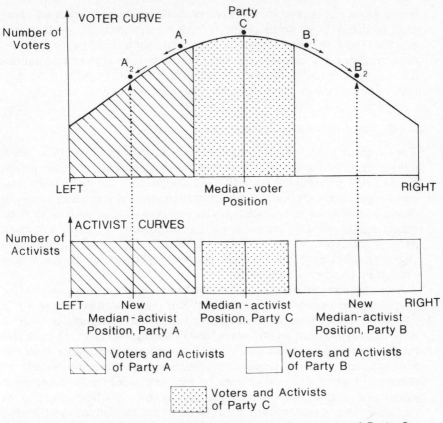

Figure 2.9 The impact of a new party (C) on the polarization of policy positions between two established parties (A and B)

ships towards 'cadre parties' has tended to increase the scope and pace of party policy change. To counteract this uncertainty, party leaders stress continuity in policy as a form of electoral insurance and try to increase the level of ambiguity in manifestos and propaganda. Activists typically seek to reduce such ambiguity and to break down the barriers that insulate leaderships from direct accountability for party strategy.

What happens if a third party can somehow be successfully established in a previously two-party system? Would it play a 'moderating' role by putting the established parties under intense competition for voters around the median on the ideological spectrum? The adversary politics model suggests a counter-intuitive result, as Figure 2.9 demonstrates. The new party *C* attracts centrist activists from both the older-established parties *A* and *B*, so that *C*'s median-activist position coincides with the median-voter position, thus allowing its leaders to maximize support simultaneously within the party and amongst voters. However, because the other two parties lose centrist activists to C, both their median-activist positions move further away from the median-voter position. Far from 'moderating' the over-polarization of the existing parties, the arrival of party C makes it worse. For party C to urge greater internal democracy on the other two parties, as the SDP has made a point of doing, is rather like advocating that they commit electoral suicide.

2.3.4 Party behaviour in government

The adversary politics model suggests that changes of party control at Westminster produce abrupt, large-scale and damaging *reversals* of public policy. Because new governments are artificially pledged to 'extreme' policies compared with those of the previous administration, many of their energies may be devoted to undoing earlier policies, creating powerful 'yo-yo' and 'stop-go' effects in issue areas of the greatest partisan controversy. With fairly frequent party alternations in government, adversary policy-making generates increased uncertainty and reduces business willingness to invest in new production facilities (Finer, 1975).

A new government puts through as much of its manifesto as it can in its first couple of years in order to appease its activists (or financial backers or MPs). This effort consolidates the leadership's position inside the party, in addition to the extra protection that the Cabinet and Prime Minister acquire by virtue of their transformed constitutional status. Having accumulated a stock of activist goodwill, and since an incumbent administration cannot realistically be removed by party activists (or even by back-bench MPs), the government gains room for manoeuvre and adopts more pragmatic policies closer to the median-voter position without harmful party dissent. Government leaders still have to enunciate the ideology that activists hold dear and let the party's manifesto be redrafted for the next election in line with median-activist views. Thus, the party of government almost always seeks re-election with an ambiguous campaign strategy, hoping that its unadvertised pragmatism in policy-making is sufficiently obvious to voters to counteract the effect of its apparent continued dogmatism.

2.4 The radical model

Until very recently there has been no developed radical model of the process of party competition in liberal democracies. Some left authors have used the responsible party model to argue that the leaders of reformist social democratic parties always become deradicalized, losing contact with membership interests and (because they control the party organization) 'selling out' manifesto policy when in government (Miliband, 1973; 1982, pp. 21–76; Coates, 1975). Prescriptively the approach argues that, because working-class voters are initially more alienated from 'normal' politics, their votes cannot be mobilized simply by accommodating their existing opinions. Instead, left-wing parties need a radical programme and cast-iron guarantees of its implementation by the party leadership. If these changes are pushed through, working-class alignments can be transformed and the majority support that was not available for a reformist programme can be created for a socialist transformation.

Other authors on the left have accepted that under capitalism two-party competition produces minimal differentiation in the choices offered to citizens. A left-wing party that attempted to stand out against the dynamic of convergence on median-voter views would simply be marginalized and replaced by a new, more 'bourgeois' channel for more liberal sentiment (Ross, 1983). Political advances cannot be won via party competition but rather in a series of ideological changes brought about by social movements in different spheres of everyday life, for the most part outside the formal political process. This approach culminates in the view that elections and party competition are simply rituals of primarily ideological significance (Lukes, 1975, pp. 304–5).

The radical model set out here argues that party competition is not primarily an ideological debate sustained by the parties' overt campaigning activities. Instead, it provides the central dynamic of regime changes in liberal democracies and the real focus of study should be on the use that parties make of their temporary control over state power. Party competition has real material implications of considerable significance for social development and is in no sense simply a ritual, chiefly because voters are crucially dependent upon parties and other social institutions to define the political agenda (Section 1.3).

2.4.1 Party organization

Political parties of all kinds are grossly imperfect democratic organizations, normally run by parliamentary leaders plus élite members of social interests backing the party financially or with other support. Leaders are insulated from significant influence from members for long periods of time. Like voters, party members and activists rely heavily upon their leadership to define what is politically feasible and to set the party's issue agenda.

None the less, open membership policies, local candidate selection and episodic grass-roots influence in national party organs all make parties respond in a fashion to shifts in activist views. The primary mechanism for change is less self-conscious campaigning by party members than it is long-run trends in the patterns of membership recruitment. Fluctuations in recruitment are rarely explicable simply in terms of the party's internal affairs but reflect broader social movements elsewhere in the economy and social system, spilling over into specific political implications. This is especially clear where a party is overtly linked with a major interest into a single social movement, as with the Labour Party and the trade unions. It occurs in other parties as well.

A measure of internal democracy, however slender, means that party policies do respond in a very mediated way and perhaps after a lengthy time-lag to changes in the party's social base. Frequently the same social changes that cause a restructuring of party memberships also produce more general ideological changes which exert direct influence upon top-level party policy-making.

2.4.2 Party leaders' strategy

Party leaders are heavily constrained by their own and their membership's ideological convictions, by voters' and activists' perceptions of what the party stands for, by its history and by its record in government. None of these inheritances can simply be wished away by leaderships for the sake of accommodating voters' preferences, even if party leaders wanted to. Nor do they compete exclusively or even primarily via variations in campaign positions and tactics. Even if we envisage an almost permanent campaign period, it is implausible that what parties say can make that much difference to election outcomes, even allowing for some opinion leadership of voters by parties.

The radical model argues that the process of party competition simultaneously defines what it is feasible for voters to want, as well as reflecting party efforts to promise voters what they want. Of course, political parties are by no means the only social institutions involved in defining feasible options and in structuring voters' preferences. Business organizations individually and collectively exert an enormous influence in this respect (Galbraith, 1972; Lindblom, 1977, pp. 135–236). So do established or traditional institutions, the trade union movement and newer social movements, such as the peace and women's movements (Byrne and Lovenduski, 1983). Most important of all in the political sphere are the mass media, which devote a great deal of their time to party political issues. The involvement of these other key social institutions means that, if party leaders sought to persuade voters to support them simply in terms of campaign competition or 'presenting a case' (Robertson, 1976, pp. 12–16), they would have little influence as one among many voices in defining a societal consensus. Hence, instead of looking for ways in which the party can deliver what voters want, party leaders look for sources of power that can be deployed to persuade voters to want what the party has to offer. The most obvious is the control over state power held by the party of government but various sources of party power are also important.

2.4.3 Party system behaviour

In the radical model no general predictions can be made about whether competing parties' policy positions converge or diverge over time. Much depends on the kinds of state and party power resources that can be used by different leaderships. The constraints imposed on party strategies by the reactions of other key social institutions to their statements and actions are also significant. In particular, the degree of congruence between a party's overall ideological message and values promoted by dominant institutions influences its freedom of action. Where this congruence is low, especially where sections of the mass media have an unfavourable partisan bias, pressures on the leadership to 'fudge' its policy commitments are especially intense.

However, in a two-party system both parties may support provisions that insulate them from third-party competition where their mutual interests are strong enough to generate a cross-party consensus on 'acceptable' uses of state power for party advantage. This may produce values and norms that constrain governments of both parties over quite long periods of time. Where these arrangements are breached, however, the parties may move rapidly apart in policy terms.

2.4.4   Party behaviour in government

The process of party competition is not a running race in which the victor is given a medal or allowed to keep some specially prestigious cup in his or her boardroom for a year or two. Nor do party leaders want to become ministers because of the entertainment value or social kudos of driving round in ministerial cars or holding up red boxes on television. On the contrary, the central purpose of party competition is to decide for a limited period which personnel should occupy key roles in the state apparatus and which ideology should guide the formulation of state policy.

Acknowledging the intrinsic involvement of state power in party competition undermines at a stroke the issue voting claim that citizens' preferences are exogenously fixed outside the process of party competition itself (Section 1.2). For, as rational choice writers admit, if any social institution has the capacity to change people's preferences, it is the state apparatus. 'If [the economic model of party competition] is to be internally consistent, the government in it must be at least theoretically able to carry out the social functions of government' and 'in the real world, governments in fact do almost everything which an organization conceivably can' (Downs, 1957, pp. 21–2; discussed in Dunleavy and Ward, 1981, pp. 352–65). If party leaders are rational actors, then state power is a free good for them to use for partisan advantage and it would clearly be irrational for them not to exploit it.

Using state power for partisan advantage allows party leaders to keep their existing policy commitments and instead to devise public policy measures that will change in a direction favourable to their party the shape of the curve showing the aggregate distribution of voter preferences; this is depicted in Figure 2.10.

Four major strategies are involved (Dunleavy and Ward, 1981, pp. 371–4). First, the government can try to engineer favourable changes in the social structure. For example, in the postwar period many Labour councils vigorously built council houses, partly with the expectation that this would increase local electoral support. Herbert Morrison, when leader of the London County Council, pledged to 'build the Tories out of London'. Similarly, after 1979 Conservative legislation forced councils to sell off properties to tenants at a large discount, partly because these measures could produce a major growth in Conservative voting amongst manual worker households.

Secondly, even if the size of particular social groups is not altered, the government may intervene to alter their relative social and economic positions in order to strengthen support for its policies among a target group. For example, Conservative administrations have rarely been able to demonstrate that they have actively improved the welfare of home-owners. On the other hand, they have consistently moved to make council tenants worse off, by

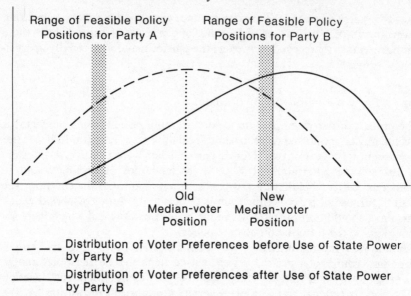

Figure 2.10   The impact of preference-shaping strategies on the distribution of voter preferences

raising rents to 'economic' levels, but cutting public-housing subsidies and by reducing the pool of new council housing available (Community Development Project, 1976). Home-owners' *relative* position thus improves, and any danger that they would be attracted by alternative housing policies is lessened since other choices are made decreasingly attractive. Governments do not have to increase the absolute well-being of voters in order to gain increased loyalty, a potent fact in times of recession and fiscal crisis. A particularly extreme form of this strategy is represented by government attempts to increase or exploit for partisan advantage social tensions within a society, by stigmatizing some group associated with support for its rival party or by bringing this group into conflict with the law. Here it is hoped that provoking the group into illegal action may encourage voters to extend 'guilt by association' to the rival party; it may also promote to particular prominence previously less important elements of the preferences or attitudes of ordinary voters. One may argue that the approach to trade union affairs and industrial relations policy used by Conservative governments at times in 1970-4 and since 1979 is to be understood in such terms.

Thirdly, state power confers on the party of government an ability to change what voters want or what they see as feasible; it does this by altering the objective situation of the polity as a whole. For example, the creation of internal crises and the conduct of external foreign policy crises have often been used by governments in ways that will boost their flagging electoral popularity. In the run-up to the February 1974 election Heath put most of Britain's manufacturing industry on a three-day week, calling the election at the height of a confrontation with the miners' union, one which on some views the government itself had largely engineered. In crisis conditions, of course, government can legitimately exert exceptional control over voters' lives, dramatically expanding the short-run potential for manipulating state power for party ends. Small, non-threatening and speedily concluded wars and foreign policy crises are almost always good news for the party of government, causing public opinion to rally round the incumbent administration as part of a broader patriotism. We shall see below that the Falklands war constituted a crucial turning-point in the electoral fortunes of the first Thatcher government (Chapters 3 and 7).

Fourthly, because of the doctrine of parliamentary sovereignty, any party with a secure Commons majority can alter existing institutional arrangements in ways that confer partisan advantage. The local authority reorganizations put through by successive Conservative governments in London (in 1965), in the rest of the United Kingdom (in 1974) and in Greater London and the metropolitan counties (1984–6), have all been fairly explicitly designed to maximize the party's control over local government (Sharpe, 1978; Dunleavy, 1980a, pp. 86–97). By the 1980s 56 per cent of people in England and Wales lived in 'safe' Conservative-controlled areas at the most important tier of local government, compared with less than 20 per cent in 'safe' Labour areas and only 25 per cent in areas where the major parties may alternate in power. Local government boundaries also influence the reorganization of parliamentary constituencies by the Parliamentary Boundary Commissioners, whose most recent efforts have produced a set of constituencies that in most electoral circumstances over-correct the acknowledged anti-Conservative bias in the previous boundaries, *pace* the assertions of equity advanced by some commentators (e.g., Waller, 1983b).

Three sources of party power are also available to major parties with a potential to become the next party of government (alone or in coalition). First, party leaders have the ability to support or aggravate social tensions in their society for partisan ends. A political leader 'becomes a symbol of some or all the aspects of the state; its capacity for benefitting and hurting, for threatening and reassuring' (Edelman, 1964, p. 73). This is especially true when one leadership decides to break out of a previous élite consensus between the parties against introducing a social tension into the process of party competition. The advantages in 'following the crowd' and legitimizing unethical or undesirable populist attitudes may be considerable. For example, in January 1978 Margaret Thatcher remarked in a television interview that because of immigration people were afraid of being 'swamped' by 'an alien culture'; this produced a sizeable (if temporary) surge in the Conservatives' opinion-poll ratings (Husbands, 1983).

Secondly, major parties have some influence on the institutional arrangements of party competition. This may not offset the incumbent party's control on issues that divide the major parties, although an opposition party can threaten to respond in kind when next in office (for example, by attacks on its opponents' finances or on its established power bases in local government). Such considerations kept Conservative governments from attacking the trade unions' political funds that were linked to the Labour Party between 1945 and 1983; they feared that legislation against company donations could be enacted under Labour governments. (However, following its re-election in 1983, the government grew bolder in its attacks on Labour finances.) More important is the extent to which major parties collaborate to skew the 'rules of the game' in ways unfavourable to new-party entrants, as with the established parties' defence of plurality-rule elections.

Thirdly, major parties can try to alter voters' perceptions of policy feasibility. For example, pledges by an opposition party to reverse current government legislation when returned to office are often used to obstruct policy implementation. In 1947, 1967 and again in 1975 Labour governments introduced various systems for trying to tax speculative profits from the sale of land. In each case the Conservatives promised to scrap the legislation and advised landholders not to sell to the government's land purchase bodies; landholders thereupon withheld land temporarily from the market and prevented public landholdings from increasing to viable levels (Blowers, 1982). Similarly, in the winter of 1982/3 the Labour Party published proposals to devalue sterling when it next took office, reputedly by something like 30 per cent. This announcement was credited by some observers with producing part of a subsequent fall in sterling's value. More generally, of course, opposition parties may try to influence voters' perceptions of current government performance by bidding up their expectations of what is feasible. Such a strategy is risky because higher public expectations are used to evaluate the current opposition if it gains power. In the long term, bidding up voters' expectations may not produce a lasting advantage for any party, instead creating greater cynicism about all party pledges. However, for the individual party acting in the short term and needing to win votes, it is none the less a rational thing to do.

If both parties were free to accommodate voter preferences, attempts to change the shape of the overall curve showing voters' aggregate preferences would be of little use. Figure 2.10 also depicts this situation. If a different curve were created by party *B* using state power or party power, but its rival *A* could instantly counteract its effect by moving towards the new median-voter position, any favourable effect for *B* would be transient. However, the radical model argues of course that parties *cannot* so easily accommodate shifts in voter preferences in view of the severe constraints on party leaders' freedom of manoeuvre. Because parties are locked in to their existing positions, preference-shaping strategies are much more attractive to party leaders than changing party policy to fit what voters currently want. With preference shaping leaders can simultaneously preserve continuity with past policy, satisfy their own ideological convictions, prevent damaging divisions inside their party and try to create increased electoral support.

PART II

Competing for Votes

3 The Run-Up, May 1979 to May 1983

The fortunes of governments reflect largely their performance in office over the preceding four or five years, as set against the effectiveness of the opposition parties. Of course, later events replace earlier experiences and so the second half of a government's term of office is normally the most important influence on 'public opinion' at the subsequent general election. The 1979–83 period was no exception to this general rule. However, it was characterized by some dramatic changes of party fortunes; we examine these for two periods, before and after the Falklands war. For each period we review the changes in government policy and the developments inside the opposition parties that affected the parties' relative standings in the opinion polls.

3.1 The fortunes of the parties, May 1979 to April 1982

3.1.1 The Conservatives' stagnation and decline

The key importance ascribed to the Conservative economic strategy by Thatcher, her opponents and outside commentators meant that it became the primary focus of public evaluations of government performance during this period. During the 1979 election campaign Labour spokesmen had charged that the Conservatives' economic programme would entail doubling Value Added Tax to pay for income tax reductions, an allegation flatly rejected by the Conservatives. However, within a month the government's first budget increased the VAT rate from 8 per cent (on most goods and services) to 15 per cent, an increase of 88 per cent. Although basic income tax rates fell from 33 to 30 per cent, the VAT change immediately boosted the rate of inflation by over 4 percentage-points. Perhaps because much larger income tax reductions were

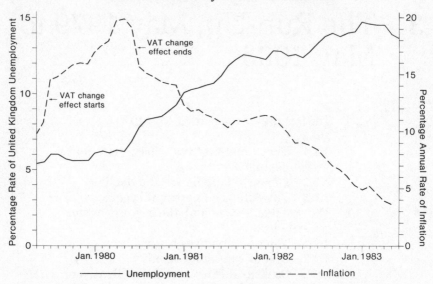

Figure 3.1   Trends in the rates of unemployment and annual inflation, 1979 to 1983

given to those in higher tax brackets, only 44 per cent of Gallup's respondents in June 1979 thought it a 'fair' budget, while 49 per cent saw it as 'unfair' (*GPI*, June 1979, p. 6).

The annual rate of inflation was running at 10 per cent in May 1979 but rose steadily higher in the next twelve months to peak at 20 per cent in May 1980; Figure 3.1, showing the trends in inflation and unemployment throughout the 1979–83 period, makes this point very clearly. The government succeeded to some extent in blaming the previous administration for its difficulty in controlling inflation. At the same time, however, Howe's first measures of financial restriction – forcing up interest rates and setting a restrictive target growth for the money supply – all implied strong government efforts to deflate the 'real' economy. Although these measures began to bite only in mid-1980, they contributed to a pervasive gloom about British economic prospects. Consequently, Conservatives' opinion-poll support fell behind Labour's within two months of the general election and stabilized around 37 to 40 per cent of the electorate until late 1980, as Figure 3.2A shows.[1] Figure 3.2B is a 'median-smoothed' version of the same data showing support for the three major parties.[2] Also shown in this figure is the timing of various important events that are related to changes in party popularity.

In other policy areas the government began to implement its proposals in a variety of ways, restricting local government spending and increasing Whitehall powers over local authorities. The Housing Act 1980 compelled districts to sell off council houses to sitting tenants at heavy discounts. At the same time the government raised rents for those council tenants who remained (in many cases by 80 to 90 per cent over two years) and drastically cut the level of local authority housebuilding. However, in other social programmes the

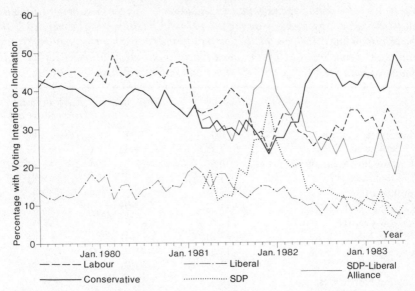

Figure 3.2A   Trends in party support, 1979 to 1983 (actual Gallup monthly data)

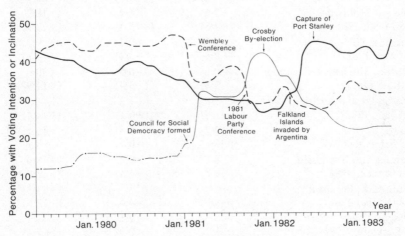

Figure 3.2B   Trends in party support, 1979 to 1983 (median-smoothed Gallup monthly data)

government moved much more cautiously, imposing cuts where they could be implemented quickly and with relatively little impact on most voters – for example, in higher education, where student numbers were reduced and fees for overseas students increased. Yet on core social security programmes it took a lot longer to produce feasible changes. The government's first year also saw a major foreign policy triumph, largely against the Prime Minister's wishes, in the convening and successful conclusion of the Lancaster House conference

Table 3.1 *Percentage-point gains (+) and losses (−) by the three major parties in all parliamentary by-elections during the 1979–83 Parliament, as compared with the corresponding 1979 general election result, and (in parentheses) national gains and losses being recorded by the immediately preceding published Gallup Poll compared with the 1979 general election result in Great Britain*[1]

	Labour	Conservative	Liberal/Social Democratic Party
Manchester Central	−0·1	−10·1	+8·8
(27 September 1979)	(+7·2)	(−4·4)	(−2·1)
Hertfordshire South West	0·0	−8·8	+7·4
(13 December 1979)	(+4·2)	(−6·9)	(+3·9)
Southend East[2]	+6·5	−19·3	+12·0
(13 March 1980)	(+11·7)	(−7·9)	(−2·6)
Glasgow Central	−11·7	−7·6	—
(26 June 1980)	(+7·2)	(−4·4)	(−2·6)
Warrington	−13·2	−21·7	+33·3
(16 July 1981)	(+2·7)	(−14·9)	(+12·4)
Croydon North West	−14·1	−18·9	+29·4
(22 October 1981)	(−9·8)	(−15·4)	(+25·9)
Crosby	−15·9	−17·1	+33·9
(26 November 1981)	(−8·8)	(−18·4)	(+27·9)
Glasgow Hillhead	−8·5	−14·4	+18·9
(25 March 1982)	(−4·8)	(−13·4)	(+18·9)
Beaconsfield	−9·8	+0·1	+9·7
(27 May 1982)	(−9·8)	(−3·4)	(+14·9)
Merton, Mitcham and Morden	−20·8	−0·5	+20·6
(3 June 1982)	(−9·8)	(−3·4)	(+14·9)
Coatbridge and Airdrie	−5·8	−1·3	—
(24 June 1982)	(−12·8)	(+0·1)	(+14·4)
Gower	−9·7	−8·5	+16·1
(16 September 1982)	(−7·3)	(−0·9)	(+8·9)
Birmingham Northfield	−8·8	−9·8	+18·0
(28 October 1982)	(−8·8)	(−4·4)	(+12·9)
Southwark, Peckham	−9·5	−15·7	+25·3
(28 October 1982)	(−8·8)	(−4·4)	(+12·9)
Glasgow Queen's Park	−8·3	−12·1	—
(2 December 1982)	(−3·3)	(−2·9)	(+7·4)
Southwark, Bermondsey	−37·5	−19·4	+50·9
(24 February 1983)	(−1·4)	(−5·3)	(+7·9)
Darlington	−6·0	−8·5	+14·3
(24 March 1983)	(−9·3)	(−5·4)	(+14·9)

Notes:
[1] These data have been calculated upon the total number of votes cast in each contest concerned. In the case of the Liberal/Social Democratic Party results the comparison is with the May 1979 Liberal result. The dash '—' means that there was no Liberal candidacy in May 1979.
[2] Gallup's fieldwork for its March 1980 published political poll took place on 11–17 March; the results may therefore have been affected to some extent by the publicity surrounding the result of the Southend East by-election.

on Rhodesia/Zimbabwe, which brought to an end the civil war and the country's illegal white-dominated regime.

In December 1979 the Conservatives had retained a by-election seat, albeit with some loss of votes to the Liberals, as can be seen from Table 3.1. However, in March 1980 Teddy Taylor – having lost Glasgow Cathcart in the general election – held the Southend East seat by only 430 votes against Labour. Taylor's 'carpet-bagger' status clearly lost him votes, while for Labour the result was a disappointing near-miss. The Liberals achieved an increase of 12 percentage-points in their vote, a harbinger of the by-election pattern that was to dominate the government's mid-term.

Geoffrey Howe's 1980 budget affirmed 'the Government's financial and monetary strategy for the medium term', which relied on stabilizing the growth of the money supply as a way of 'squeezing' inflation out of the economy. In areas of social policy, prescription charges were raised in phases that effectively quintupled the 20p level which the Conservatives had inherited from Labour. In industrial policy, a small number of Enterprise Zones were set up, whose success on most criteria has been uncertain (Roger Tym and Partners, 1983). Not until the summer of 1980 did the government's financial measures begin to deflate the economy but their impact was unexpectedly savage, chiefly because the publicly proclaimed measures were allied with a largely implicit policy of maintaining a very high value for sterling on foreign exchange markets. The combined effect of monetarist deflation and a strong pound was to bring much of British manufacturing industry lurching sharply into loss. Bankruptcies and plant closures began to rise sharply and even industrial giants such as ICI went into the red for almost the first time. Wholesale restructuring of industrial capacity began in the private sector, adding to the drastic measures that the government itself had initiated in the state-owned steel industry and British Leyland car plants. Union resistance was crushed, most notably in a seven-week steel strike. The unemployment figures began to rise dramatically from mid-1980, as redundancies coincided with an age-bulge of young people coming on to the labour market for the first time; Figure 3.1 clearly shows this sharp increase in unemployment.

By the time of the 1981 budget there was considerable hope, among some even an expectation, that Howe would allow a modest reflation of the economy. Instead, to the consternation of many even in the Cabinet, the Chancellor unveiled a £2 billion net increase in taxes, achieved by not inflation-proofing income tax allowances and by higher tax rates on alcohol, petroleum, tobacco and vehicles. Social Security benefits rose by 1 per cent less than the rate of inflation. All these provisions aimed to reduce demand and maintain the medium-term financial strategy (Hopkin, 1983) but they created dismay in the Conservative ranks. Thatcher and Howe accepted some small changes and also conceded that in future the Cabinet should have the opportunity to discuss the budget in advance, which had not been the practice hitherto. In public opinion terms only 22 per cent of respondents thought the budget 'fair'; 73 per cent thought it 'unfair'. Only 24 per cent said Howe was doing a 'good job' as Chancellor, while 61 per cent said a 'bad job' (*GPI*, March 1981, p. 19).

March 1981 also saw the official launch of the Social Democratic Party, so that the massively unpopular budget coincided with the new party's arrival in a dazzle of media euphoria (Husbands, 1982a). However, because the SDP did not officially contest the May county council elections (since it was still creating a set of local organizations), these contests provide the last straight two-party fight of Thatcher's first term. In the previous county council polls in 1977 Labour had won control in just three of the forty-seven non-metropolitan counties in England and Wales. Now, however, it made sweeping gains, winning control of fourteen shire counties. Even solid Conservative counties such as Berkshire and Cheshire were reduced to the status of no overall control. Even more significantly, Labour now controlled all the big-city metropolitan county councils in England, regaining the four lost in 1977 and the Greater London Council from the Conservatives, although the victory in London was more muted than had been widely anticipated (Husbands, 1981). In all these areas the new Labour groups promptly set about introducing policies that were in opposition to the government's desire to see a reduction in local government spending. For the Liberals, the county council elections were disappointing in the extreme. They were unable to convert the nominal 29 per cent opinion-poll support for a possible Liberal–SDP coalition into any equivalent result in local ballots and had to be content with scattered increases in their seats.

The spring and summer of 1981 brought further difficulties for the government as serious urban riots broke out in many cities. In the spring of 1980 there had been disorder in the St Paul's area of Bristol and a year later even more violent scenes – widely attributed to excessively heavy policing – took place on 10–12 April in Brixton in London (Scarman, 1982). In July there was more rioting in Brixton and in some thirty other places in London and other cities, especially Toxteth in Liverpool, Manchester and Leicester. In many cases a majority of the rioters were black youths, so that the ethnic dimension to the disturbances gave them a particularly threatening appearance. These events provoked predictably authoritarian rhetoric from some quarters but for once liberal arguments linking the riots to government economic policy in creating mass unemployment achieved some general credence.

Approval of the government and satisfaction with the Prime Minister reached unprecedented troughs in middle and late 1981, as Figure 3.3 shows.[3] The primary reason for this was undoubtedly the popularity of the Social Democratic and Liberal Alliance, now consolidated with the recruitment by the SDP of 60,000 members and its creation of a local party organization. The new grouping took support in the polls from both the Conservatives and Labour. Both parties suffered badly in the series of by-elections that characterized the Alliance surge at its peak. The Conservatives lost Croydon North West to a little-known Liberal candidate, despite a pre-poll row over Shirley Williams's claim on the seat. Williams went on in November to overturn the massive Conservative majority at Crosby. Both contests showed increases of 30 or more percentage-points on the 1979 Liberal share of the vote, as Table 3.1 shows.

In the first months of 1982 some observers began to detect a slight improvement in the government's standing with the public. The change was very small, however, and seems to have been in response to a short-term

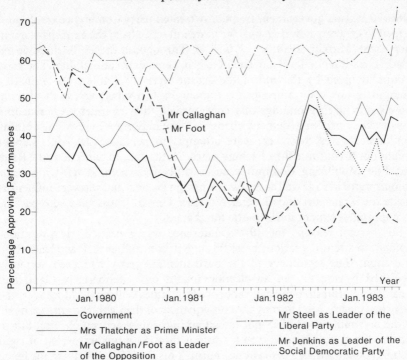

Figure 3.3   Trends in approval of government and of party leaders, 1979 to 1983
(Gallup monthly data)

amelioration of the unemployment situation, which soon worsened again
(Husbands, 1985). Thus the sudden invasion of the Falkland Islands by
Argentina came at a time when the Conservatives still stood at a very low point
in the opinion polls, with no apparent option for bringing about a dramatic
improvement in the party's fortunes.

3.1.2   Labour's 'false dawn' and decline

The scale of Labour's defeat in 1979 was a serious blow. However, when the
party overtook the government in the polls in the aftermath of Howe's first
budget and maintained a significant lead until the end of 1980, longer-term
lessons were widely discounted. Given the seemingly self-destructive policies
being pursued by the Thatcher government, many MPs and activists hoped
that Labour could simply bounce back at the next election on a tide of
anti-Conservative feeling. One key reason why such expectations proved
unfounded was the party's internal divisions over proposals for constitutional
change.

There had been a significant divergence between the views of Labour
activists and the PLP, not to mention those of the ordinary Labour voter, since
the late 1960s (Whiteley, 1983, pp. 21–52). The contempt with which the

1966–70 Wilson government frequently treated party Conference resolutions helped to generate new demands for more influence from the extra-parliamentary party (Minkin, 1980, pp. 290–314). Throughout the 1970s there developed a constituency-level movement to bring greater accountability. The main groups involved by the end of the decade were the Labour Co-ordinating Committee and the Campaign for Labour Party Democracy, both of them loosely organized groupings that concentrated their energies on persuading constituency parties to demand changes. More important in terms of winning Conference votes, however, were attempts to persuade the large Labour unions not to continue their backing for the status quo. In particular, the Rank and File Mobilising Committee successfully incorporated left-wing trade unionists and MPs as well as the two campaign groups, and was very influential inside the Transport and General Workers' Union, whose bloc vote became an important element in the battle for change.

For several reasons the 1979 Conference was a particularly propitious moment to attempt a serious breakthrough in controlling PLP and leadership discretion. The legitimacy of the parliamentary party had been seriously tarnished by the loss of an election fought on a deliberately bland and pragmatic manifesto personally approved by James Callaghan. Moreover, the party had clearly been hurt by the consequences of the Cabinet decisions made in the late summer of 1978 not to call an immediate general election but to continue in government and to try to put through a further period of rigid incomes policy with a 5 per cent pay norm. This latter led directly to the fierce industrial conflicts of the 'winter of discontent'. The push for reform centred on three issues:

1 the lack of accountability of MPs to their local parties, which led to the demand for mandatory reselection;
2 the method of selecting the party's leader and deputy leader, hitherto the preserve of the parliamentary party alone;
3 who was to have final approval of the content of the party's election manifesto.

The 1979 Conference accepted by 4,008,000 votes to 3,039,000 the principle of mandatory reselection of MPs by constituency Labour parties. However, proposals for a revision of the leadership selection procedures were narrowly defeated and the search for a mechanism to settle the manifesto issue was postponed until 1980, when the NEC was to report back on how it alone, after the widest possible consultation with all sections of the movement, would take the final decision on the content of the party's general election manifesto.

In the 1980 Conference all the same issues re-emerged in one form or another. An amendment to the mandatory reselection issue was passed, although the principle was not affected. The Conference rejected the NEC's proposal that it should decide the content of the manifesto 'after consultation with the leader of the party and the parliamentary committee of the Parliamentary Labour Party'. Although the 1979 Conference had thrown out proposals for changing the leadership selection procedure, this was one of the matters considered by a wide-ranging commission of inquiry into the party's constitution that had begun work in late 1979. The commission's basic innovation was to create an electoral college for choosing the party leader and deputy leader, in which the PLP, the trade unions and the constituency parties would all have some share of the overall vote. This idea became the basis of a proposal from the NEC to Conference. The principle of an electoral college won a clear majority of Conference votes. However, three separate suggestions concerning the college's composition and mode of operation ran into fierce controversy. As a result, it was agreed to reconvene the Conference at a later date to discuss that issue alone.

Shortly after the Conference season finished, in the middle of October 1980, James Callaghan announced his long-anticipated resignation as the Labour Party's leader. It was widely assumed that his successor would be Denis Healey, who certainly commanded most public support in opinion polls. Yet Healey was particularly blamed by the left and by many trade union leaders for the disastrous decision in 1978 on a 5 per cent pay norm. He was also seen as too closely aligned with the party's right wing, many of whom were already complaining vociferously both about the substance of the constitutional changes put through and contemplated and also about the manner in which activist left groups were campaigning for them. Realizing the gulf opening up between the PLP and a majority of activists, Labour MPs made a collective attempt to heal the divisions within the party by eschewing Healey's claims to the leadership in favour of a compromise candidate. Pressure of this kind brought Michael Foot quite late into the leadership race and in the PLP ballots the votes of the four candidates were:

	First ballot	Second ballot
Denis Healey	112	129
Michael Foot	83	139
John Silkin	38	Eliminated
Peter Shore	32	Eliminated

The run-off between Healey and Foot was required under the elimination ballot system, since the Silkin and Shore votes failed to equal Foot's first-ballot total. Unless there was a dramatic amount of switching between Foot and Healey, most of the Silkin and Shore votes must have transferred to Foot, who thereupon beat Healey by ten votes. Almost immediately, as Figure 3.3 shows, Foot's public rating fell. He had only the shortest of honeymoon periods; even some slight public agnosticism about his performance lasted only a month or so. Foot was never expected to become leader by the public and even just before he was elected he was little known and poorly regarded.

The special Conference on the electoral college met at the Wembley Conference Centre on 24 January 1981. The proceedings looked something of a shambles to even the more objective media reporters, chiefly because of the complex system of elimination ballots used. The Conference was faced with seven variations of apportionment between the PLP, the Constituency Labour Parties, and the Trade Unions and other affiliated organizations. Four possibilities were eliminated on a first ballot. The three remaining options were respectively 'equal shares' of 33:33:34 per cent of the electoral college vote (the NEC's suggestion); 'union preponderance' with 30:30:40 (proposed by the Union of Shop, Distributive and Allied Workers); and 'PLP preponderance' with 50:25:25 (proposed by the National Union of General and Municipal Workers and reportedly Michael Foot's preference). A second ballot produced the following votes for each option:

PLP preponderance	2,685,000
Union preponderance	1,813,000
Equal shares	1,757,000

The 50:25:25 formula therefore failed to achieve the necessary majority. The NEC's proposal for equal shares was then eliminated before the third ballot, whose results were:

Union preponderance	3,375,000
PLP preponderance	2,865,000

Almost all who had supported the equal shares proposal – chiefly trade unions willing to accept an equal weighting for their group but not to acquiesce in a further reduction of the trade unions' apportionment – switched to the union preponderance option (30:30:40) rather than to 50:25:25. The 30:30:40 formula was then accepted in a final confirmatory ballot by 5,252,000 votes to 1,868,000. There was considerable unhappiness about this outcome. Michael Foot made it clear that he personally wanted it altered. On 29 January 150 Labour MPs – over half the PLP – signed a statement rejecting the Wembley decision and calling for the 'rectification' of the 'mistake'.

The Limehouse Declaration by Jenkins, Owen, Williams and Rodgers, which established a Council for Social Democracy, was published amid great publicity on 25 January, only a day after the Wembley Conference. Its proceedings may have been the catalyst of this development but the evidence assembled by Bradley (1981) and Stephenson (1982) suggests strongly that it would have eventually happened anyway. The event makes it difficult to assess how uniquely damaging the Wembley Conference was for Labour's support. According to Gallup, Labour support slipped 11 points between mid-January and mid-February but other polls placed the decline at well under half this figure. In the aftermath of Wembley and the Limehouse Declaration a Labour Solidarity Campaign was launched, associated with the centre and right of the PLP, many of whom were keen to show that they did not intend to defect to the newly emerging SDP. At the end of March the party's NEC accepted the 30:30:40 formula.

While 'resolving' with a minimum of intra-party consensus the matter of how leader and deputy leader were to be elected, the party embroiled itself in other disputes that culminated in a further loss of support after the 1981 party Conference. In March 1980 Lord (Reg) Underhill, formerly the party's national agent, had personally released his hitherto secret 1975 report on the Militant Tendency (and other Trotskyite groups) inside the party. Early in

1981 he made public more material on this subject, which became a running sore for the next two years as the party's NEC moved reluctantly to grapple with the nettle of alleged 'entryism'. Then, at the beginning of April (in the early hours of the morning) Tony Benn announced that he would be a candidate for the deputy leadership at the forthcoming September Labour Conference, in competition with the incumbent Denis Healey. Despite calls from Foot, Clive Jenkins and others that he withdraw his candidacy, Benn persisted in his campaign, which rumbled on through the party machinery for nearly six months and later drew in John Silkin as a further contender. At the party Conference in September Healey received little support from the constituency parties, around 40 per cent of the union votes and the bulk of the PLP share, retaining his position by an overall wafer-thin margin. Particularly important here were the votes of the PLP 'inside left'. Led by Neil Kinnock, some thirty-seven MPs voted for Silkin on the first ballot but, when he was eliminated, switched their votes to Healey on the second ballot. Benn's defeat opened a week of fierce policy wrangles that did nothing to enhance the party's public image. Conference committed Labour finally and unequivocally to opposing the continued presence of any nuclear weapons (whether under British or American control) on United Kingdom soil and a large majority reaffirmed the party's commitment of a year's standing to take Britain out of the European Economic Community within the lifetime of the next Labour government. Between September and October 1981 Gallup reported a decline of 8·5 points in Labour's support, as Figure 3.2A shows – a slide confirmed by other polls. From October 1981 until the 1983 general election the party's recoveries in popularity were fleeting and short-term. In ten of the following eighteen months its support, as reported by Gallup, was below 30 per cent.

3.1.3   The Alliance's apparent hegemony

Although the Liberal Party's 1979 vote fell by 4·5 points from its October 1974 level, its leader David Steel emerged from the campaign with a public approval rating of around 60 per cent (as measured by Gallup), some 20 points higher than his rating before the election.[4] Steel's personal popularity consolidated his position inside the party and later gave him the confidence to encourage the emergence of the SDP as a separate party. It was also critical in persuading the SDP 'gang of four' that there was some prospect of political survival outside the ranks of the Labour Party.

However, in 1979 David Owen and William Rodgers were still Labour front-benchers and Shirley Williams was one of the more prominent casualties of the pro-Conservative swing in the general election. Roy Jenkins was considerably removed from day-to-day British politics in his job as President of the European Commission, but he none the less initiated the first moves towards the emergence of the SDP in his November 1979 Dimbleby Lecture (reprinted as Jenkins, 1982). Stephenson (1982, p. 20) calls this 'the single most important event (between May 1979 and March 1981) in placing on the agenda for serious discussion the idea of some new party or grouping in the middle ground of British politics'.

In addition to Jenkins's speech the major influence on the emergence of the SDP was events inside the Labour Party. Owen, Williams and Rodgers reacted most vigorously to the manner in which the Labour Co-ordinating Committee and other would-be party reformers organized their campaign, complaining of personal rudeness and intimidation in various party forums. Rodgers's outspoken right-wing views additionally created difficulties for him in his relations with his local constituency party. Their possible secession as a group was first signalled publicly in mid-1980, although it was not until the autumn that Owen's probable defection became clear-cut. Opinion-poll questions about the electoral prospects of a new grouping began to demonstrate the extent to which voters could be attracted to a break-away party.

By January 1981 the formation of a new party was almost a foregone conclusion in terms of the four principal actors, although the number of Labour MPs whom they would carry with them remained in doubt. At the Wembley Conference Owen was angered by the derisory reaction given to his own proposal for a 'one man, one vote' leadership selection procedure drawing on the whole Labour Party membership. The following day Owen, Jenkins, Williams and Rodgers finalized contingency plans that had been prepared over several months to break with the Labour Party (Bradley, 1981, pp. 82–9). The 'Limehouse Declaration' claimed that 'a handful of trade union leaders can now dictate the choice of a future Prime Minister' and announced the establishment of a 'Council for Social Democracy'. On 26 January nine Labour MPs declared their support for the new Council. In a survey conducted in mid-February Gallup reported 36 per cent of respondents supporting a new Social Democratic Party in alliance with the Liberals, compared with only 22 per cent for the Conservatives and Labour, and the remainder uncommitted (*GPI*, February 1981, p. 4). On 26 March the Social Democratic Party was formally launched with extensive media coverage (Stephenson, 1982, p. 6). Much attention was given to its distinctive 'cadre party' organization, especially the supposed efficiency implied by its central computerized list of members, the use of areas instead of constituencies as the local units of organization and the intention to have direct election of the party's leadership by members.

The party accumulated a string of successes throughout the rest of 1981. A succession of MPs and a few peers announced their defections to the SDP so that by October 1981 the party could claim thirty-one members in the Commons, all but one formerly Labour MPs. In July Roy Jenkins narrowly failed to beat an unprepossessing Labour candidate, Douglas Hoyle, in the Warrington by-election, recording an increase in the SDP vote of over 33 percentage-points compared with the 1979 Liberal figure. Owen, Williams and Rodgers all published widely reviewed books setting out their views on the intellectual foundations of a new centre-left grouping. Plans for an Alliance between the SDP and the Liberals were formalized over the summer by Steel and the 'gang of four'. A complicated network of joint committees of the two parties was to draft policy agreements and to apportion constituencies between them. In mid-September the Liberal Assembly in Llandudno voted by a sixteen-to-one majority to accept Steel's proposals for the Alliance. The first

SDP 'rolling conference' turned out to be a very disorganized affair, involving the party leaders and the media travelling between three separate locations. Following the Croydon North West and Crosby by-election victories in Conservative seats, Gallup gave the Alliance 50·5 per cent of public support in December 1981.

The alliance between the Liberals and the SDP was not totally harmonious from either's point of view. During 1981 the SDP saw itself as commanding the larger share of the Alliance's opinion poll support and as more successful in a string of council by-election victories. The influential Liberal MP Cyril Smith was persuaded to accept the Alliance only because it seemed far more successful as a vote-catcher than the Liberal Party alone. Within the SDP former Labour MPs such as Michael Thomas were concerned that the new party was losing some of its identity and *raison d'être* by too close a contact with the Liberals. None the less, early 1982 saw the Alliance as an apparently dominant force in shaping public opinion and the machinery of joint campaigning working well.

3.2   The Falklands war and the run-up to the general election

On 1–2 April 1982, after only a couple of weeks of crisis signals, Argentina invaded the Falklands Islands, a British South Atlantic dependency of some 1,400 people over 8,000 miles from the United Kingdom mainland, which had been the subject of a long-running dispute with Argentina over sovereignty. These events seriously embarrassed the government, chiefly because the intelligence and diplomatic failures involved left no opportunity to prevent the loss of the islands. On 5 April all the Foreign Office ministers involved, headed by Lord Carrington, resigned following a furious parliamentary debate in which Labour leaders demanded strong action to rectify the situation. The government dispatched a large military task force to recapture the islands, a strategy that the opposition parties had perforce to accept, given their earlier reactions to the invasion.

3.2.1   The Conservatives bounce back

Governments generally benefit in public opinion terms from the onset of acute foreign policy or defence crises, as people rally round an incumbent administration if basic patriotism is at stake. Thus, once the initial damage to the government had been absorbed by Carrington's resignation, it was always likely that the Conservatives would be able to exploit their traditional association with strong defence policies. Indeed, within three weeks of the decision to send the task force the Conservatives began to reap opinion poll dividends. NOP's published and unpublished polls show that government support rose by 5 percentage-points to 38·5 per cent by the last week in April. The only short-term slippage in the growth of government support followed the sinking of the Argentine cruiser, *General Belgrano*, on 2 May and the subsequent Argentine destruction of HMS *Sheffield* on 4 May (Worcester and Jenkins

1982). Only one poll recorded this dip but, if it actually occurred, it may have limited Conservative successes in the local elections held on 6 May (Husbands, 1982b).

The onset of full hostilities with a substantial loss of life for both Argentina and Britain left the opposition parties (especially Labour) hopelessly wrong-footed. The government at no stage voiced public qualms or hesitation about resorting to military force to win back the islands. Indeed, Thatcher seemed at times to exult in military activity, as in her famous 'Rejoice, rejoice!' remarks in Downing Street when the uninhabited island of South Georgia was retaken. Controversy continues to surround the decision made at Chequers to sink the cruiser *General Belgrano*, an act that finally scotched all hopes of a negotiated peace settlement. Labour leaders were increasingly forced into inescapably timid efforts to dull the escalation of military involvement in the war, while the Alliance leaders found themselves hopelessly upstaged by ministers in preaching support for British forces. Only a small section of the Labour left unequivocally opposed the conflict and the casualties. The government exten-sively manipulated the mass media throughout the campaign, justifying its behaviour by the need to keep information useful to Argentina out of the public domain. However, two useful corollaries of this blanket news manage-ment and morale-building exercise were to prevent the development of any major anti-war feeling – despite the eventual loss of 260 British servicemen's lives – and to foster a widespread national chauvinism sympathetic to Con-servative values and policies (R. Harris, 1983; Hobsbawn, 1983; Nairn, 1983).

The recapture of the Falklands' capital, Port Stanley, in mid-June boosted Gallup's Conservative poll support to 46·5 per cent in July, as Figure 3.2A shows. Other surveys for June included two NOP polls giving the Conserva-tives 49·5 and 51 per cent, and a MORI figure of 48 per cent. Overall public approval of the government's performance reached 48 per cent in June (according to Gallup) and their measure of Thatcher's approval rating was 52 per cent in July, both peaks for the 1979–83 period. The military victory was undoubtedly a personal triumph for the Prime Minister, since she took control of the war through a small inner Cabinet. Milked for all it was worth by sympathetic newspapers, this 'war record' became a central element in consolidating her 'resolute' image, allowing a generalized Churchillian aura to be applied to monetarist economic policies, an aggressive stance on Europe, and so on. Yet there is little evidence that the 'Falklands factor' ever turned into a generalized 'Thatcher factor' with positive consequences for continuing Conservative support. Public approval of Thatcher at the height of her popularity was below the level that Callaghan enjoyed as Prime Minister during much of 1978 or during most of his time after 1979 as Leader of the Opposition. Her approval rating was also consistently below the level given by Gallup respondents to David Steel after 1979, as Figure 3.3 shows clearly. Public approval of Thatcher, even at the height of Falklands euphoria, has always been tempered by more negative components. During the summer of 1982, as Table 3.1 shows, the Conservatives performed in by-elections at close to national-poll predictions, retaining a safe seat in Beaconsfield and defeating

Bruce Douglas-Mann (a Labour defector who had quixotically resigned to fight a by-election under the SDP label) at Mitcham and Morden.

Thatcher was urged by party sources to hold a general election in the autumn of 1982, a strategy that would almost certainly have won her a large majority. However, the Conservatives felt that it could just backfire, as with earlier single-issue campaigns (such as February 1974) or previous premature elections (such as Wilson's 1970 decision). In addition, an autumn election would have been unpredictable; the Alliance was performing badly in the polls but its successes were still quite recent, while Labour was still trailing but had recovered somewhat from its mid-summer low point. Moreover, the government had little evidence of economic success to which to point.

However, a number of government initiatives began to create the climate for an election in 1983. Central Office made pre-emptive campaign plans for the spring or summer of 1983 as well as the conventional later dates. In July 1982 controls on hire purchase were removed, stimulating demand by letting money circulate faster, while keeping the volume of money within government targets. 'Though not against the letter of monetarist policy it was not easily reconciled with its spirit' (Hopkin, 1983). By the end of the year new consumer credit reached record levels, creating a consumption boom largely satisfied by imports rather than domestic goods. The monthly visible trade balance averaged a £297 million surplus in the second half of 1982 but a deficit of £166 million in the first six months of 1983. Although the money supply did not expand dramatically, it ceased to fall in line with inflation, making a remarkable break with the government's previous monetary strategy.

By late 1982 the government was very actively influencing short-term economic indicators such as the mortgage interest rate, which had been reduced by 1·5 per cent in September. Ministerial pressure on the building societies for a further 2 per cent reduction intensified in the ensuing weeks (The Times, 24 October 1982, p. 1; 4 November 1982, p. 17) and was successful in December. In early 1983 press speculation suggested major new tax concessions for home-owners, although in the event the budget simply increased the entitlement to tax relief on mortgage interest by £5,000 to £30,000. However, this was the first such increase in ten years. Howe's fourth budget also increased personal income tax allowances by over three times the rate of inflation, setting the scene for a government popularity boost in April and May as the effect of these concessions worked through to people's pay.

The government made major changes in the way unemployment statistics were calculated. From November 1982 people looking for work but not claiming state benefits were omitted from official figures, reducing the unemployment rate by almost 1 per cent at a stroke. In March 1983 other ameliorations were introduced involving the exclusion from the figures of men aged 60 and over. Together with more vigorous youth training programmes to take 16- and 17-year-olds from the dole queues, these manipulations kept official unemployment figures hovering around the salient 3 million mark when they would otherwise have shown a continued increase.

These background changes of style complemented the government's first real economic success, a rapid fall in the rate of inflation to below 4 per cent, largely because of favourable changes in the United Kingdom's terms of trade with the rest of the world and a general decline in levels of world inflation as the recession bit more deeply; Figure 3.1 shows the trend in inflation. Business opinion also decided that the specially intense British recession had bottomed out by the start of 1983, creating expectations of a boom, at least in stock market values if not in real manufacturing output.

From the start of the new year the government went out of its way to encourage speculation about an imminent dissolution. In early January Thatcher made a highly publicized air trip to the Falklands, where her itinerary included visits to war graves, firing an artillery gun for the benefit of television and being enthusiastically acclaimed by crowds of servicemen. On her return, she refused to rule out the possibility of an impending general election and was reported to be under some pressure from many back-benchers to go to the country sooner rather than later. There was a short period in March and early April 1983 when the pundits' speculation shifted in favour of the autumn. However, by May the bandwagon would have been difficult to stop without creating an appearance of uncertainty.

After peaking in the summer of 1982, the Conservative performance in by-elections and council polls settled into a consistent pattern that evoked a quiet confidence in Central Office. In particular, rising unemployment never seemed likely to bring any major change in popularity, even in areas worst affected. At Birmingham Northfield in October 1982, despite a large increase in local unemployment since 1979, Labour was held to a swing of less than 1 per cent, far less than was needed to displace the Conservatives from government. By January 1983 the Conservatives' Gallup-measured support was 44 per cent, Alliance support had gone down to 22·5 per cent, while Labour had sluggishly recovered to run a poor second with 31·5 per cent. Labour's crawl back to viability was apparently jeopardized in February when it lost the inner London seat of Bermondsey to a sudden Liberal surge. However, the danger of any general revival in Alliance popularity was quickly squashed when Labour retained the Darlington seat against a weak Alliance challenge in March 1983. Even here the Labour swing from the Conservatives was barely 1 per cent in a contest where unemployment was a substantial issue.

3.2.2   Labour's quest for stability

In the immediate aftermath of the Falklands war Labour and the Alliance were both trailing badly behind the Conservatives in the opinion polls. Labour's leaders first egged on the government to drastic measures when the crisis broke and then recoiled in distaste from the loss of life and chauvinistic moral climate that the war occasioned. During the summer of 1982 there was nothing for the party to do but lie low and hope that the Falklands enthusiasms would wane. The autumn party conference marked the first stage in a long fight-back organized by Foot, the big Labour union leaderships and people on the right and centre-left of the PLP. In a secret session Conference accepted an NEC report proposing that all groupings inside the party should be registered and have to prove that they were not 'a party within a party', for example, by declaring their sources of finance. This was directed chiefly at the Militant Tendency, supposedly no more than a newspaper operating with the help of 'supporters' within the party but widely believed to be a Trotskyite entryist organization, the Revolutionary Socialist League. Many on the left – though not themselves Militant supporters – worried that the register could bring a return to the witch-hunt era characteristic of the party during the 1950s. Militant applied for registration. When the NEC turned this down in mid-December, five members of the editorial board contested the decision in the High Court but had their motion denied. The actual expulsion of the five members from the party was agreed at the NEC's meeting on 23 February, the day before the Bermondsey by-election.

The second key Conference decision was the election of a right-wing-dominated NEC, after the General Secretary of the National Union of Railwaymen, Sidney Weighell, cast his union's vote against his executive's instructions for one of the successful right-wing NEC candidates. Although Weighell was subsequently forced to resign, amidst much anti-Labour publicity in the Conservative press, his action gave Foot an NEC that would line up behind his lead. 'Outside left' NEC members, such as Tony Benn, lost key committee chairships and the various left campaign groups saw their previous gains slipping away as the big unions changed tack and demanded that Labour should have no further sudden changes in its policies or constitution. Reselection, for example, rumbled on through the autumn and winter of 1982/3 with far less fuss than might have been expected. Union support for Foot was confirmed at two important meetings between the PLP leadership and the Trade Unions for a Labour Victory grouping in late 1982. Various rumours about plots to unseat Foot circulated in the autumn but, after he remained unchallenged at the 1982 Conference, union leaders seem to have accepted that they must perforce enter the next election with the Foot–Healey team at the helm.

These various stabilization manoeuvres restored Labour's fortunes only in a superficial way. Small incidents, such as Tariq Ali's application for Labour Party membership (subsequently turned down by the NEC) were still blown up into major *causes célèbres* by Conservative newspapers. The events that preceded and accompanied the Bermondsey by-election were perhaps the most damaging of all the factors affecting the party's popularity from late 1981. There was the credence initially given in the party to the attitude of the sitting MP, Robert Mellish, about events in the Bermondsey party and towards his prospective successor, Peter Tatchell, including allegations of entryism and Trotskyite affiliations. Mellish had alienated Labour activists by becoming vice-chairman of the London Docklands Development Corporation, a quango which had been established by the Conservatives to foster private enterprise inner-city renewal and which the inner London Labour boroughs and the Greater London Labour Party strongly opposed. The Labour Party was also seriously damaged by the about-turn on the issue of Tatchell's candidacy; in late 1981 he had been rejected as candidate by the NEC after a personal parliamentary intervention by Foot that had been stimulated by Tatchell's support for extra-parliamentary action against the Thatcher government.

Mitchell (1983, p. 96) dismisses one theory that in his parliamentary statement Foot mentioned Peter Tatchell but had intended to say Tariq Ali. Mellish announced his intention not to stand again for Parliament as early as July 1981 but he was dissuaded by Foot from resigning for over a year. Mellish eventually resigned in November 1982 at a time – according to Tatchell (1983, pp. 112–13) – intended to inflict maximum damage on the Labour Party. Tatchell was thereupon chosen yet again as candidate by the Bermondsey party and his candidacy was reluctantly accepted by Foot and the NEC in January 1983. Tatchell became the focus of unprecedented media harassment, with smear stories about his personal life and political leanings being given wide credence. An anti-Tatchell 'Real Bermondsey Labour' candidate stood with Mellish's endorsement. Following the tactical collapse of the Conservative vote, Liberal support jumped 51 percentage-points to 57·7 per cent, which brought their candidate Simon Hughes the seat with a 9,319 majority.

Labour was very lucky to have another by-election in the offing. A month later at Darlington, the right-of-centre Labour candidate Ossie O'Brien held a much more marginal seat against both Alliance and Conservative challengers in a contest that had been widely touted in the media as a touchstone for Foot's leadership. As it was, Labour battened down the hatches and tried to dismiss Bermondsey as an aberrant result produced by specific local circumstances.

3.2.3   Back to third place: the Alliance in the doldrums

Roy Jenkins won the Glasgow Hillhead by-election in March 1982, just three weeks before the onset of the Falklands crisis, coming from behind to take the seat on 33 per cent of the vote in a close four-party contest including the Scottish National Party. Less sensational in terms of swing than earlier results, Jenkins's success was none the less vitally needed reinforcement for an Alliance that could not afford to see their senior figure lose again, as he had at Warrington in 1981. Jenkins duly assumed leadership of the SDP in Parliament but he found it hard to adapt to the Commons under persistent barracking by Labour left-wingers nor did he react at all effectively to the Falklands war so soon after re-entering the Chamber. Indeed Jenkins, like Shirley Williams before him, became less visible after his return to Parliament than before. In contrast, David Owen was generally agreed to have 'had a good war', almost the only figure on the Alliance benches who did. In the summer of 1982 the SDP held their first leadership elections, which resulted in Jenkins beating Owen by a ratio of five to four for the post of leader and Williams winning easily against Rodgers and the right-wing fringe candidate Stephen Haseler to become the party's president, a post created to head the party outside Parliament.

The Alliance, especially the SDP, had seen their opinion poll ratings slide even before the Falklands boost to Conservative support began. Part of this decline may also have reflected the public surfacing of strains inside the Alliance. In early January 1982 William Rodgers semi-publicly criticized the manner in which the Liberals were interpreting the guidelines for deciding who was to fight which constituency on behalf of the Alliance at the next general election (Stephenson, 1982, pp. 190–2). These gave the Liberals first crack at the top fifty seats in terms of 1979 Liberal votes, with the SDP contesting its existing seats plus many of the 'second best' hundred seats (Curtice and Steed, 1983). Although the cracks produced by Rodgers's tactics were publicly patched up, they resurfaced at the Liberal Assembly, strengthening pressures on Steel not to 'sell out' legitimate Liberal expectations in seats where they had put in years of work. Similar tensions were apparent in Islington, where a majority of the Labour council group defected to the SDP in late 1981 and then attempted to dominate the local SDP organization and to secure their own candidacies in the forthcoming local elections. This tactic aroused particular ire amongst local Liberals, for whom they represented all that was most discredited in old-style Labour 'machine' politics (Stephenson, 1982, pp. 158–62).

The first nationwide test of the Alliance's electoral standing was the district council elections in May 1982. The Alliance, especially the SDP, had been preparing for just this test for almost a year, sorting out candidacies and organization at the grass roots. By most judgements (e.g., Curtice, Payne and Waller, 1983; Husbands, 1982b), their performance was disappointing. The Conservatives, boosted by the Falklands conflict, hung on to the gains they had made four years before, while Labour did not do as badly as they might have feared. Although the Alliance gained more council seats nationally, they did not gain control of a single local authority. Some commentators suggested that Liberal candidates did better than SDP ones but there is some evidence from London for equivalent contests that suggests the contrary (Husbands, 1982b).

Following the recapture of Port Stanley, Alliance support in the Gallup polls drifted down to 22 per cent by December 1982. The decline clearly jeopardized their chances of winning a significant number of parliamentary seats because of the combined effects of a constituency-based, plurality voting system and the relative lack of geographical concentration in Alliance support, the latter a reflection of its general lack of social distinctiveness (Crewe, 1982a; Husbands, 1982a). The SDP and Liberals did successfully negotiate a single candidate in all but three reorganized constituencies (see Chapter 8). Even so, Alliance tensions continued up to polling day. For example, the defeat of the SDP's Bryan Magee in Leyton was partly attributable to the boycott of his campaign by some local Liberals, heartened about Liberal prospects there following 1982 council victories in two wards in the Leyton constituency.

Coming on top of this chequered performance in the months since April 1982, the Liberals' success at Bermondsey in winning their first inner-city seat since the 1960s, quickly followed by the SDP candidate's failure at Darlington, contributed to a general uncertainty about the Alliance's prospects. Their poll successes in council by-elections, especially in southern England, tended to run ahead of their national opinion poll ratings in the period from December 1982 to April 1983. Their leaders retained the confidence characteristic of the Liberals since the early 1970s that they would perform better in a general election campaign than in a period of 'normal' politics, when it is hard for third parties to maintain their public image at a high profile. However, the failure to create a bandwagon effect from the Bermondsey result must count as an important missed opportunity.

4 The Election Campaign of May and June 1983

4.1 An overview of the campaign

The general election campaign began on Sunday 8 May when a meeting of senior Conservative ministers and party officials at Chequers considered a Central Office computer analysis of the local elections held three days earlier, as well as the results of two private opinion polls. Although the media judged the local elections as fairly inconclusive, with the Conservatives perhaps looking strongest overall, both the Conservatives' analyses showed that they had at least a 10-point lead over Labour in terms of votes cast and intending support. The decision to call a general election was clear-cut and most discussion centred around how it could be fitted into the Prime Minister's immediate timetable, which included an EEC summit and a Western economic summit in the United States. Neither could easily be missed without damage to Thatcher's reputation for defending British interests. The decision to dissolve Parliament almost immediately left just thirty-one days of formal campaigning in which the opposition parties could try to claw back some of the commanding Conservative lead.

4.1.1 The basic chronology of the campaign

We concentrate here on the overall character of each week's campaigning. Appendix A contains a day-to-day chronology of the major events that made the headlines on the evening's broadcast news and in the following day's newspapers.

The first week of the election period (8–15 May) had the character of a 'phoney war'. Although television quickly swung into election overdrive, the newspapers reacted more slowly. The Conservatives tried further to curtail the already restricted campaign by not beginning formal electioneering or publishing their manifesto until 18 May. Labour reacted most vigorously to the election announcement on the morning of Monday 9 May, decrying Thatcher's insistence (repeated with a straight face on the preceding day's lunchtime television) that she would do what was 'best for Britain' by scheduling any election in order not to clash with her international commitments. However, attempts to make a 'cut and run' jibe stick were never very successful. Labour announced a punishing schedule of walkabouts, visits and speeches of a highly traditional kind for Michael Foot and later in the week he began his engagements, at first meeting with an enthusiastic response from Labour audiences and crowds at his walkabouts. In the Commons Labour MPs led by Peter Shore obstructed the government's attempts to push through a skeletal Finance Bill to cover the budget needs until after the general election, in order to force withdrawal both of the tax concessions to higher-income people and also of the raising of the mortgage interest threshold. In mid-week the party's NEC met and unanimously adopted as the election manifesto a lengthy policy document called *The New Hope for Britain* (Labour Party, 1983), first issued two months earlier and perhaps somewhat unfortunately titled since it enabled the Conservatives to dub it *No Hope for Britain*. Some media speculation that defining a manifesto would cause further splits in the party proved unfounded. The decision also committed Labour to its 'alternative economic strategy', launched the previous November by Shore, and designed to reduce unemployment by 2 million within five years. The mood of enforced stabilization in the party's public affairs maintained by the NEC since the previous autumn was thus continued.

Both Labour and the Alliance began their early-morning press conferences on Thursday 12 May, their timing reflecting a now traditional competition to try and 'set the agenda' for later conferences to answer. The Alliance announced economic plans to reduce unemployment by 1 million within two years without increasing inflation. On Friday Parliament was dissolved and Thatcher made her first big speech of the campaign – to a conference of Scottish Tories that had conveniently been going on in Perth all week. This captive audience had earlier provided ministers such as Norman Tebbit with a platform from which to begin the attack on Labour. Thatcher's set-piece address was a blistering attack upon the alleged threat to freedom contained in the Labour manifesto and it secured live coverage on the main evening television news.

The second week (16–22 May) began, after the quiet weekend characteristic of British elections, with concerted attacks on Labour's economic plans by Conservative ministers, a theme also pursued by David Owen in vigorous fashion at the Alliance's Monday press conference. The Conservatives sorted out Thatcher's engagements by persuading the EEC to postpone by several weeks its summit planned for June and by arranging an abbreviated stay for Thatcher at the Western economic summit in Williamsburg, Virginia. The Conservative manifesto was launched at their first press conference on Wednesday and attracted much more attention than those of its two rivals, partly because the media confidently expected it to be the one that would be implemented (Conservative Party, 1983). Its main innovations were firm pledges to abolish the Greater London Council and the metropolitan county councils, whose Labour majorities had been a thorn in the government's side, and proposals to 'cap' local authorities' powers to raise local property taxes (the rates) (Boddy and Fudge, 1984). There were also promises of further union 'reforms': secret ballots before strike decisions; election of union leaders; and ballots about whether political funds should be paid to the Labour Party. Labour's main counter-attack on the following day was the unveiling by Denis Healey of a leaked paper written in 1981 by the Central Policy Review Staff (CPRS). He claimed it showed that, if they secured a second term, the Conservatives were planning to dismantle large parts of the welfare state in the late 1980s. On Friday the monthly inflation figures showed annual price rises at 4 per cent, the lowest level for fifteen years, making headline news on television and in the press and undoubtedly consolidating the Conservatives' dominant lead as a party able to control inflation. Another quiet weekend was marked by the publication of a cluster of polls showing little change in the parties' standing since campaigning began, except perhaps some marginal Labour improvement.

The third week (23–29 May) began badly for Labour with persistent media demands at its morning press conference to know the party's exact stance on nuclear disarmament. Journalists had picked up remarks made by Denis Healey at the end of the previous week in which he had suggested that Labour's commitment to scrapping Britain's Polaris nuclear missiles was dependent on the outcome of negotiations with the Soviet Union about mutual force reductions. The Labour Party's head office in Walworth Road and Michael Foot himself tried at first to brush the matter aside but eventually issued a statement to the effect that Labour was unequivocally committed to removing the British deterrent within the five years of a new Parliament, the basic implication being 'come what may'. Scarcely had this damage-limitation exercise been belatedly wheeled out on Tuesday than the former Labour Prime Minister James Callaghan made a speech in which he attacked as unrealistic the party's unilateralist position. Foot struggled again in his statements on Thursday to insist that Labour's defence policy was coherent, unambiguous and supported by the whole leadership. On Tuesday 24 May, in the middle of the media excitement over Labour's difficulties, the House of Commons Treasury Committee, chaired by the prominent Conservative MP Edward du Cann, issued a draft report on international monetary arrangements, which was generally interpreted as attributing more than half the increase in unemployment since 1979 to the government's monetary policy rather than to world recession. This largely escaped attention. Instead, at the end of the week Thatcher claimed in a major speech that the Conservatives were the 'real peace party' and she used the Friday press conference to launch a plea for an 'unusually large majority, an unusually large authority' in order to consolidate her government's standing in world affairs, already (she said) so dramatically improved since the Falklands war. On the Saturday the Prime Minister flew to the Williamsburg summit, which provided a quota of the weekend's restricted news coverage. The other main story was rumours of conflict in the Alliance camp brought about by Jenkins's apparently ineffective leadership of the SDP and his flagging popularity compared with that of David Steel. The 'gang of four' met at the Liberal leader's Scottish home at Ettrick Bridge, under the massed lenses of the news media. However, Jenkins, Williams and Rodgers fought off demands from some Liberals (supported by Owen) for dramatic changes. Instead, the Alliance leaders began a series of initially unsupported public claims that their previously stagnant poll ratings were beginning to increase. The saturation coverage given to the Ettrick Bridge 'summit' plus Thatcher's Williamsburg trip meant that little attention was accorded to a major speech by Enoch Powell, in which he attacked the idea of an independent British nuclear deterrent as 'a delusion'.

The fourth week (30 May to 5 June) began with Thatcher's early departure from Williamsburg, orchestrated around a special press conference in advance of a summit communiqué. Both Foot and Jenkins attacked its deliberately vague tone as indicating that the summit had been a failure, with no solution for rising Western unemployment. On her return, Thatcher countered Powell's speech by stating unequivocally her readiness to use the British deterrent if the country was attacked, challenging other party leaders to say the same. Foot rather miserably pledged he would not press the nuclear button if he were Prime Minister. Labour tried desperately to shift the focus of the campaign, launching an assault on the Conservatives' policies for the National Health Service and suggesting that a new Conservative government would initiate wholesale privatization of NHS activities. However, any potential this theme might have had was shattered by two front-bench speeches on Wednesday night. One, by Neil Kinnock, demanded an inquiry into the government's decision to sink the Argentine cruiser *General Belgrano* during the Falklands war. The other, by Denis Healey, included passages accusing the Prime Minister of 'wrapping herself in the Union Jack' and 'glorying in slaughter' during the Falklands war, while behaving with 'stupefying hypocrisy' in allowing British banks to go on funding Argentina. Such intensely partisan comment gained blanket and predictably hostile media coverage, which continued as Healey was forced publicly to withdraw his remarks. The week ended with the publication of unemployment figures, reduced by various government statistical wheezes to just over 3 million and showing another slight fall due to counting changes. At the weekend Powell made another largely unremarked speech urging a vote against the EEC – of course, Labour was the only party committed to withdrawing Britain from the Common Market. However, the main weekend story was the first solid indications of a growth during the week of Alliance support, largely at Labour's expense. The *Sunday Mirror* even published a Marplan poll showing the Liberals and Social Democrats running half a percentage-point ahead of Labour.

The final week of just three days' campaigning plus polling day (6–9 June) was marked by universal predictions of a huge Conservative majority. The Tories' campaigning started with an American-style youth rally featuring a host of sport and entertainment stars including Kenny Everett, who excited his audience to rapturous applause by the supposedly comic suggestions, 'Let's bomb Russia!' and 'Let's kick Michael Foot's stick away!' When attacked by Owen at the Alliance press conference, Thatcher was forced to minimize the incident. The week started quietly with all the party leaders talking to an audience of 500 'representative' people assembled by Granada Television. However, on a small Southern Television talk show an exhausted Neil Kinnock was startled by heckling from a hostile studio audience into a remark about the Falklands war, regretting that 'so many people had to leave their guts at Goose Green' (where seventeen British soldiers died in an assault on Argentine positions) in order to prove that Mrs Thatcher had 'got guts'. The following day Kinnock was exposed to the same kind of intensely hostile press coverage that had greeted Healey's 'glorying in slaughter' speech the previous week. Yet he refused to withdraw his comment, instead writing a letter of explanation to the relatives of servicemen killed at Goose Green and going on to make a forceful attack on the government's record and future policies in a speech at Bridgend. The final day of (traditionally more subdued) campaigning saw the publication of a cluster of opinion polls showing Labour and the Alliance neck and neck in terms of popular support and the Conservatives with an unchanged commanding lead.

4.1.2 Movements in public opinion during the campaign

There were an unprecedented fifty published polls conducted between 9 May and polling day, plus numerous regional and constituency investigations. Appendix A contains details of all national poll findings by the last day of their fieldwork. Figure 4.1 shows both the parties' median poll scores from week to week during the campaign and the spread of results for each party around these medians.

Conservative support at the start of the campaign was around 46 per cent (although a Harris poll on 11 May put it as high as 52 per cent). In the second week there was a range of poll findings around the figure of 46 per cent and in the third week, with the start of Labour's defence difficulties, Conservative ratings rose slightly on average to the 45-52 per cent range. In the last two weeks the Conservative Party's rating drifted down slightly to a 41-47·5 per cent range.

Labour started the campaign with around 33 per cent support, although a single Harris poll on 6 May had given them 5 points more than this. In the second week Labour's rating improved very slightly with a maximum of 37 per cent reported in two MORI polls, one on 16 May and the other on 19 May, the

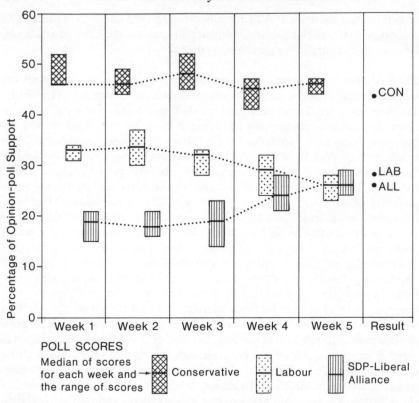

Figure 4.1 Trends in party support in the opinion polls during the campaign

former meaning that the Conservative lead was reduced to 7 points – a finding given front-page treatment by the *Daily Star*. In the third week Labour support fell back; a new low of 29 per cent was recorded by MORI on 26 May and by the end of the week the party's rating stood near the 30 per cent level. In the fourth week only five of fourteen published polls had Labour at or above this psychologically important figure, while Marplan charted a low of 27 per cent and Audience Selection, using the discredited technique of telephone polling, had a result as low as 24 per cent.[1] In the final days of the campaign all polls placed Labour in the 23–28 per cent range. Scores of 24 and 23 per cent were produced by Audience Selection using its dubious telephone method. On 8 June, the day before polling day, MORI was alone in giving the party 28 per cent. Labour therefore finished with barely four-fifths of the net support that it had held at the beginning of the campaign. At its lowest point Labour had less than three-quarters of the support that it had had at a temporary peak only three weeks earlier; this amounts to a net loss of perhaps 3 million votes.

The Alliance started at a low 19 per cent in the polls, with two MORI surveys recording figures of 15 and 22 per cent support during adjacent periods of fieldwork. In the second week the range declined very slightly and the median actually fell 1 point. Alliance support became more uncertain in the third week, NOP recording a low of 14 per cent and MORI one of 15 per cent on 23 May; however, another MORI poll on 24–25 May produced a high of 23 per cent, as did Gallup on 25–30 May. Only in the fourth week did there materialize a clear upward trend in the aftermath of the Ettrick Bridge 'summit'. One Harris poll suggested 24 per cent, a MORI one 25, and a Marplan one 27·5 (although another Marplan poll just two or three days earlier had produced only 22 per cent). In the last week two Audience Selection telephone polls placed Alliance support at 29 per cent, NOP still rated them lowest at 24, but all the other polls were in the 25–26 per cent range.

As a whole, the final week's polls overestimated Conservative strength by 2·5 points, underestimated Labour strength by a similar magnitude, but measured the Social Democratic-Liberal support exactly right.

4.2   The Conservatives' election campaign

We look at four main aspects of the Conservatives' campaign: the handling of economic issues, references to the Falklands, divisions inside the party, and themes in their national-level electioneering.

4.2.1   The great escape on economic issues

There is considerable evidence that the government's pre-campaign efforts to manipulate the economic environment continued throughout the campaign period. The dissolution of Parliament was timed to take advantage of the lowest point in the run of inflation statistics. Interest rates were more of a problem. While the Conservatives' election broadcasts emphasized that interest rates were coming *down* with inflation, there were already strong pressures at work for increases in the home loans market, where queues of prospective borrowers were growing dramatically. However, government efforts persuaded the building societies to delay announcing a 1 percentage-point increase in the mortgage interest rate until the day *after* polling. On unemployment the Conservatives accepted the advice of Saatchi & Saatchi, their advertising agency, and reiterated in all their propaganda that unemployment had never fallen over the term of a Labour government. Although factually wrong, this simple message secured widespread coverage. Further counting changes in the unemployment figures produced a drop of nearly 120,000 in the statistics published a week before polling day. The Labour Party and trade union campaigns emphasized a 'real' unemployment figure in excess of 4 million. Inevitably, however, in a contest for legitimacy with government statistics, such unofficial estimates had little chance of becoming established in the public's mind. On 17 May the latest industrial output figures showed a 1 per cent decline, raising doubts about government claims of an economic 'recovery'. By announcing Thatcher's travel plans on the same day, the Conservatives pushed the output figures well down the headline ratings and discounted their fall as a one-month aberration.

Finally, the government started the campaign by making warning noises to the Common Market about a list of budget rebates totalling £800 million. In early May the Foreign Secretary, Francis Pym, was reported as wanting the budget issue settled before 9 June and hints were dropped that Britain would veto any settlement unless its budget demands were met. Signs of Conservative dissent surfaced after this story was placed with two newspapers and Edward Heath publicly warned against too ready a resort to the veto. When the EEC summit was postponed, the Conservatives dropped all mention of the budget problem. Instead, they concentrated on promoting a positive attitude to the EEC by claiming in press advertisements that Labour's policy of withdrawal would put 'two and a half million' jobs at risk. Labour's weakly argued case for disengaging from Europe was portrayed as rebuilding tariff walls against British goods in what had become their largest overseas market since entry to the EEC in 1973.

4.2.2　The Falklands factor

Margaret Thatcher's speech on 13 May to a flag-waving audience of the party faithful at Perth made maximum play with the Falklands conflict as a basis for Conservative support. She claimed that Britain had recovered its own self-respect as a result of the government's 'resolute approach', both on economic policies and on defence:

> We have regained the regard and admiration of other nations. We are seen today as a people with integrity, resolve and the will to succeed. This is no small achievement.

She contrasted the 'defeatism' of the women demonstrators at Greenham Common with the 'swift and sure response of our brave young men in the South Atlantic a year ago':

> If today we are able to walk a little taller – and I believe we do – then it is those brave young men who deserve the praise.

Together with an assertion that defence should be the nation's priority, this was a potent attempt to hijack patriotism for the Tory cause:

> What we have begun here tonight will end not only in victory for our party but in fulfilment of our nation's destiny.

For some Conservatives the mix was altogether too heady. John Nott, who was Secretary of State for Defence during the Falklands war, made a strong plea in a *Times* interview to keep the Falklands out of the election. By the time that the Conservatives launched their manifesto, the official party line was very similar to Nott's and for two weeks the issue receded into the background. It was revived in a uniquely favourable way for the Conservatives by Healey's 'glorying in slaughter' speech on 1 June. Thatcher described Healey's claim as:

beyond all bounds of public and political decency. It has given offence to many, many people in this country, and beyond that I do not think it is worth discussing.

Even after the 'glorying in slaughter' phrase had been withdrawn, the Conservative Party chairman Cecil Parkinson stressed:

> Not by design, not because we had any order, but by unspoken understanding we have not exploited the Falklands conflict. We did not bring the subject into the election. Mr Healey did. And he did it in a contemptible fashion.

Equally, Kinnock's call for an inquiry into the *General Belgrano* affair allowed Thatcher to evoke memories of the Falklands. On 2 June she told a television interviewer: 'You had the luxury of knowing that we came through all right. I had the anxiety of protecting the *Hermes* and the *Invincible*, our air cover and the people on the vessels going down there.' Only once during the campaign was this response shaken, when Thatcher was questioned live on a phone-in programme by a Bristol teacher who refused to be put off from a list of detailed questions about the *General Belgrano* sinking. Again, the Falklands issue was revived three days before polling day by Kinnock's unscripted 'guts at Goose Green' remark, which was denounced by the Defence Secretary Michael Heseltine in a televised speech as the 'politics of the gutter'.

Finally, the Falklands war became involved in the campaign through Conservative propaganda at a local level. Despite Parkinson's claims, over 200 Conservative candidates made explicit references to the Falklands war in their election addresses, mostly in terms strikingly similar to Thatcher's Perth speech. In the unrecorded conduct of election meetings and of canvassing, such references were probably greatly multiplied.

4.2.3 Divisions inside the party

The Conservatives have traditionally conducted their internal conflicts in private. However, during the 1983 campaign, divisions inside the government were a prominent media theme, even in the Conservative press. The election started well with Heath's decision to campaign actively and make some equivocal endorsements of the government's new-found economic pragmatism. Yet rumours of a post-election reshuffle began to circulate almost immediately, suggesting that William Whitelaw (the Deputy Prime Minister and Home Secretary) would be made a peer and moved to a non-departmental Cabinet job and that Francis Pym (who had been Foreign Secretary for only a year) was to be replaced. At the launch of the Conservative manifesto Pym said little, except to respond optimistically to a question about future relations with Argentina. Thatcher intervened to 'clarify' Pym's answer as relating only to 'commerical relations', her brusque style raising eyebrows among journalists present. The following day Pym was asked about the prospects of a landslide Conservative victory on the television programme 'Question Time' and replied that landslide victories rarely produced good government. Next morning Thatcher dismissed Pym's remark as the natural caution of a former Chief Whip, adding that they were 'very unusual people, you know' and declaring: 'I want as many Conservatives to win as I possibly can get . . . . I think I could handle a landslide majority all right.' The Sunday newspapers carried details of an 'ultimatum' by Pym saying that he would not be moved to another Cabinet job in a reshuffle. Thatcher publicly denied this story but Pym did not. In due course it proved to be perfectly accurate.

Another isolated 'wet' in the Cabinet, James Prior (sent to the Northern Ireland Office in the autumn of 1981 after his disagreements with economic policy) made a major speech on 17 May arguing that strong leadership was 'not enough'.

> We need to show by our actions that we care about the hearts and minds of our people. They must be reassured that we understand their problems, the concern they have about jobs and a decent life for their children and grandchildren. . . . If I sometimes urge my colleagues along the road of growth, it is because we all share the intense anxiety which unemployment engenders.

At the same press conference where she welcomed a landslide Thatcher responded to Prior's point in a dismissive fashion that was said by the *Daily Mirror* to be 'humbling' him.

Both Labour and the Alliance tried to exploit evidence of Conservative dissent. Healey described the 'public humiliation' of Pym and Prior as the Cabinet's few remaining 'wets' 'throwing coded messages through the bars of their prison cell, as fast as autumn leaves in a gale'. David Steel commented on Thatcher's curtness: 'If she does that on her present majority, what would she be like if she got a bigger one?' Roy Jenkins declared that 'the liberal wing in the Tory party' would be weaker in another Thatcher administration than at any time since 1938. This anxiety was fuelled later in the campaign, partly by Labour's spluttering attempt to make the 'secret manifesto' charge stick but, more importantly, by speculation in the Tory press about who would be promoted in a post-election reshuffle. Norman Tebbit, attacked by Denis Healey as one of 'the hard core of the hard men, the Provos of the Tory party', was at one stage rumoured for the Home Office. Similarly, it was suggested the likely new intake of Conservative MPs would favour the reintroduction of the death penalty and stood solidly on the right. The candidate in Stockton South turned out to have been a National Front parliamentary candidate and the *Daily Mirror* gave front-page prominence to a story about fascist infiltration of the party (broadly confirmed after the election by a Young Conservative report to Central Office). In these circumstances Thatcher's repeated calls 'to vote Conservative for the biggest victory of all time' probably began to generate more alarm than they added to a bandwagon effect. The SDP and Liberal leaders stressed throughout the last week that only a large Alliance vote and an effective presence in the Commons could 'moderate' the direction of the new Conservative government. The strongest Labour variant of this theme was in Kinnock's Bridgend speech.

4.2.4   Key themes in the Conservatives' national campaign

By far the most radical departure in Conservative electioneering was the attempt to portray the Labour Party as dominated by 'Marxists' and hence outside the scope of legitimate politics. In the first week Thatcher denounced Labour's manifesto as 'the most extreme put before the electorate in modern times' and ministers' speeches were designed to demonstrate that 'under Labour's soft face, there is a very hard man' (*Daily Telegraph*, 11 May 1983, p. 1). Thatcher's Perth speech set the tone:

> The choice facing the nation is between two totally different ways of life. And what a prize we have to fight for – no less than the chance to banish from our land the dark divisive clouds of Marxist socialism and bring together men and women from all walks of life who share a belief in freedom and have the courage to uphold it.

Whitelaw suggested on television that a Labour government would introduce something akin to a police state and Peter Walker declared that the Labour programme 'delights the Kremlin'. Tebbit joined the chorus in the second week by accusing Labour of 'bringing Communism into its policies for British industry':

> No party except the Communist Party has ever published such a wholesale attack on businesses which employ British workers. No party except the Communist Party has ever shown such contempt for British management.

In the later weeks of the campaign the press and television news found these attacks too generalized to be continuously newsworthy. However, the Conservatives maintained the 'guilt by association' attack through press advertising, using a full-page spread with the headline 'Like your manifesto, Comrade'. This showed two leaflets labelled 'Labour Party Manifesto 1983' and 'Communist Party Manifesto 1983' with the same ten points listed underneath. Labour condemned this 'smear' tactic on the grounds that support for these policies (such as withdrawal from the EEC, cancelling Trident or the reintroduction of exchange controls) either individually or collectively could not be identified with communism. The Conservatives blandly replied that they were simply informing the public of similarities in Labour and Communist proposals.

Interlocking with the 'red menace' argument, the Conservatives attacked the alleged threat to freedom contained in *The New Hope for Britain*. In a speech at Cardiff on 23 May Thatcher counted forty-seven ways in which Labour's proposals would reduce British citizens' freedoms, many of them economic 'freedoms' to use capital but with some personal freedoms also, such as indulgence in 'cruel sports'. She also named six major companies liable to be nationalized if Labour won the election, including improbable candidates such as Barratt, the housebuilding firm. Economic ministers stressed that Labour's plans for state investment entailed a 'raid on savings', which could endanger pensions. Again, all these arguments were followed up with a press advertisement during the second week of the campaign that featured fifteen contractual-looking clauses and claimed: 'PUTTING A CROSS IN THE LABOUR BOX IS THE SAME AS SIGNING THIS PIECE OF PAPER'. Eight clauses were 'freedoms' already mentioned in ministers' speeches, including the rights to buy a council house, to private schooling or to private medicine. Five were general policy issues, such as a lower exchange value for sterling (which it was claimed would 'reduce immediately . . . the value of my savings') and higher rates of inflation.

Underlying the overt themes in the Conservative campaign was basically a minimalist strategy. The Conservatives contributed no new issues to the campaign period. Even the manifesto proposals for introducing more union 'democracy', capping the rates and abolishing the metropolitan county councils, had been extensively 'trailed' in the press before being issued. The Conservatives concentrated throughout on moving debate and media scrutiny away from the government's record and on to Labour's proposals. Almost all aspects of the Conservative campaign meshed into this minimalist and reactive stance. The party accepted a suggestion from their advertising agents to cut down the length of their television broadcasts to five minutes, halving their air time since they gained no additional slots. However, their party election broadcasts (PEBs) were correspondingly slicker than in previous years, making much use of animated text further to break up the broadcasts into commercial-length segments. Thatcher's election campaign was organized around a minimum number of carefully orchestrated inspections of private factories, restricted public visits (with heavy police presence to keep away demonstrators) and speeches to the party faithful. As in 1979, her advisers concentrated on getting her picture on to the television news and into the newspapers.

The Conservatives religiously ignored the Alliance parties, except to dwell from time to time on the record of the SDP leadership as former Labour politicians (and hence architects of nationalization proposals) and to argue that an Alliance vote could 'let Labour in'. This stance obviously became less credible during the last three weeks of the campaign as the Conservative lead over Labour lengthened and was to some extent replaced by positive advocacy of a large majority as restoring Britain's place in the world. Some commentators detected a move by the Conservatives to sustain Labour as Alliance support surged in the last days of the campaign. Thatcher, for example, denied that Labour would be eliminated or endangered as a party by its forthcoming defeat. This certainly reflected a concern to ensure that the party's heavily anti-Labour campaign did not lose bite and some concern about a potential Alliance bandwagon. Even then, however, the strategy was to talk only about the Conservative/Labour choice.

For as long as possible the Conservatives also ignored Labour's criticisms of the government, such as the 'secret manifesto' charge, and rarely reacted strongly. Many Labour claims rested on leaks of past Cabinet discussions and ministers stressed that these were unauthorized records of isolated discussions in a whole series of meetings that looked at possible options, most of which were never pursued. The only exception to this general immune response was on the NHS, which the Conservatives' own research showed to be a 'Labour issue'. On the same day (31 May) that Labour made this the central feature in its morning press conference, Thatcher declared that she 'despised' those who put out 'scare stories to alarm the sick and the elderly' and added that she 'would no more run down the National Health Service than I would run down the nation's defences'. Conservative spokesmen stressed watertight funding for the NHS in current public expenditure plans and increased staffing since 1979. Given the government's public stance of refusing to make pledges 'to buy votes', these assurances were undoubtedly effective.

4.3 The Labour campaign

One of the best press summaries of Labour's campaign described it as 'disaster snatched from the jaws of defeat' (Linton, 1983). We look at how Labour handled three key issues: its economic strategy, the 'secret manifesto' charge and the confusion over defence policy. We then discuss its national campaign.

4.3.1 The alternative economic strategy

As unemployment began to soar from mid-1980 onwards, Labour developed a rhetoric in which an embattled Britain, ravaged by the drastic economic experiments of monetarism, would look to the party for a radical remedy. This 'alternative economic strategy' (AES) was the product of extended debates in diverse contexts. First, the most important influence was union pressure for high industrial subsidies to cushion declining industries and to pump-prime the development of new activities. Much of this pressure was overtly protectionist and the largest unions were firmly opposed to remaining inside the EEC. Secondly, Labour academics and economists, especially the Cambridge Economic Policy Group, emphasized the difficulty in reducing mass unemployment. They argued that an effective devaluation of sterling, tariff protection for British manufacturing and other actions breaching the Common Market's open trading rules, would be needed if any progress on jobs was to be achieved. Thirdly, Labour's economic spokesman Peter Shore gave the policy a strong macro-economic emphasis, particularly in launching the AES publicly in November 1982, when he was widely interpreted as implying the necessity of a devaluation of up to 30 per cent in the current value of sterling. He always disclaimed any precise figure but the idea certainly influenced financial markets, where sterling's value was set to decline for other reasons.

Fourthly, many of the changes in Labour's economic thinking since 1979 were not apparent in the presentation of policies. For example, Labour local enterprise boards in the Greater London Council, the West Midlands, Sheffield and other areas used equity stakes in private companies to save and create jobs, completely rejecting old-style nationalization as a way forward. However, at the national level the proposals for state investment banking could easily be read (as they were by the Conservatives) as a further programme of conventional nationalization.

Lastly, Labour became committed to reducing unemployment by 2 million in a single parliamentary term. Although Shore repeatedly claimed that this target had been set after sophisticated economic modelling (and the party's election broadcasts duly wheeled out a couple of economics dons to agree that the figure was realistic), such an ambitious and specific commitment was widely seen as implausible (Chapter 7) and as requiring the sacrifice of other economic objectives if it was to be achieved. In particular, the party's proposals for controlling inflation involved only a vague voluntary social contract with the trade unions, now relabelled as a 'national economic assessment'. However, since the last social contract had ended in the winter of discontent (a theme in Conservative election broadcasts) and since trade union power had apparently dwindled so quickly in the anti-corporatist climate of the Thatcher government, these delphic pronouncements were insufficient to refute the Conservative and Alliance charges that a Labour administration would be unable to control inflation. Given the united hostility of the business community and the scepticism of the media, the Labour–trade union plan seemed isolated and implausible throughout the campaign.

4.3.2 'The secret manifesto'

Labour made a number of efforts in its electioneering during the campaign to exploit leaked documents. On 19 May Healey claimed on breakfast television that a 1981 Central Policy Review Staff report demonstrated that Thatcher and her Cabinet had 'lied' in presenting joblessness as an unanticipated consequence of the world recession. Labour leaders also tried to strengthen the message in the Commons Treasury Committee draft report attributing half the growth in United Kingdom unemployment since 1979 to government policy. At the beginning of the fourth week a special Labour press conference, run by Healey, was devoted to the prospects for Britain under a second Thatcher government. The existence of a 'hidden manifesto' was explicitly asserted and the following day was given over to a letter from the Department of Health and Social Security to the chairmen of regional health authorities that appeared to place renewed emphasis on the privatization of some NHS services. Roy Hattersley claimed that the government was intent on dismantling the NHS piecemeal, beginning with the privatization of ancillary services. This well-orchestrated presentation did at least trigger the firmest Thatcher assertion that the NHS was safe in Conservative hands.

Foot and Shore started Labour's final week by unveiling documents sent to the Chancellor of the Exchequer by the National Economic Development Office (NEDO) in March 1983; they dealt with the long-run prospects for the economy and unemployment. Labour suggested on this basis that up to 6 million people could be jobless by the end of the decade unless government policy was reversed. Government ministers denied that the NEDO projections were novel or official and claimed that they were not secret but intended for a relatively open consultation meeting between the government, the CBI and the TUC.

One of the side-effects of the preoccupation with the 'secret' manifesto was a lack of sustained criticism of the Conservatives' public proposals. Foot dismissed them early on as 'more of the same, shameful disastrous policies as before', a blanket condemnation reflected throughout Labour's campaign. Conservative proposals for local government were given some attention but Labour was almost silent on the trade union law proposals, except for a statement by the party chairman for 1982–3, the leader of the National Union of Seamen Sam McCluskie, to the effect that the Conservatives' proposals could precipitate a general strike. This claim was naturally interpreted by ministers as asserting that the unions would refuse to accept the general election's outcome.

4.3.3   Defence and the nuclear deterrent

In 1981 and 1982 Labour Conference resolutions unequivocally rejected the siting of American Cruise missiles on British territory, committed the party to scrapping purchase of a new Trident missile system and committed the next Labour government to disposing of Britain's existing Polaris deterrent within one parliamentary term. In addition, all American nuclear bases in the United Kingdom would be closed. All these points were set out clearly enough in the manifesto, although the dismantling of Polaris was linked to talks with the Soviet Union designed to reduce nuclear weapons stocks overall and there was a clear assertion of support for Britain's continued membership of NATO in a non-nuclear role.

However, from the outset of the campaign the leading Labour right-wingers, Healey, Hattersley and to a lesser extent Shore, came under pressure to explain how they reconciled support for Labour's manifesto with their belief in the effectiveness of nuclear deterrence strategies. At the start of the second week Healey suggested on television that Labour would get rid of Polaris only in the context of Soviet concessions of equivalent significance, although he was confident that such concessions would be forthcoming. He also claimed that abolition of the nuclear deterrent would go hand in hand with increases in conventional defence spending, possibly as much as doubling this in the short term. At the following morning's press conference he 'rubbed salt in the party's wounds' by repeating this analysis (*The Times*, 18 May 1983, p. 1). At the end of the week Hattersley was reported to be coming out against complete unilateral nuclear disarmament, while Healey made the most committed noises yet on an obscure Radio Leicester phone-in programme to the effect that, if Soviet arms concessions were *not* made, the Polaris deterrent would be retained. At the weekend Labour's defence spokesman, John Silkin, outlined a theme which he developed throughout the campaign, that with a non-nuclear defence policy Britain could assume a strong 'Navy of NATO' role, which would 'help widen Western strategy'.

The beginning of the third week's campaigning saw intense pressure from journalists about the need to clarify Labour's defence policy. Walworth Road drew up a statement on Sunday 22 May reiterating Labour's unequivocal commitment to scrap Polaris and other existing nuclear weapons within five years of gaining office. However, the statement was not released the following day, despite the run of questions at the press conference and to Michael Foot on his campaign tours. The party's General Secretary, Jim Mortimer, briefed journalists that Healey's interpretation was not party policy and Foot claimed simply that Labour's policy was perfectly clear in the manifesto. Healey and Shore were hinting semi-publicly that Labour had changed its stance on Polaris. *The Times* reported that Foot had accepted Healey's version of how the shift to a non-nuclear defence policy would take place, after the Deputy Leader had delivered an ultimatum to withdraw his campaign support unless a concession was made. At last, on the Tuesday, Foot authorized release of the Walworth Road clarification and repeated it in his evening speech. He attacked the *Times* report as 'malicious'. His efforts were wrecked by Callaghan's Cardiff speech doubting whether any Soviet concessions would be made if a Labour government were committed in advance to scrapping nuclear weapons. The pressure continued on Labour to clarify exactly how scrapping Polaris would be achieved, with some journalists interpreting the stance of 'moving' to a non-nuclear defence policy as a retreat from the Conference decisions. Forceful Labour criticisms of Healey and Callaghan for disloyalty and attempting to muddy waters quickly emerged. Some of Callaghan's local constituency workers withdrew their support from him. McCluskie attacked Healey for trying to fudge party policy.

During the fourth week the defence issue left the centre of the media stage, since journalists' suspicions of an attempted policy coup by the Labour right were no longer being fuelled by individual statements and front-bench spokesmen at last adhered to the Walworth Road line. However, by this time massive damage had been done to Labour's appearance of unity. It seems clear that Healey, Hattersley and Shore did engage in a more or less concerted effort to shift public perceptions of Labour's policies away from a 'come what may' abandonment of Polaris (which we shall see in Chapter 7 was unpopular with a large majority of voters) and towards a policy of putting Polaris into talks on mutual force reductions, which did have majority public support. Labour's panic-laden reaction to media pressure once this distinction had been revealed is harder to explain. It is difficult to see why the party accepted as valid the insistence of the media that it lay down a hard and fast commitment on an issue which was simultaneously so momentous and so difficult to anticipate in advance.

Lastly, public perceptions of Labour's policies were probably complicated by a series of actions against American nuclear missile bases mounted during the election period by the Campaign for Nuclear Disarmament. Demonstrations, arrests and property incursions featured frequently on television news and Conservative ministers (especially Michael Heseltine) associated

Labour with the policies of the demonstrators and, by implication, with support for their methods.

4.3.4 Labour's national campaign

Nine months' work by the right-wing NEC plus the stabilization in Labour's support at Darlington meant that Foot could successfully appeal for election funds to the affiliated unions. In general, the party was not short of money during the campaign and was able to afford private polling (carried out by MORI), some expensively produced election broadcasts and a bit of national press advertising. In other respects, however, the party's campaign was a retrogression from earlier elections, chiefly because there was no effective system of campaign co-ordination. In 1974 and 1979 Wilson and Callaghan had exercised direct control over the daily pattern of party activities, including scrutiny of the speeches of front-bench colleagues and decisions about themes in press conferences (Butler and Kavanagh, 1975, pp. 110–15; 1980, p. 174). However, Foot's extensive itinerary of speeches and visits meant that his role in campaign control was much reduced; he attended fewer than two-thirds of Labour's press conferences, for example. In addition, Jim Mortimer was a relative novice at political campaigning, having come into his post from the Advisory, Conciliation and Arbitration Service (ACAS) and the union world. Control devolved on to a large and unwieldy campaign committee, attended by as many as twenty people from the Shadow Cabinet; the NEC and the party's head office. This committee met daily. The key figures at these meetings were very much the same people who had dominated the NEC since the previous October, particularly Healey, Hattersley, Shore and John Golding – a right-wing union MP and NEC member who had been the main architect of the change in character of the National Executive. Foot, of course, was influential when he was present. However, other prominent party spokesmen were wholly absent (such as Tony Benn, enmeshed in a difficult election in Bristol East) or weighed down with a heavy burden of speeches in the constituencies (especially true of Neil Kinnock).

The campaign began badly for Labour, with little real mileage out of their earlier start of formal electioneering, although the response from the constituencies in the first two weeks was reasonably enthusiastic. At the start of the third week, with no overall reduction in the Conservatives' national lead, some campaign committee members pressed for a greater concentration of the party's efforts in marginal seats, but without getting an explicit decision on such a switch. Both the campaign committee and morale at Walworth Road weakened visibly during the uncertainty and press harassment over Labour's defence policy. On the morning after Callaghan's speech Jim Mortimer blurted out to the press conference that Michael Foot was 'still the party leader' and revealed that the campaign committee had passed a 'unanimous' vote of confidence in him – both statements that might have been calculated to increase rather than assuage speculation about Foot's leadership position.

At the start of the fourth week some changes were made. A small action committee was established in order to expedite implementation of the campaign committee's decisions. Healey relaunched the 'secret manifesto' charge and extensively outlined again the party's manifesto, a move interpreted by the *Daily Express* (31 May 1983, p. 1) as indicating that *de facto* party leadership had passed to him. Visual aids were introduced, securing somewhat better coverage on television of the party's press conferences. A supposedly tighter control was imposed upon themes to be raised by Shadow Cabinet members in their speeches. All of these efforts vanished into the dust storms created by Healey's 'glorying in slaughter' speech in mid-week. The end of the week saw powerful press and opinion poll backing for the Alliance policy of 'talking up' their level of support. Yet Walworth Road issued no statement at all in response to the Alliance 'hype' until on 6 June they denied that any increase in Alliance support was indicated by Labour's own *canvass returns*. The party's own private polls were apparently too depressing for even a spark of comfort. The reaction to Kinnock's 'guts at Goose Green' remarks was for once fairly competently handled. However, by this time two weeks of the broadcast media's equal coverage of the Labour campaign had been dissipated on examining divisions inside the party leadership and counter-productive abuse of Thatcher.

For the rest, Labour's campaign seemed ineffective. The press advertisements reiterated the forlorn slogan, 'Think Positive, Act Positive, Vote Labour', and were often small and inconspicuous. Far more eye-catching campaigns, not explicitly linked to support for Labour, were run by some of the trade unions, such as the advertisement of the National and Local Government Officers' Association (NALGO) featuring a jet fighter firing an air-to-air missile surmounted by the headline: 'BANG GOES ANOTHER KIDNEY UNIT'. There was no apparent co-ordination of Labour frontbench speeches, advertising or PEBs, and no clear development of themes during the campaign. Just about the only problem that did not revive much during the campaign was the Militant affair, although twelve professed members of the Tendency were Labour candidates – most famously Pat Wall in Bradford North, who was opposed by Ben Ford, the deselected incumbent MP standing as an Independent Labour candidate. Foot's itinerary involved his sharing a platform with four of the Militant candidates in Bradford, Liverpool and Brighton. The *Daily Express* (2 June 1983, p. 17) duly produced a list of seventy Labour left-wingers under the headline: 'SPOT THE TROTS', which included people such as Neil Kinnock with a three-star 'Trot' rating.

4.4   The Alliance campaign

Apart from their plan for cutting unemployment, the Alliance did not manage to promote any specific policy stance on to the front pages of the newspapers or the lead stories of the evening news. Their campaign overwhelmingly stressed the themes of 'moderation', reasonableness and an absence of bigotry. On virtually all policy issues their solutions lay somewhere in between those of the other parties. As practised by Steel and by Jenkins – the 'Prime Minister designate' in a putative Alliance government – this style did probably consolidate the loyalties of existing Alliance supporters. However, the elements of the Alliance campaign that brought them to the notice of uncommitted voters were chiefly reactions to daily events in the campaign itself. The master of these tactics was David Owen, who repeatedly formulated snappy criticisms of what other politicians were saying. His contributions were pointedly anti-Labour, reflecting his belief that the Alliance should go all out to take the fragmenting edges of Labour's support.

The difference between the Steel/Jenkins line and the Owen approach reflected a fundamental quandary for the Alliance. Throughout the campaign Labour voters looked more likely to be attracted, especially in southern England and in some constituencies where the MP had defected to the SDP. However, across the country as a whole, the operation of the plurality-rule election meant that a further reduction in the Labour vote would simply deliver huge numbers of seats to the Conservatives, but without giving the Alliance sufficient concentrations of support to elect more Liberal or SDP MPs. Alliance leaders were under no illusion about the probably miserable scale of their parliamentary representation after the election. Most poll predictions in the first two weeks suggested that the SDP could be virtually wiped out. Because of the areas where they hoped to win seats, the Liberals were more concerned to put over an anti-Conservative message, while Jenkins also stressed a reassuring and experienced image designed to appeal to Conservative voters. The public visibility of both messages was limited because the Conservative press picked up from the Alliance's output chiefly the attacks on Labour that fitted their own editorial line. For example, on 11 May the *Daily Mail* gave almost its entire front page to a fairly routine attack by Shirley Williams on the Labour Party, which was barely reported in other newspapers.

There were considerable problems in producing collaborative working between two distinct party organizations. Almost all campaign activities had to be approved by both parties and a large and somewhat disorganized campaign committee met daily for this purpose. The SDP, however, were paying for the Alliance's election broadcasts and private telephone polling by Audience Selection (whose published results consistently favoured the Alliance). Liberal control over the election broadcasts was firmer than over polling, which they had never used in previous general elections. The SDP imported an American film producer to advise on election broadcasts; he generated the ideas for a 'running mates' programme in which David Steel and Roy Jenkins talked in glowing terms about each other. One television critic thought that the result 'resembled nothing so much as an advert for a gay dating agency' (*Observer*, 22 May 1983, p. 40). The SDP also engaged an advertising firm (Gold Greenlees Trott) to advise on the presentation of the Alliance campaign; the firm found it difficult to liaise with their fragmented Alliance 'client'. The joint offices of the two party leaders, imitating Jenkins and Steel themselves, got on well together. However, much of the dynamism in the campaign was consistently provided by Owen, who operated on his own, talking extensively to the television news on his constituency tours but keeping away from campaign committee meetings.

By the third week Alliance anxieties about their median support of 19 per cent in the polls surfaced in pressures for a thorough review by Steel and the 'gang of four' of where they stood. Although Alliance leaders vigorously denied any concern about Jenkins's role in the campaign as 'Prime Minister designate', less official Liberal voices complained to the press about his low standing in the public's eyes compared with that of Steel. A trip to Wales by Jenkins in the third week to 'rediscover his roots' merely emphasized his remoteness from most voters. The Ettrick Bridge 'summit' was preceded by Owen's well-trailed suggestions of a major rethink of Alliance strategy, leading the media to speculate that Jenkins was about to be deposed from his nominal overall leadership role. Some Conservative newspapers duly reported this as the outcome, whereas the meeting was in the end largely cosmetic, skilfully designed to lure the television cameras up to Scotland on a quiet campaign weekend. Steel and Owen became more prominent in the Alliance's press conferences and their presentation began to stress that only a strong group of their MPs could successfully moderate the future policies of the coming second Thatcher administration.

Following the 'summit' the Alliance strategy of 'talking up' opinion poll support, together with Labour's 'own goals', showed handsome dividends in the fourth week. In addition, the Liberals and Social Democrats were buoyed by the journalistic imperative to find an angle to inject interest into an apparent walk-over election, which duly became whether the Alliance could beat Labour into second place. However, the attitudes of the Conservative news-papers hardened noticeably in the last few days before polling, with increased prominence for the likely fate of all but a handful of the SDP's 'turncoat' MPs. This may help to explain why, despite these bandwagon effects, the only last-minute swing was back towards Labour, squeezing the Alliance into a psychologically important third place in their national share of the vote.

5 Voting, Party Images and the Media in 1983

This chapter examines three aspects of voting behaviour that are directly related to the changing party fortunes during the first Thatcher government and to the campaign of June 1983: the relationship between short-run voting decisions and citizens' longer-term party loyalties, the way in which party organizations and leaders were perceived by voters, and the evidence for mass media influences on political alignments.

5.1 Party loyalties and voting in 1983

Any single election result provides only a snapshot of voters' political sympathies, a picture that may be especially unrepresentative following a campaign as one-sided as that in May and June 1983. The conventional tool for analysing the longer-term basis for political alignments has been that of 'party identification'. We are sceptical of the meaning that should be attached to this concept, especially when voting decisions and 'party identifications' are often inconsistent, as in our survey. None the less we asked our respondents: 'Generally speaking, do you think of yourself as closer to one of the parties than to the others? IF YES: Which party is this? (and) Is there a party you like second best?' Comparing responses with the way in which people actually voted reveals that most people did vote for the party to which they felt closest. Table 5.1(a) shows these data. However, people feeling closest to Labour were twice as likely as those closest to the other major parties to vote inconsistently, overwhelmingly favouring the Alliance. People close to no party were much more likely to stay at home on polling day but, when they did vote, the largest proportion opted for the Alliance. Looking at the distribution of second-party preferences shows an interesting picture, as Table 5.1(b) makes clear. About three-fifths of those closest to the Conservatives or Labour had a second preference for the Alliance, while just over one in three were 'loyalists' to their

Table 5.1 *Voting in the 1983 general election and second-preference party among those feeling closest to one party or none (in percentages)*

	Labour	Party felt closest to Conservative	Liberal/SDP	No party	Total sample
(a) 1983 General election vote					
Labour	79	1	2	12	25
Conservative	1	83	3	22	37
Alliance	10	5	81	38	24
Did not vote	10	12	14	29	14
Total:	100	101[1]	100	101	100
N:	264	369	140	165	938
(b) Second-preference party					
Labour	—	3	31	—	6
Conservative	7	—	27	—	6
Alliance	57	62	24	—	42
No party	36	35	18	100	46
Total:	100	100	100	100	100
N:	242	384	138	188	952

Note:
[1] Some of the percentage totals in this and later tables in the chapter contain rounding errors.

party alone. Amongst those closest to the Liberals or Social Democrats a quarter had a second preference for the other Alliance party and just over half for one of the other major parties.

Analysing the composition of each major party's votes shows many more significant differences between the older parties and the Alliance. Nine out of ten Conservative or Labour voters felt closest to that party, as Table 5.2(a) shows. However, barely half of all Alliance voters gave a consistent response to this question. A fifth of Alliance voters actually felt closest to one or other of the two major parties, while over a quarter felt close to none of the parties. Most of the non-voters in our sample felt close either to no party or to the Conservatives. Looking at first- and second-preference parties in Table 5.2(b) shows that again Conservative and Labour voters were similar to each other. Around one in three of their voters felt closest to them alone, while around half felt closest to the party for which they voted and second-closest to the Alliance. Yet only one in five Alliance voters felt closest only to the Liberals or SDP, almost as many as expressed a first preference for the Conservatives or Labour. Alliance voters to some extent resemble non-voters in the fragmentation of their feelings of closeness to the parties.

Another way of assessing the meaning of votes cast in 1983 is to place them in the context of respondents' earlier voting record. As with any cross-section survey we are dependent on people's subjective recall of their earlier votes, which may well be erroneous, so that these data need to be treated with some caution. Labour seems to have fared worst in holding on to its vote, a reversal of the situation in 1979 when the Liberals' ability to retain support was well

Table 5.2   *The first and second preferences of those eligible to vote in the 1983 general election (in percentages)*

	Vote in 1983				Total
	Labour	Conservative	Alliance	Did not vote	sample
(a) Closest party					
Labour	89	1	12	19	28
Conservative	1	88	9	32	39
Liberal/SDP	1	1	52	14	15
No party	9	10	28	35	18
Total:	100	100	101	100	100
N:	234	348	221	135	938

(b)   *Combinations of first and second closest parties*

Vote in 1983

Labour		Conservative		Alliance		Did not vote	
1 LAB 2 LSD[1]	46	1 CON 2 LSD	54	None	29	None	37
1 LAB 2 None	37	1 CON 2 None	30	1 LSD 2 None	21	1 CON 2 None	16
1 None	10	1 None	11	1 LSD 2 LAB	16	1 CON 2 LSD	16
1 LAB 2 CON	5	1 CON 2 LAB	3	1 LSD 2 CON	13	1 LAB 2 LSD	9
Others[2]	2	Others	2	1 LAB 2 LSD	11	1 LAB 2 None	6
				1 CON 2 LSD	8	1 LSD 2 LAB	6
				Others	2	1 LSD 2 None	6
						1 LSD 2 CON	3
						1 LAB 2 CON	2
Total:	100		100		100		100
N:	210		328		213		127

Notes:
[1] 'LSD' in this table means the Liberal Party *or* the Social Democratic Party.
[2] 'Others' includes all other permutations of preferences.

Table 5.3   *Vote in the 1983 general election by vote in 1979 (in percentages)*

	Vote in 1979					
	Labour	Conservative	Liberal	Other	Did not vote	Too young
Vote in 1983						
Labour	66	4	6	11	33	27
Conservative	8	80	17	50	37	42
Alliance	26	16	78	39	31	32
Total:	100	100	101	100	101	101
N:	286	331	71	18	49	41

Table 5.4   *The level of consistent voting between the 1979 and 1983 general elections amongst those feeling closest to one or more parties*

Parties felt closest to		Percentage voting in both 1979 and 1983 for party felt closest to	Percentage not voting in either 1979 or 1983 elections	N
1 Labour	2 None	81	15	87
1 Labour	2 Alliance	58	15	139
1 Labour	2 Conservative	44	31	16
1 Conservative	2 None	70	24	120
1 Conservative	2 Alliance	67	16	216
1 Conservative	2 Labour	33	33	12
1 Alliance	2 None	35	31	58
1 Alliance	2 Labour	35	19	43
1 Alliance	2 Conservative	16	19	37
No party preference		NA[1]	37	188
Total sample		NA	23	916

Note:
[1] 'NA' in this and other tables in this chapter means 'not applicable'.

below that of the two major parties (Dunleavy, 1983, pp. 46–7). Table 5.3 presents the 1979 and 1983 comparison. The Conservatives continued to do best in attracting consistent support across two elections.

Analysing the consistency of voting patterns according to the parties to which people felt closest shows an interesting pattern, which is revealed in Table 5.4. People who felt close to Labour, without a second preference, were much more likely to have voted for it in both 1979 and 1983 than were 1983 Labour supporters who had a second-party preference. On the other hand, Conservative supporters with an Alliance second preference were as consistent between 1979 and 1983 as those feeling close only to the Conservatives. Consistent voting amongst the smaller group feeling close to the Alliance was much less than for Conservative and Labour supporters. People feeling close only to the Alliance were rather likely to have been non-voters in at least one of the elections.

The large surge in Alliance support during the 1979–83 period and the substantial movement towards them during the campaign clearly raise questions about where their support came from and went to. We asked our respondents whether they had 'ever *seriously* considered voting' for parties other than their eventual choice, either in the inter-election period or during the campaign itself. These data are presented in Table 5.5. Nine out of ten eventual Labour or Alliance voters claimed not to have considered voting differently. However, over a quarter of eventual Conservative supporters remembered seriously considering a vote for the Alliance, chiefly during the inter-election period, but with some echoes of this earlier dalliance during the June 1983 campaign.

Finally, it is important to try to assess how voters construed their decisions

Table 5.5 *Whether people had seriously considered voting for another party, by vote in the 1983 general election*

| | Vote in 1983 | | |
	Labour	Conservative	Alliance
Percentage considering party before campaign			
Labour Party	NA	3	4
Conservative Party	4	NA	2
Liberal Party/SDP	1	23	NA
Percentage considering party during campaign			
Labour Party	NA	2	4
Conservative Party	3	NA	1
Liberal Party/SDP	3	10	NA
Percentage considering no other party	91	69	92
Total:	102[1]	107	103
N:	234	348	221

Note:
[1] These percentage totals exceed 100 because some respondents had considered voting for another party both before and during the campaign.

at the end of the campaign – what they saw as the reasons that led them to choose one party rather than another. Our survey question for this purpose was: 'In choosing how to vote, which of these would you say you were influenced *most* by? And what would you say was the *second most important* influence on your decision how to vote?' Options, offered on a showcard after initial piloting, were:

• the positive attractions of the party you voted for
• the national policy issues in the campaign
• the personalities of the party leaders
• the costs and benefits of the party programmes for you personally
• a commitment or loyalty to the party you voted for
• how people around you were intending to vote
• a wish to prevent some other party from being elected
• a wish to prevent a Conservative landslide
• some other influence.

We also asked those who had wanted to prevent some other party from being elected: 'Which party did you particularly wish to prevent from being elected?' Obviously, direct questions of this kind, using precoded answers, need to be interpreted with caution. However, some results are clear-cut. For example, only 2 per cent of our respondents said that they were influenced by people around them, a level consistent with our findings in Table 5.15 below on the

Table 5.6   *Percentages of voters for the three major parties in the 1983 general election who cited various reasons for their voting decision*

Labour voters

Preventing a Conservative victory or landslide	45[1]
Party loyalty or commitment	34
National policy issues	34
Labour Party's positive attractions	25
Personal costs and benefits	19
Personalities of leaders	8

Conservative voters

National policy issues	56
Conservative Party's positive attractions	42
Personalities of leaders	25
Preventing a Labour victory	24
Party loyalty or commitment	20
Personal costs and benefits	17

Alliance voters

Preventing (another party's) victory or landslide	48[1]
National policy issues	39
Preventing a Conservative victory or landslide	36
Positive attractions of Alliance and/or Liberal Party/SDP	29
Personalities of leaders	24
Preventing a Labour victory	16
Party loyalty or commitment	12
Personal costs and benefits	8

Note:
[1] These figures eliminate the double-counting of those mentioning a victory and a landslide as first and second reasons. For Alliance voters both preventing a Conservative victory and preventing a Labour one are included in 'preventing (another party's) victory or landslide'.

relatively minor role played by personal contacts in structuring people's political information. If interpersonal relations do affect people's voting behaviour, this must be an objective process rather than one operating through self-conscious attitude formation.

The most striking aspect of the answers is the variation between the different parties' voters in the influences that they cited; Table 5.6 gives some of our results. Labour and Alliance supporters were much more likely to give a 'negative voting reason' than were Conservative ones. More Labour supporters specified defeating the Conservatives (28 per cent) rather than just stopping a landslide (23 per cent). However, Alliance voters distributed their reasons differently, 25 per cent trying to avoid a Conservative landslide against 16 per cent wanting a Conservative defeat. One in six Alliance supporters voted to prevent a Labour victory and 4 per cent voted negatively against both the Conservatives and Labour. Conservative voters were much more positive, stressing national policy issues in the campaign and the positive attractions of their party far more than anti-Labour sentiment. By contrast, Labour supporters mentioned loyalty to the party more than did any other group and de-emphasized the positive attractions or personality factors. Alliance voters rarely cited party loyalty as an influence, understandably enough since it was a new political formation. They were also less likely to cite personal costs and benefits as having influenced their voting decision, perhaps indicating the expressive quality of Alliance support.

5.2   Voters' images of the parties in 1983

The role of generalized voter images of parties and their leaderships in structuring voting decisions remains the focus of considerable controversy. Attitudes of this kind tend to be quite closely interrelated with voting behaviour but it is difficult to establish in which direction (if any) the causal influences run. Someone who has voted for a party may well adjust his or her responses to attitude questions about its image or leadership in order to produce a consistent response. Nor has any existing literature unequivocally established the salience of particular 'image' components with the public at any given time, not least because the context of public evaluation may change rapidly from one period to another. We cannot say what precise level of importance should be ascribed to voters' attitudes in this area. They obviously play some role but they do not seem to be dominant influences on how people vote.

We asked our respondents five questions about the party leaders (Foot, Thatcher, Steel and Jenkins) and seven about the parties themselves. Because responses on party images or perceptions of leaders (like all data on attitudes) are very sensitive to question wording, we have clustered our response items into four groups: the relationship between the parties/leaders and 'ordinary people'/'people like me'; the parties and 'the national interest'/'the interests of the country as a whole'; the conduct of parties' internal affairs; and the competence and style of party leaders. All the response items were designed to tap dimensions of evaluation that had been suggested as important influences on public opinion during the 1979–83 period. Each question sought responses on the four-point scale: Agree strongly/Tend to agree/Tend to disagree/ Disagree strongly.[1] Because people with uncertain views tend to choose the weak 'Tend to agree/disagree' options, we focus first on those giving agree/ disagree strongly answers on individual items and second on those who *consistently* agree or disagree with the three questions in each cluster. By alternating the 'slant' of the response items irregularly – with half the items favourable and half critical of the parties or leaders – we tried to avoid leading respondents. Finally, we have analysed all the attitude data in this section using respondents' most preferred party rather than their 1983 vote, since on these dimensions of public appraisal the notion of longer-run party attachments may make more of a difference to attitudes.

5.2.1   *The parties and 'ordinary people'*

We asked our respondents to agree or disagree that each party leader 'Cares for the concerns of people like me', or 'Acts in the interest of ordinary people', and

Table 5.7 *Percentages of respondents agreeing/disagreeing strongly with three response items on 'ordinary people'/'people like me' concerning parties and party leaders*

(a) *Leader . . . 'Cares for the concerns of people like me'*

	Agree strongly (+)	Disagree strongly (−)	Balance	N
Steel	16	5	+11	852
Foot	20	16	+4	917
Jenkins	8	13	−5	751
Thatcher	16	24	−8	930

(b) *Leader . . . 'Acts in the interest of ordinary people'*

	Agree strongly (+)	Disagree strongly (−)	Balance	N
Steel	20	4	+16	874
Foot	22	13	+9	932
Jenkins	8	12	−4	768
Thatcher	17	24	−7	938

(c) *Party . . . 'Couldn't care less about people like me'*

	Disagree strongly (+)	Agree strongly (−)	Balance	N
Liberal Party	19	4	+15	846
Labour Party	24	12	+12	920
SDP	17	6	+11	797
Conservative Party	17	22	−5	953

that each party 'Couldn't care less about people like me'. In general, the Conservative and Labour parties and leaders evoked much stronger responses and fewer 'don't knows' than did the Alliance parties, as Table 5.7 demonstrates. The Liberals and Steel obtained the most favourable balance of agree strongly minus disagree strongly responses. Labour won most strong disagreement that it could not care less and that its leader was the one most identified as caring for the concerns of ordinary people. Jenkins attracted more strong criticism than support but the SDP itself gained similar responses to the Liberals. Despite having the largest number of party supporters in our sample, the Conservatives attracted more strongly negative answers than strongly positive ones on all three statements.

It is not very useful to present all agree/disagree responses on individual items, for we should then run the serious risk of attributing to people views that they do not really hold. However, we can bring weaker responses into the analysis by looking at those who consistently agree that a party leader 'acts in the interest of ordinary people' and 'cares for the concerns of people like me', while disagreeing that the party 'couldn't care less about people like me'. By contrast, a consistently unfavourable response pattern involves disagreeing with the first two statements and agreeing with the last. Even if someone gives a weak response on one item, we may legitimately see it as seriously held if it is

Table 5.8   *Overall perceptions of parties and party leaders on the three response items in Table 5.7 (in percentages)*

	Consistently favourable	Consistently unfavourable	Balance	N
Whole sample				
View of Liberal Party/Steel	70	6	+64	748
View of SDP/Jenkins	49	15	+34	633
View of Labour Party/Foot	46	19	+27	826
View of Conservative Party/Thatcher	35	33	+2	867
View of Liberal Party/Steel				
Alliance supporters	88	1	+87	131
Conservative supporters	68	5	+63	273
Labour supporters	65	7	+58	149
No partisan loyalty	65	9	+56	128
View of SDP/Jenkins				
Alliance supporters	77	6	+71	119
Conservative supporters	45	17	+28	237
No partisan loyalty	45	18	+27	128
Labour supporters	36	18	+18	149
View of Labour Party/Foot				
Labour supporters	82	3	+79	229
No party loyalty	44	20	+24	179
Alliance supporters	42	17	+25	121
Conservative supporters	20	40	−20	297
View of Conservative Party/Thatcher				
Conservative supporters	70	3	+67	323
No party loyalty	23	39	−16	191
Alliance supporters	17	36	−18	122
Labour supporters	6	68	−61	231

matched by similar or stronger responses on closely related questions. Table 5.8 presents these analyses. Again, voters took an overwhelmingly favourable view of the Liberals, while the SDP's rating was significantly less favourable – similar in fact to that of the Labour Party, which also has a fairly healthy balance of opinions on these issues. The Conservatives gained the consistent support of barely a third of respondents and virtually the same proportion of criticism. Clearly, the basis for their electoral appeal in 1983 was not a populism based on being identified with ordinary people's interests.

As we might expect, the parties attracted consistently favourable responses from people who felt closest to them. In addition, however, the Liberals were seen in a favourable light by supporters of other parties, although far more people did not know what they thought of the Alliance parties than was true of Conservative and Labour parties. By contrast, the SDP attracted relatively few consistently favourable reactions from Labour supporters. Labour was seen quite favourably by those closest to no party and by Alliance supporters but very unfavourably by those closest to the Conservatives. Even here, however,

Table 5.9 *Percentages of respondents agreeing/disagreeing strongly on three response items on 'national interest'/'country as a whole'/'promise anything to win votes' concerning party leaders and parties*

(a) *Leader . . . 'Is genuinely concerned about the national interest'*

	Agree strongly (+)	Disagree strongly (−)	Balance	N
Thatcher	37	8	+29	970
Foot	27	9	+18	967
Steel	26	8	+18	953
Jenkins	16	15	+1	924

(b) *Party . . . 'Acts in the interest of the country as a whole'*

	Agree strongly (+)	Disagree strongly (−)	Balance	N
Conservative Party	26	10	+16	940
Liberal Party	14	3	+11	825
SDP	12	5	+7	775
Labour Party	17	15	+2	920

(c) *Party . . . 'Will promise anything to win votes'*

	Disagree strongly (+)	Agree strongly (−)	Balance	N
Liberal Party	9	16	−7	866
SDP	8	17	−9	835
Conservative Party	14	26	−12	950
Labour Party	9	36	−27	954

one in five Conservatives gave consistently favourable responses. On the other hand, in terms of caring about ordinary people the Conservatives were regarded very unfavourably by everybody except their own supporters. Twice as many people close to the Alliance or to no party took a consistently unfavourable view of the Conservatives as took a favourable view, while amongst those closest to Labour the ratio was more than eleven times as many unfavourable reactions.

5.2.2   The parties and 'the national interest'

We asked our respondents whether each party leader 'Is genuinely concerned about the national interest', and if each party 'Acts in the interest of the country as a whole' or 'Will promise anything to win votes'. On these items the distributions of strong agreement and disagreement clearly favoured the Conservatives and disadvantaged Labour, as Table 5.9 shows. The Conservatives obtained a healthy positive balance on the first two items but attracted criticism on their 'promising' – as did all the parties to some degree. The Alliance parties did moderately well on all the questions, except that Jenkins's concern for the national interest evoked little strong agreement and almost as much dissent. Foot outperformed Jenkins on concern for the national interest

Table 5.10   *Overall perceptions of parties and party leaders on the three response items concerning parties and party leaders in Table 5.9 (in percentages)*

	Consistently favourable	Consistently unfavourable	Balance	N
Whole sample				
View of Liberal Party/Steel	42	5	+37	759
View of SDP/Jenkins	34	9	+25	709
View of Conservative Party/Thatcher	38	15	+23	888
View of Labour Party/Foot	21	22	−1	872
View of Liberal Party/Steel				
Alliance supporters	66	0	+66	124
Conservative supporters	42	6	+36	290
No partisan loyalty	35	4	+31	152
Labour supporters	32	7	+25	193
View of SDP/Jenkins				
Alliance supporters	60	0	+60	123
No partisan loyalty	31	8	+23	139
Conservative supporters	30	12	+18	266
Labour supporters	25	13	+12	181
View of Conservative Party/Thatcher				
Conservative supporters	69	0	+69	343
Alliance supporters	31	15	+16	130
No party loyalty	25	14	+11	185
Labour supporters	8	38	−30	230
View of Labour Party/Foot				
Labour supporters	49	2	+47	238
Alliance supporters	18	18	0	126
No party loyalty	14	20	−6	180
Conservative supporters	6	40	−34	328

but Labour's ability to act in the interest of the country as a whole provoked almost as much dissent as agreement. On the last item, Labour's performance was markedly poor, with over a third of people strongly agreeing that the party will promise anything to win votes.

As Table 5.10 shows, over 40 per cent of respondents took a consistently favourable view of the Liberals, agreeing that Steel is genuinely concerned about the national interest and that the party acts in the interest of the country as a whole, while disagreeing that it will promise anything to win votes. Only one in twenty reversed their stance on all three propositions. The SDP attracted rather less agreement and slightly more dissent. However, far fewer people ventured a view about the two Alliance parties. One in five respondents with the full range of views about the Conservatives or Labour had no views about the SDP on at least one of the response items. The Conservatives came close to the Liberals in being consistently seen as oriented to the national interest (and they certainly attracted the largest number of favourable statements). However, they also evoked three times as much consistent dissent,

Table 5.11 *Percentages of respondents agreeing/disagreeing strongly with three response items on the conduct of party affairs*

(a) *Party . . . 'Operates its own affairs in a democratic manner'*

	Agree strongly (+)	Disagree strongly (−)	Balance	N
Conservative Party	21	7	+14	840
Liberal Party	16	3	+13	762
SDP	15	4	+11	711
Labour Party	13	20	−7	842

(b) *Party . . . 'Acts in favour of the groups that finance it'*

	Disagree strongly (+)	Agree strongly (−)	Balance	N
Liberal Party	5	13	−8	609
SDP	5	13	−8	585
Conservative Party	4	32	−28	816
Labour Party	4	38	−34	834

(c) *Party . . . 'Has policies approved by party members but not by most of the general public'*

	Disagree strongly (+)	Agree strongly (−)	Balance	N
Liberal Party	7	7	0	711
SDP	7	8	−1	662
Conservative Party	8	19	−11	833
Labour Party	5	29	−24	828

reducing their favourable balance to a level below that of the SDP. By contrast, barely a fifth of respondents consistently saw Labour as acting in a publicly interested manner. A majority saw Labour as promising anything to win votes, chiefly because of its ambitious but implausible alternative economic strategy (Chapter 7).

Labour was the party seen in the most unfavourable light by the supporters of other parties. In addition, fewer than half of all *Labour* supporters consistently defended their party. On these statements the Conservatives evoked much more loyalty from those close to the party and they secured a balance of favourable responses from Alliance supporters and those close to no party. Labour respondents were predictably more critical, although without the unanimity shown in Table 5.8. The Alliance parties attracted a balance of consistently favourable responses, despite far more people being without any substantive opinion. Labour supporters were rather more favourable to the Liberals than to the SDP.

5.2.3 Parties' conduct of their own affairs

We asked respondents to agree or disagree that each party 'Operates its own affairs in a democratic manner', 'Acts in favour of the groups that finance it', and 'Has policies approved by party members but not by most of the general

Table 5.12   *Overall perceptions of parties on three response items in Table 5.11 on the conduct of party affairs (in percentages)*

	Consistently favourable	Consistently unfavourable	Balance	N
Whole sample				
View of Liberal Party	25	5	+20	491
View of SDP	23	7	+16	457
View of Conservative Party	13	19	−6	678
View of Labour Party	5	42	−37	682
View of Liberal Party				
Alliance supporters	33	3	+30	110
Conservative supporters	26	4	+22	268
Labour supporters	19	5	+14	112
No partisan loyalty	21	10	+11	101
View of SDP				
Alliance supporters	33	0	+33	95
No partisan loyalty	19	5	+14	88
Labour supporters	17	4	+13	100
Conservative supporters	22	10	+12	174
View of Conservative Party				
Conservative supporters	23	4	+19	268
Alliance supporters	5	24	−19	111
No party loyalty	9	28	−19	137
Labour supporters	5	34	−29	162
View of Labour Party				
Labour supporters	13	12	+1	169
No party loyalty	4	41	−37	135
Alliance supporters	1	43	−42	110
Conservative supporters	0	61	−61	268

public'. However, some Labour supporters (especially those in trade unions) clearly interpreted the party's acting in favour of the trade unions as a positive rather than a negative feature, so that this item needs to be cautiously interpreted for this group.

The Conservatives did best overall in terms of being seen to conduct their own affairs in a democratic manner, as Table 5.11 shows. The Alliance parties evoked less strong agreement and dissent, giving all parties except Labour favourable balances of opinion. Labour was quite widely seen as not democratically run, despite all the public agonizing since 1979 about internal party democracy. In terms of favouring the groups that finance it, Labour also did rather worse than the Conservatives, despite the equivocal meaning of the question for some of its supporters. The established parties are clearly seen as beholden to their financial backers, while the Alliance attracted only a generalized cynicism about all parties rather than anything specific to their operations. Finally, in terms of having policies approved by party members but not by most of the general public, the Liberals and SDP were the most favourably perceived, while Labour attracted especially unfavourable responses. The Conservatives' poorish rating on this item is interesting when set against their plurality support at this time. This must rank as one of several indications in these data that party image is not a major determinant of voting; many people vote for a party despite, rather than because of, certain important components of its image.

Table 5.12 shows that the Alliance parties attracted a healthy balance of consistent positive responses, although again fewer voters had views about them. More people took a steadfastly adverse view of the Conservatives. Labour was seen by more than two out of every five voters in a consistently unfavourable light, placing the party well behind all the others in public esteem. There is no great tendency for party supporters to take a consistently favourable view of 'their' party. A third of Alliance supporters and fewer than a quarter of Conservative ones made no criticisms of their own leaderships. Because of the ambiguous meaning of the interest group question for Labour supporters, their high incidence of consistently *unfavourable* answers is the most significant indicator. Both Alliance parties attracted more favourable than unfavourable reactions even from their non-partisans, although far fewer people had any sort of view about them. People not close to the Conservatives tended to see them adversely but Tory and Alliance supporters were much more likely to have an unfavourable view of Labour.

Table 5.13 *Percentages of respondents agreeing/disagreeing strongly with three response items on party leaderships*

(a) Party ... 'Has leaders capable of running the country'

	Agree strongly (+)	Disagree strongly (−)	Balance	N
Conservative Party	53	5	+48	972
Liberal Party	24	7	+17	886
SDP	14	15	−1	820
Labour Party	13	38	−25	931

(b) Leader ... 'Thinks his/her viewpoint is more important than that of anybody else'

	Disagree strongly (+)	Agree strongly (−)	Balance	N
Thatcher	3	53	−50	950
Foot	12	21	−9	896
Steel	8	14	−6	841
Jenkins	9	13	−4	760

(c) Leader ... 'Presents problems as being more simple than they really are'

	Disagree strongly (+)	Agree strongly (−)	Balance	N
Steel	9	10	−1	775
Thatcher	15	18	−3	882
Jenkins	7	12	−5	682
Foot	7	27	−20	862

Table 5.14   *Overall perceptions of parties on three response items in Table 5.13 on party leaderships (in percentages)*

	Consistently favourable	Consistently unfavourable	Balance	N
Whole sample				
View of Liberal Party/Steel	25	9	+16	699
View of Conservative Party/Thatcher	10	9	+1	838
View of SDP/Jenkins	15	17	−2	572
View of Labour Party/Foot	8	32	−24	785
View of Liberal Party/Steel				
Alliance supporters	46	3	+43	114
No partisan loyalty	23	10	+13	145
Conservative supporters	22	10	+12	269
Labour supporters	21	11	+10	171
View of Conservative Party/Thatcher				
Conservative supporters	19	0	+19	317
Alliance supporters	11	7	+4	124
No partisan loyalty	7	11	−4	185
Labour supporters	1	18	−17	215
View of SDP/Jenkins				
Alliance supporters	23	3	+20	104
Conservative supporters	15	20	−5	224
No partisan loyalty	15	22	−7	109
Labour supporters	10	18	−8	135
View of Labour Party/Foot				
Labour supporters	20	14	+6	202
Alliance supporters	7	30	−23	112
No partisan loyalty	6	38	−32	177
Conservative supporters	2	42	−40	294

5.2.4   Party leaderships

We asked our respondents whether each party 'Has leaders capable of running the country', and if each party leader 'Thinks his/her viewpoint is more important than that of anybody else' or 'Presents problems as being more simple than they really are'. Table 5.13 shows that Conservative leaders were clearly seen by most respondents as capable. The Liberals secured only half this level of agreement and the SDP failed to gain a favourable balance of strong responses. Nearly 40 per cent of voters strongly disagreed that Labour had capable leaders, doubtless reflecting widespread public uncertainty about Foot (Chapter 3). Thatcher was perceived by over half of respondents as thinking her own views more important than anyone else's but the other party leaders also attracted more criticism than support on this item, with Foot polarizing views far more than the Alliance leaders. All the leaders were seen as presenting problems as more simple than they really are, again with Foot coming off worst.

Steel did best among the party leaders in projecting a consistently favourable image, as Table 5.14 shows. By contrast, Jenkins generated more criticism than consistent support, as well as startlingly high numbers of 'don't know' responses. Only a tenth of respondents had no critical view of Thatcher but equally few were consistent detractors of her leadership. Foot undoubtedly came off worst in attracting a large net balance of consistently critical opinions.

Party supporters were quite discriminating in their views of leaders. Only a quarter of people closest to the Alliance took a consistently favourable view of Jenkins and only one in five of those close to the Conservatives or Labour had no unfavourable view of their leaders. Steel was the only leader to attract more favourable than unfavourable reactions from all groups. Foot still evoked consistently favourable responses from those closest to Labour. His overall unpopularity stemmed chiefly from the hostility of Conservative supporters and uncommitted people towards him.

5.3   Media influences on voting in 1983

Our analysis of media influence differs from other approaches in being informed by a wider range of theoretical perspectives, in particular, the radical approach to media analysis that stresses the importance of the overall climate of media values in influencing citizens' views into convergent patterns of thinking (Glasgow University Media Group, 1976, 1980; Philo *et al.*, 1982). From this perspective we should be less concerned about trying to gauge the political impact achieved by any one media source – such as a single newspaper – and focus attention instead upon the overall climate of media influence to which people have been exposed.

A first stage is to determine where voters obtain their political information. Table 5.15 shows that watching television was cited as their most important source of political information by more than twice as many respondents as referred to newspapers. However, if we broaden attention to include the top two sources of political information, and control for those respondents who do not read a daily newspaper, the apparent hegemony of television disappears. Almost the entire sample included television news in their top two sources of information. However, the same is true of newspaper readers as a group, once allowance is made for the 16 per cent of respondents who do not read a daily newspaper. On the other hand, radio serves as a primary source of news chiefly for people without television sets and as a secondary source for non-readers of newspapers. Only a small minority of people seem to use personal sources as an important way in which to obtain their information about politics, despite our inclusion of three prompts about friends and neighbours, people at work and other members of the family.

There are no strong associations between people's major sources of political information and their political alignment. Those who cited newspapers as their most important channel of such information are slightly more Conservative and disinclined to vote for the Alliance than those who cited television. However, for a more useful analysis we need to know in much finer detail which elements of media output structure people's political cognitions, infor-

Table 5.15   *Voters' major sources of political information*

Media source	Percentages citing source		Percentages citing source in top two media sources	
	As most important media source	In top two sources	Amongst newspaper readers	Amongst non-readers
Television	63	88	88	85
Newspapers	29	73	80	35
Radio	4	14	11	29
Personal contacts	3	12	9	27
Other	1	3	—	—
Total:	100	NA		
N:	1,009		849	160

Major combinations of media sources (in percentages)

Primary source	Secondary source	
Television	Newspapers	45
Newspapers	Television	25
Television	Radio	8
Television	Personal sources	8
Newspapers	Radio	2
Radio	Television	2
All other combinations of sources		10
Total:		100

mation that is hard to obtain about television sources using survey methods. Most television presentation is so similar that there are few differences in political attitudes among those who rely on one programme source rather than another (Seymour-Ure, 1974).

By contrast, newspapers' highly partisan coverage of the election campaign and the events of the preceding four years (culminating in direct advice to their readers on how to vote) clearly creates a potential for political influence (Harrop, 1984). There is, in addition, a sparsely researched tradition of trying to gauge the influence of single newspapers upon their readerships (e.g., Miller, Brand and Jordan, 1982). However, even if an association is established between reading a newspaper and adopting a congruent alignment, it is not clear which of these pieces of behaviour should be seen as the cause and which as the effect. People may use political criteria in deciding which newspaper to read in the first place, or they may decide what to buy on other grounds and be influenced by the newspaper's coverage into seeing political affairs from its perspective, or both processes may be involved in an observed association. Most studies have shown a linkage between press readership and voting behaviour, but not one strong enough to suggest that the partisan slant of news reporting is a dominant causal factor, after making allowances for a plausible level of self-selection into readership. Only Butler and Stokes (1969, pp. 265–300) followed through the development of newspaper readers' political views over time. They argued that there was a pronounced tendency for readers with views inconsistent with their newspaper's political slant to shift their allegiance so as to bring them into line.

From a radical perspective, however, the preoccupation with whether or not a single newspaper can influence its readers' politics is unjustified. It is unlikely that a gross effect such as a change in voting behaviour would correlate very closely with a finely graduated variable such as newspaper readership. Rather, our concern should be with the overall level of pluralism in the mass media messages to which voters are exposed. Given the increasing tendency for readers of 'popular' newspapers to read more than one title regularly (either because they buy two newspapers or because they swap papers with work colleagues), we can distinguish in quite a sophisticated manner between those press readers involved with a homogeneous or undifferentiated stream of political information from the press and those exposed to more mixed stimuli.

We may distinguish four types of press message:

1   The Tory press proper consists of those Fleet Street titles that consistently supported the Conservative government against other parties throughout its term and advocated voting Conservative in June 1983, namely, the *Sun, Daily Express, Daily Mail, Daily Telegraph, The Times* and the *Financial Times*, plus the London evening newspaper the *Standard*.

2   The Labour press consists of the *Daily Mirror* and in Scotland the *Daily Record*, the only titles consistently to criticize the Conservative government's record and directly to advocate voting Labour in 1983.

3   The 'non-Tory' press includes two Fleet Street titles that mixed their messages to readers over this period. The *Guardian* was broadly anti-Conservative throughout the period but did not clearly advocate either an Alliance or a Labour vote. The *Daily Star* was fairly clearly anti-Conservative in 1980–1, still critical in 1982–3 but reluctantly concluded that they could not support Labour (as too extreme) or the Alliance (as too inexperienced) in 1983, somewhat ingenuously advocating a vote for Thatcher's 'leadership' capabilities.

4   The 'other' press consists chiefly of regional daily morning or evening newspapers. Many of them are owned by national chains that produce overtly Tory papers on Fleet Street and so their preponderant colouring is again Conservative. This is significantly qualified, however, by their greatly reduced partisanship. While virtually all regional newspapers do have an explicit political line (unlike local weeklies, which cultivate a frequently bogus non-partisanship), this is usually restricted to formal editorializing. It rarely extends to the highly slanted presentation of lead stories and to the incessant propagandizing characteristic of the national popular press.

Our sample's exposure to press influences conforms closely to data on newspaper circulations and common-sense expectations of how different readerships cast their votes are broadly confirmed. Amongst the Tory press the Conservatism of *Daily Telegraph* readers is very marked, but in other titles

Table 5.16   *Voting in the 1983 general election and newspaper readership*

Newspaper	Vote in 1983 (%)			CON lead over LAB	N	1983 sales[1]	% of sample
	LAB	CON	ALL				
Daily Telegraph	3	85	12	+82	67	1·28	7
The Times/Financial Times	8	60	33	+52	27	0·48	3
Daily Express	15	63	22	+48	106	1·94	12
Daily Mail	16	58	26	+42	111	1·83	13
Sun	34	40	26	+6	177	4·15	23
All Tory press	20	55	24	+35	430	9·68	43
Other daily newspaper	27	49	25	+22	196	NA	24
Guardian	45	14	41	−31	49	0·42	6
Daily Star	48	21	31	−27	48	1·31	6
Non-Tory press	46	18	36	−28	94	1·73	11
Labour press (Daily Mirror/Record)	53	24	23	−29	199	3·27	24

Note:
[1] Figures for sales are in millions of copies and are the mean of monthly Audit Bureau of Circulation figures for the full year preceding the June 1983 general election.

around six out of ten readers vote Conservative and only one in six at most vote Labour. The (large) exception remains the *Sun*, where readers' political affiliations remain balanced, despite its uncompromising political line. Readers of 'other' daily newspapers show a lesser level of Conservative predominance. Despite their very different composition in terms of social class, readers of the two non-Tory newspapers are very similar in their political views, with a healthy Labour lead over the Conservatives and stronger Alliance support. Finally, *Daily Mirror/Record* readers showed the strongest levels of Labour voting.

These data still include a good deal of multiple counting of people who read more than one daily newspaper. Controlling for mixed readership reveals that more than one in three voters read a single Tory press title. By contrast, although Labour newspapers were seen by nearly a quarter of our sample, only 11 per cent read no other daily newspaper, about the same proportion as depended on regional papers and around twice that of those who read only a non-Tory newspaper. Altogether, 58 per cent of voters depended on one daily newspaper, with 26 per cent reading two or more regularly and 16 per cent reading none. There is now an even clearer match between voters' political orientation and their press exposure, as Table 5.17 reveals. The Conservative vote and the Conservative lead over Labour are highest amongst readers of the Tory press and next highest amongst other press readers. However, both fall dramatically amongst people who either read no newspaper at all or are exposed to a Labour or non-Tory newspaper. Alliance voting increases sharply amongst people who do not read a daily newspaper and hence rely chiefly on the broadcast media. This is an especially interesting result when we consider

Table 5.17   *Voting in the 1983 general election and type of press readership (in percentages)*

	LAB	CON	ALL	CON lead over LAB	N	% of Three-party voters
Two Tory newspapers	9	65	27	+56	34	4
Mixed Tory newspapers[1]	16	62	22	+46	74	9
One Tory newspaper	16	60	24	+44	244	30
One other newspaper	20	54	26	+34	87	12
No daily newspaper	27	30	43	+3	129	16
Mixed Tory/Labour	45	32	23	−13	78	9
Mixed Labour/other	51	27	22	−24	37	4
One non-Tory newspaper	56	8	35	−48	48	6
One Labour newspaper	62	14	24	−48	84	11

Note:
[1] 'Mixed Tory newspapers' include the readerships of a Tory paper plus an 'other' or a 'non-Tory' newspaper (but not a Labour one).

the general lack of social distinctiveness in Alliance support. Readers of the non-Tory press and those taking a Labour newspaper are much the same in their political affiliations, except that Alliance voting is noticeably higher in the former group.

The relationship that we have traced seems too close to be attributable solely or even mainly to partisan self-selection into readership. We can further control for a selection effect by incorporating social background variables, of which the most important known correlate with readership behaviour is social class. We deploy a four-category measure of social class, one that is explained in more detail in Chapter 6. We have also reformulated the readership categories given above into a new four-category variable, whose categories are as follows:

1 People exposed to predominantly Tory press influences (that is, Tory newspapers alone, or a Tory title and a regional daily) [Tory Predominance].
2 People exposed to more mixed or less partisan influences (that is, reading a Tory newspaper together with a non-Tory or Labour one, or reading only a regional newspaper) [Mixed Influences].
3 People who do not read a daily newspaper [No Newspaper].
4 People exposed chiefly to non-Tory or Labour messages (that is, reading a single newspaper in this group or any combination of titles involving a Labour or non-Tory newspaper without a Tory press title) [Non-Tory Predominance].

The control on social class further sharpens the differences that exist between people who are in the same social background but who receive different sorts of mass media messages and political information. Table 5.18

Table 5.18   *Voting in the 1983 general election by press exposure and social class (in percentages)*

Social class	Collapsed press category	LAB	CON	ALL	CON lead over LAB	N
Manual workers	Tory predominance	28	45	26	+17	125
	Mixed influences	44	29	28	−15	87
	No newspaper	50	16	34	−34	50
	Non-Tory predominance	71	9	20	−62	79
Non-manual workers	Tory predominance	8	64	28	+56	78
	Mixed influences	12	67	21	+55	42
	No newspaper	13	25	63	+12	40
	Non-Tory predominance	46	20	34	−26	39
Controllers of labour	Tory predominance	3	78	20	+75	80
	Mixed influences	16	58	26	+42	43
	No newspaper	14	46	39	+32	28
	Non-Tory predominance	46	20	34	−26	35
Employers, etc.	Tory predominance	3	85	12	+82	34

shows this clearly. Within all the class categories used the Conservative vote is some 30 percentage-points lower amongst people primarily exposed to non-Tory messages than it is amongst readers of the Tory press, a high level of association that has few parallels amongst either social background or issue influences (see Chapters 6 and 7). The difference is even more marked when we compare the two extreme groups, those exposed to a predominantly Tory message and those receiving a predominantly non-Tory one; the differences in Conservative support range from 36 to 58 points.

Finally on press exposure, we need to take account of the role of the Sunday newspapers. Their potential electoral impact is clearly much less since voters saw just five issues in the 1983 campaign compared with twenty-eight daily issues. There is considerable continuity of readership habits across the two types of newspapers, produced particularly by 'family' titles. However, political news and coverage form a very small part of the output of 'popular' Sundays, especially the three largest circulation titles, the *News of the World*, *Sunday People* and *Sunday Mirror*, none of which ran the election campaign as a major lead story in more than one issue. The *News of the World* is a Conservative newspaper in editorial line but it regularly gives space to Labour and Alliance spokesmen. The *Sunday People* is chiefly 'non-political' with an anti-Conservative tinge, while the *Sunday Mirror* urged a Labour vote but without any of the elaborate propagandizing of its daily counterpart. For our analysis we have grouped all three into a 'non-political' category. By contrast, the 'quality' Sundays place a special emphasis on political coverage and weighty editorializing. The *Observer* is markedly opposed to the government and is the only Sunday title to qualify as a non-Tory newspaper in our analysis. The *Sunday Telegraph* is an equally firm Tory title. Despite some more mixed reporting and a slightly equivocal endorsement of the Thatcher government's

Table 5.19   *Voting in the 1983 general election by Sunday newspaper readership (in percentages)*

Readership category	LAB	CON	ALL	CON lead over LAB	N
Tory newspaper or Tory mix	14	59	27	+45	243
No Sunday newspaper	26	45	30	+19	186
Mixed influences	36	32	32	−4	81
Non-political newspapers only	43	32	25	−11	267
Non-Tory newspaper	41	22	37	−19	27

record, the *Sunday Times* has become consistently Tory, especially so since its change of ownership in 1981. In between are two semi-popular Tory newspapers, the *Mail on Sunday* and the *Sunday Express*, whose political coverage closely resembles that of the Tory dailies. There are therefore five Sunday titles in the Tory press. Finally, there are a number of regional Sunday titles, notably in Scotland, which constitute our final ('other') category.

The key feature of Sunday readership patterns is the dominance of the 'non-political' popular titles, and the almost complete absence of a non-Tory press, as Table 5.19 shows. Voting patterns in the 'non-political' group are very close to those we should expect, given the social class of their readers, and they certainly show no signs of a distinctive political influence from the newspapers involved. Labour had a 12 percentage-point lead over the Conservatives amongst *News of the World* readers (urged by that newspaper to vote Conservative) and only a 5-point lead amongst *Sunday Mirror* readers (urged by that newspaper to vote Labour). The other two groupings show the familiar polarization that we observed with the dailies, although again it is hard to see any specific Sunday newspaper effect when we take into account the overlap between daily and Sunday readerships produced by Fleet Street's 'stables' of titles.

The real importance of the Sunday newspapers lies in the extent to which their different composition helps to produce any pluralization of the overall press 'line' to which most people are exposed. There is little evidence that it does. We distinguish five categories:

1   People exposed to 'solid Tory' press influence (that is, reading Tory daily and Tory Sunday newspapers, or a Tory daily with no Sunday newspaper) [Tory Influence].
2   People exposed to 'mainly Tory' influence (that is, reading a Tory daily with a Sunday newspaper other than a Tory title; or a mix of daily newspapers with at least one Tory Sunday title) [Mainly Tory].
3   People not exposed to any significant press influence (that is, reading no newspapers at all or only a Sunday newspaper) [Minimal or None].
4   People exposed to 'evenly mixed' influence (that is, reading a mix of daily newspapers but no Tory Sunday, or a non-Tory daily and a Tory Sunday) [Mixed Influences].

Table 5.20   *Voting in the 1983 general election by social class and overall press exposure (in percentages)*

Overall press exposure	Social class	LAB	CON	ALL	CON lead over LAB	N
Tory influence	Non-manual classes[1]	6	74	20	+68	192
	Manual workers	30	43	27	+13	113
Mainly Tory	Non-manual classes	17	54	28	+37	46
	Manual workers	26	52	22	+26	27
Minimal or none	Non-manual classes	13	39	48	+26	79
	Manual workers	50	16	34	−34	50
Mixed influences	Non-manual classes	25	48	27	+23	85
	Manual workers	49	23	28	−26	78
Non-Tory influence	Non-manual classes	48	22	30	−26	73
	Manual workers	71	10	19	−61	72

Note:
[1] Non-manual classes are non-manual workers, controllers of labour, and employers and petit-bourgeoisie.

5   People exposed to 'non-Tory' influence (that is, reading a non-Tory daily alone or in combination with a non-political, regional or non-Tory Sunday) [Non-Tory Influence].

Nearly four out of ten voters are exposed to solid Tory press influence and 46 per cent to at least mainly Tory influence. Considering only actual newspaper readers, a clear majority fall into this latter category. On the other hand, only a fifth of the sample were exposed to evenly mixed influences and even fewer to non-Tory influences; Table 5.20 shows the distribution among the five categories. We also show a breakdown by social class within each of the five readership categories but, since the number of categories for this analysis is one more, we distinguish only between manual workers and all other classes.[2] There is again a very marked variation in political alignment according to media exposure. Eight times as many non-manual people vote Labour when exposed to non-Tory press influence as do those exposed to solid Tory influence. Amongst manual workers the level of Labour voting more than doubles across these two categories, while the Conservative vote falls by a factor of four. It is worth noting again the high level of Alliance support amongst people who read no daily newspaper or a Sunday newspaper alone. The more detailed data in Table 5.18 show that this support is concentrated especially amongst non-manual workers, over 60 per cent of whom in this readership group (out of a group of forty respondents in this class) voted for the Alliance.

PART III

The Analysis of Voters' Behaviour

6 The Social Bases of British Politics in 1983

In this chapter we explore the patterning of voter alignments at the 1983 election by social influences, by the jobs that people do, by the nature of their work-place, by the tenure of the housing in which they live, and so on. Our perspective is essentially that of the radical model set out in Chapter 1 but we draw attention as appropriate to the interpretations and sorts of evidence that would be important for other approaches. Naturally, with the fairly limited resources available to us, our survey could not cover all aspects of the complex structure of modern British society. Some of those elements that we could not cover here, such as differences in voting between white and black people, are discussed in Chapter 8 using aggregate-level data on constituency voting. Here, however, we concentrate on five major issues about the social bases of politics where we profoundly dissent from most of the existing work in the field. These are: choosing a set of 'class' categories with which to analyse voting behaviour; the impact of gender and household situation on people's voting; the importance of such work-place features as sectoral location and trade union membership; the role of consumption sectors in influencing alignments; and lastly, the political effects of unemployment or dependence upon state benefits.

6.1 'Class' and political alignment

We noted in Chapter 1 that 'class' is an important concept in at least two models of voting. For party identification models 'class' means occupational class, where people's jobs stand in a hierarchy of prestige or social status and, as a corollary of this, the kinds of life chances that they have. For the radical approach, however, 'class' means social class, defined by location in a system of production and by the level of power that people can exert over their own work tasks. The distinction is not trivial because there are some important cases where people are differently classified. For example, two plumbers, one of whom works in a factory while the other is self-employed, are in the same occupational class because of their similar job status but in different social classes because of their different degrees of control over their work tasks. In addition, social class positions are defined solely by location in the production system; the concept cannot be enlarged or extended to encompass other aspects of social differentiation in the manner of 'class-inclusive' patterns of explanation in the party identification account.

A conventional kind of occupational class schema might divide the electorate into four groups. Upper non-manual people would be those whom the Registrar-General classifies as professional workers, employers and managers. Intermediate and junior non-manual people are those in more routine white-collar jobs, such as clerical, secretarial and general office administration, as well as some semi-professional jobs. For blue-collar workers it is common to find a distinction between 'skilled' and less skilled jobs (virtually all of which are now classified in official statistics as 'semi-skilled' rather than 'unskilled'). There are considerable difficulties in all of these distinctions, brought about by the postwar trend for a blurring of income and status levels between intermediate non-manual and skilled manual jobs and by the difficulty of distinguishing arbitrarily between skilled and 'less skilled' manual occupations.

Assuming, however, that we could somehow quell our anxieties on these points, use of an occupational class schema to analyse voting behaviour reveals the fairly familiar pattern seen in Table 6.1. The proportion of people voting Labour in 1983 increases by 20 percentage-points across the non-manual/manual division, while Conservative support falls rather less than this. Across the four class categories in the table, the Conservative lead over Labour falls somewhat within the non-manual group (partly because Alliance voting is marginally higher among intermediate non-manual people) and again within the group of blue-collar workers. However, as we shall see below, the two effects within the non-manual and manual groupings are quite complex and perhaps spurious results, partly produced by different concentrations of the sexes in these occupational classes.

The alternative social class categories that we shall adopt in the rest of our analysis are defined in a more complex but robust way than are occupational classes, partly drawing on ideas developed by Wright (1978, pp. 30–110; 1979) and by Carchedi (1977). Our typology is built around three key distinctions. The first is the break between those who own some means of production and those who do not. A second distinction is between those whose work involves controlling other people's labour – who, according to some Marxists, take on part of the 'global function of capital' – and those who are simply wage-earners. The third important difference is between manual workers and those whose jobs carry 'white-collar' attributes. These three criteria apply in different ways. Ownership of some means of production separates employers and the petit-bourgeoisie (self-employed people who do not hire others) from wage-earners. Within the wage-earner category, non-manual controllers of labour are a distinct group who cannot be counted as working-class because of the predominant character of their work tasks. Finally, the manual/non-

Table 6.1   *Voting in the 1983 general election by Registrar-General's occupational class of respondent (in percentages)*

Occupational class	Labour	Conservative	Alliance	CON lead over LAB	N
Professional workers, employers and managers	12	64	25	+52	113
Intermediate and junior non-manual workers	18	51	31	+33	292
Skilled manual workers	38	35	26	−3	164
Less skilled manual workers[1]	47	27	26	−20	203
All classes	*29*	*43*	*28*	*+14*	*772*

Note:
[1] This category includes those sometimes defined as semi-skilled manual and personal service workers and as unskilled manual workers.

manual distinction is useful in separating two rather different kinds of working-class positions. Although the bases of differentiation here are fairly minor – such as the salary/wage distinction, varying prestige levels as between 'mental' and 'physical' work and differential access to employment perquisites – they are quite important in terms of lifetime career paths and earnings profiles and do merit separate consideration.

In some specialized contexts the distinction between manual workers with and without supervisory functions may be useful but for the most part we take it that blue-collar foremen are almost as powerless and dependent on their employers as are the manual workers whom they co-ordinate. Certainly, in terms of political attitudes and alignments, there is no important distinction to be made here.

In analysing our survey data we thus have a four-category social class schema:

- *Manual workers* are all wage-earners in blue-collar jobs with private firms, public sector bodies or other organizations.
- *Non-manual workers* are wage-earners in white-collar jobs whose work tasks do not involve supervising other people's labour, and again who are dependent on owners of capital, the state or another external source for employment.
- *Controllers of labour* are wage-earners in white-collar jobs whose work tasks essentially involve supervising and managing other people's labour.
- *The petit-bourgeoisie* are people in any kind of job who are working for themselves, but without employing other people's labour.
  Since the number of employers (who work for themselves and also employ others) is in any survey necessarily very small, we always include this category in the more numerous and structurally similar petit-bourgeoisie in the data analyses given below.

Table 6.2   *Voting in the 1983 general election by social class of respondent (in percentages)*

Social class	Labour	Conservative	Alliance	CON lead over LAB	N
Manual workers	46	28	26	−18	341
Non-manual workers	18	49	34	+31	199
Controllers of labour	16	58	27	+42	186
Employers/petit-bourgeoisie	14	68	18	+54	56
All classes	29	43	28	+14	782

Applying this schema to the analysis of voting, as in Talbe 6.2, shows a picture quite similar to that obtained using occupational classes. The chief difference is a strengthening of the Labour alignment amongst manual workers, as self-employed people with their more Conservative alignment are reclassified as petit-bourgeoisie rather than as skilled manual workers. This classification also enables us to distinguish rather more clearly some graduated differences in voting patterns within the non-manual categories. We shall also see that the overall similarity between political alignments considered on an occupational and a social-class basis masks some critical differences that become apparent as soon as we move away from the aggregate level, especially in looking at gender effects on voting.

6.2   Gender, class and alignment

In mainstream accounts of voting behaviour, deciding whether people's gender has any influence on their political alignment is a wholly unproblematic exercise. Most comparisons of men's and women's voting patterns do not even control for occupational class. More conscientious researchers proceed on the basis that, since the primacy of occupational class has been established, we simply compare male and female voting within the same class. A problem immediately arises, however, because 71 per cent of women are married and four out of ten of these are housewives who are neither retired nor looking for a job. How should we cope with coding women's class positions? Butler and Stokes (1969, p. 70) solve the issue in a footnote without even explicitly mentioning women:

> We have followed the practice of categorizing respondents on the basis of the breadwinner's occupation even where the respondent is working, on grounds that the occupation of the major figure in the family group tends to give the family as a whole its position in the class system.

This means in practice that all married women are assigned to an occupational class on the basis of their husband's job. This procedure has been followed by other British authors in the field (e.g., Rose, 1976, p. 30; Särlvik and Crewe, 1983, p. 106).

Table 6.3   *The classification of men and women under alternative occupational and social class schemas (in percentages)*

	Men	Women
(a) *Occupational class of head of household*[1]		
Managerial, professional or administrative workers ('upper non-manual' – AB)	19	15
Skilled or supervisory or lower non-manual ('lower non-manual' – C1)	20	23
Skilled manual (C2)	31	33
Unskilled manual and others (DE)	31	29
Total:	101[2]	101
N:	482	533
(b) *Occupational class of respondent*[3]		
Professional workers, employers and managers	22	6
Intermediate and junior non-manual workers	19	54
Skilled manual workers	39	7
Less skilled manual workers	20	33
Total:	100	100
N:	474	465
(c) *Social class of respondent*[4]		
Manual workers	53	38
Non-manual workers	13	36
Controllers of labour	24	21
Employers, petit-bourgeoisie	10	6
Total:	100	101
N:	465	506

Notes:
[1] This schema is that formulated by the Institute of Practitioners in Advertising (Reid, 1977, pp. 46–7).
[2] Some of the percentage totals in this and later tables in the chapter contain rounding errors.
[3] This schema is the scale – also called 'socio-economic class' – that is derived from the fifteen socio-economic groups of the Registrar-General (Reid, 1977, pp. 37–9) and used in Tables 6.1 and 6.4.
[4] This schema is that employed in most of this book and was used in Tables 5.18 and 6.2. Twenty-six married women who had *never* had a paid job were allocated to the manual worker or non-manual worker class on the basis of their husband's social class.

Using a husband's class measure to categorize a married woman has a number of useful implications for conventional explanations. For one thing, it produces a very evenly matched spread of men and women across occupational classes, as Table 6.3(a) shows. Mainstream authors using the conventional opinion-poll occupational classes of 'heads of household' occasionally notice the greater proportion of women in the lower non-manual grade (Rose, 1976, p. 38; Blondel, 1981, p. 34). However, they certainly do not have to confront any glaring evidence of sex discrimination in terms of employment. Thus, they are not surprised to find that male/female differences in voting behaviour are in general slight. In 1983 the Conservative vote in our sample was 5 percentage-

Table 6.4 *Voting in the 1983 general election by gender and Registrar-General's occupational class (in percentages)*[1]

Occupational class	Gender	Labour	Conservative	Alliance	CON lead over LAB	N
Professional, etc.[2]	Men	9	65	26	+56	85
	Women	8	57	36	+49	76
Intermediate and junior non-manual	Men	26	40	34	+14	70
	Women	19	55	26	+36	115
Skilled manual	Men	39	32	29	−7	134
	Women	33	43	24	+10	138
Less skilled manual	Men	42	29	30	−13	77
	Women	53	28	19	−25	92
All classes	Men	30	40	30	+10	366
	Women	29	45	25	+16	421

Notes:
[1] As explained in the text, married women have been coded by their husband's occupation.
[2] 'Professional, etc.' includes professional workers, employers and managers.

points greater at Labour's expense amongst women compared with men. However, looking at the breakdown between occupational classes shows evidence of greater differences, as Table 6.4 reveals. It seems on this basis that upper non-manual women are less likely to vote Conservative and more likely to vote for the Alliance than comparable men. Amongst intermediate non-manual and skilled manual people, women are markedly more Conservative and less likely to vote for either of the other parties. Finally, in the 'less skilled' manual category, women are more likely to vote Labour and less attracted to the Alliance than are similar men.

There are two critical problems with this conventional approach. First, it seems obviously and offensively sexist to reclassify half of all female respondents into an occupational class that bears no relation to their current or past position in a job prestige hierarchy but relates instead to their husband's work. Such a step has been justified only in terms of empirically dubious assumptions about the role of men as 'breadwinner', 'major figure in the family group', 'head of household', and so on, for which no developed argument has ever been put forward. There is a simple alternative to this approach, namely, to assign women to a class category on the basis of their own current job or their last job if they are not at present gainfully employed. Since almost everyone has had some kind of paid job, this approach reduces to a negligible level the number of cases where people's labour-market position is completely obscure.

The second problem is more serious; it is very dangerous to try to assess the impact of gender on voting behaviour by looking at how men and women in the same occupational class vote. This is because there is ample evidence that in British (and other Western) society, gender differences are a critically important influence in determining who occupies particular sorts of job positions. Two effects are crucial here:

1 Women who enter the labour market with equivalent educational levels and individual attributes to men are much less successful in attaining major career advancement if they get married and stop working for a period in order to have children. It is difficult to re-enter the labour market after being inactive at a crucial career stage. The major burden of child-rearing, plus the prevalent division of labour within households, frequently pushes married women into jobs with restricted prospects of career development, especially routine and part-time work.

2 Women additionally underachieve within the educational system, and later in terms of career development, compared with equivalent men because of strong and prevailing sexism in dominant social attitudes.

It therefore follows that gender positions are logically and empirically prior to occupational class. We can demonstrate this graphically by looking back to Table 6.3(b), which shows how women and men are distributed across the Registrar-General's occupational classes when categorized by *their own* jobs. Five out of every six women fall into the intermediate non-manual and less skilled manual classes, while the skilled manual workers and the upper non-manual class are very largely male. The point about conceptions of occupational class is that they crystallize people's social positions in terms of status rankings. In a society disfigured by sexism any class schema expressed in this way is inherently likely to produce clusters of occupations whose overall social prestige reflects the predominance of particular sexes in that kind of job, rather than factors specific to the work tasks, skills or incentives of that position. It is invalid to assess gender effects on voting *within* a class schema where people's sex has as great an influence as this on their class categorization and where the categorization schema itself embodies reference to gender in the rankings of occupations.

Our approach is to drop occupational class categories altogether for the analysis of political alignments because they are so contaminated by gender effects. Instead, we use the notion of social class defined above, which applies from the outset to both sexes in a more even-handed way, as Table 6.3(c) shows. The concentration of women in the non-manual worker group is still pronounced but the majority of both men and women are clearly working-class. Because social class categories do not aim at ranking occupations in a hierarchy of prestige, but rather try to provide a summary measure of how much power people have within the production process, they are much less vulnerable to distortion by gender effects.

Applying this categorization illuminates some promising new aspects of the interrelationship of social class, gender and political alignments, as Table 6.5 shows. First, the Labour vote is 11 percentage-points higher amongst women manual workers than among men, largely because support for the Alliance is less. Secondly, male non-manual workers are much less Conservative than are women in the same position, and much less Conservative than non-manual controllers of labour (whether men or women). There is an additional effect in the employer/petit-bourgeois group, where women's Conservatism is less pronounced than among men. This is chiefly because far more of the men are

Table 6.5 *Voting in the 1983 general election by gender and social class (in percentages)*

Social class	Gender	Labour	Conservative	Alliance	CON lead over LAB	N
Manual workers	Women	52	27	20	−25	147
	Men	41	29	30	−12	191
Non-manual workers	Women	15	53	32	+38	156
	Men	26	36	38	+10	42
Controllers of labour	Women	16	61	24	+45	84
	Men	15	56	29	+41	99
Employers, etc.[1]	Women	20	64	16	+44	25
	Men	10	71	19	+61	31
All classes	Women	29	46	25	+17	412
	Men	30	41	30	+11	363

Note:
[1] In this table and in later ones in the chapter where the same abbreviation is used, 'employers, etc.' includes the petit-bourgeoisie.

employers of other people's labour. Looking at the summary statistic for the percentage-point Conservative lead over Labour, the stronger Labour alignment of women manual workers is apparent, as is the exceptional behaviour of male non-manual workers. More fundamentally, however, if we look at both gender and class *simultaneously* (rather than concentrating on gender effects within classes) we can see that there is an important difference between men and women in the patterning of major breaks in political alignment by class. For women it is the manual/non-manual distinction that is critical, with the Conservative lead increasing 63 percentage-points in the non-manual group. For men this distinction is much less significant than is the gap between controllers of labour and (non-manual) workers.

We can obtain some insights into the patterning of these gender effects by looking at variations in voting patterns across different household situations. Table 6.6 presents data for different sorts of households. Because of the limited numbers of respondents in our data-set we have to use a collapsed version of social class in this table, which simply distinguishes between manual workers and all other classes. Non-manual housewives are amongst the most Conservative of all groups, while manual worker housewives are by far the most Labour-inclined. Working couples are more differentiated in alignment terms by the split between manual workers and other classes than are husbands with non-working wives. Amongst single people in work, the dichotomized class measure had very little impact. Retired people are noticeably Conservative-inclined in both class groupings, while non-manual retired people also show a lower level of Alliance support than any other household type. Reading back from these results into Table 6.5, we can partly explain the two key points of interest distinguished above. Male non-manual workers are distinctively non-Conservative largely because they are younger people at an early transition

Table 6.6   *Voting in the 1983 general election across different household groups by social class (in percentages)*

Social class and type of household	Labour	Conservative	Alliance	CON lead over LAB	N
All manual workers	46	28	26	−18	341
Housewives	52	15	33	−37	27
Unemployed	56	22	22	−34	45
Others	57	26	17	−31	35
Working couples	49	26	26	−23	82
Working husbands	32	26	42	−6	31
Retired people	39	37	24	−2	87
Working singles	35	35	29	0	34
Unemployed	28	41	31	+13	32
Working singles	25	46	30	+21	61
Working husbands	24	50	27	+26	34
Others	17	54	29	+37	35
Working couples	13	53	34	+40	129
Housewives	7	59	35	+52	58
Retired people	14	69	17	+55	92
All non-manual classes[1]	16	55	29	+39	441

Note:
[1] In this table and in later ones in the chapter where the same term is used, non-manual classes are non-manual workers, controllers of labour, and employers and petit-bourgeoisie.

stage in their career; they often have a wife at home looking after young children or are single people living alone. Women manual workers are distinctively Labour-inclined where the household is dependent on a single income (because one member is unemployed or the woman is not working); 63 per cent of women in this category voted Labour in 1983, a higher level than any other household grouping. One important reason for this distinctiveness may be that women are more involved than men in consuming welfare state services and hence more vulnerable to cut-backs in social expenditures. Edgell and Duke (1983) demonstrated this effect but found no related differences in political attitudes. Our results suggest a need for further investigation.

6.3   Class, trade union membership and production sectors

We noted in Chapter 1 that the mainstream party identification model has developed a pattern of class-inclusive explanation in which 'class corollaries' such as trade union membership and housing tenure have been progressively incorporated into the definition of occupational class. In these accounts union membership has always figured as the most important work-place effect on voting behaviour. It has been almost universally interpreted by political scientists as a variable that simply mediates part of an overall occupational class influence. Yet there is *no* reliable evidence to show that occupational class is a major determinant of whether people join trade unions. The variation in rates

Table 6.7   *Trade union membership by production sector and social class in 1983 (in percentages)*

Social class	Production sector	Percentage rate of unionization[1]	Union members	Not union members	Those not working	N
Manual workers	Public	66	41	21	38	124
	Corporate	78	46	13	42	132
	Market	19	9	38	54	112
Non-manual workers	Public	72	49	19	32	69
	Corporate	27	16	43	41	58
	Market	11	6	46	48	67
Controllers of labour	Public	82	52	11	37	97
	Corporate	41	20	29	52	66
	Market	18	12	53	35	34
Employers, etc.	Market	15	12	71	17	41
All classes	Public	73	46	17	36	292
	Corporate	57	31	23	45	262
	Market	16	9	47	44	257

Note:
[1] The rate of unionization shows the percentage of people *in work* who are union members.

of unionization across sectors of production throughout the postwar period suggests that there could not be any simple association of occupational class and degree of unionization (Price and Bain, 1976, pp. 342–3). This has not been clear to mainstream authors, however, because they invariably proceed by working out the influences on trade union membership *within* their own data-sets. Since until very recently election surveys never collected data about production sectors, they were able to conclude that class and unionization are correlated (Särlvik and Crewe, 1983, p. 97).

This might still be shown to be accurate for the 1950s and 1960s. However, by the mid-1970s the link was a classic case of spurious association. Dunleavy (1980b) demonstrated that, with a control for production sector, there is no overall association between social class and trade union membership – that is, there is no significant additive effect. Instead, the relationship between class and union membership varies very markedly from one sector to another. However, there is one significant interaction effect, restricted to corporate sector manufacturing industry, where manual workers are particularly likely to join a trade union – a phenomenon that almost certainly reflects the importance of the closed shop. Our data in Table 6.7 strongly confirm these earlier findings. Wage-earners in the public sector are at least three and a half times more likely to join a trade union in every social class than those in the market sector. Manual workers in the public sector are less likely to be in a trade union than those in corporate sector firms. However, amongst non-manual workers and controllers of labour the position is reversed. Public sector wage-earners in these classes are twice as likely to be unionized as those in large private firms.

Table 6.8   *Trade union membership by gender, production sector and social class in 1983 (in percentages)*

Social class	Sector	Gender	Unionization	Union members	Not union members	Those not working	N
Manual workers	Public	Women	50	32	32	37	57
		Men	81	50	12	38	66
	Corporate	Women	50	11	11	77	35
		Men	81	57	14	29	96
	Market	Women	14	6	34	60	53
		Men	23	12	41	47	58
Non-manual classes	Public	Women	70	37	16	47	94
		Men	84	68	13	20	71
	Corporate	Women	29	12	31	57	65
		Men	37	24	41	35	58
	Market	Wome	12	6	48	45	95
		Men	16	13	70	17	46

A second key influence on trade union membership is gender, a variable not explored by Dunleavy (1980b) since his data-set was restricted to men of working age. As we have seen, the inter-correlation of gender and occupational class is such that any residual association of occupational class and union membership present in Table 6.7 is partly a submerged gender effect. Looking at a breakdown by social class and production sector, as in Table 6.8, shows that gender influences do affect union membership. In every sector and social class trade union membership among women is less than among men.[1] Women's greater reluctance to join a trade union is especially marked among manual workers in the public and corporate sectors. Female unionization rates are far higher among public sector non-manual people than in any other group. Lower membership levels chiefly reflect much more extensive part-time working amongst women than amongst men.

Only when we have correctly analysed union membership as overwhelmingly determined by production sector and by gender, rather than by class, can we move on to understand its political implications. Almost all estimates previously made of how union membership affects voting have simply contrasted people in households that contain one or more union members against everyone else. These sorts of figures are unhelpful for two reasons. First, they continue with an implicitly sexist strategy of classifying a sizeable net balance of non-unionized married women as in 'trade union families' because of their husbands' membership. Secondly, within the non-member category, no distinction is made between those in work (who can potentially join a union) and the non-working population (almost all of whom in practice cannot). A more accurate estimate should look at the difference that membership makes among working people in similar jobs, comparing these differences against the

Table 6.9 *Voting in the 1983 general election by trade union membership and social class (in percentages)*

Social class	Trade union membership	Labour	Conservative	Alliance	CON lead over LAB	N
Manual workers	Member	46	26	28	−20	96
	Non-member	34	34	31	0	70
	Not working	50	25	25	−25	148
Non-manual workers	Member	27	33	40	+6	45
	Non-member	15	47	38	+32	60
	Not working	15	58	27	+43	74
Controllers of labour	Member	24	43	33	+19	63
	Non-member	7	71	22	+64	45
	Not working	14	60	26	+46	73
Employers, etc.	Non-member	10	73	17	+63	30
	Not working	21	57	21	+36	14
All classes	Member	34	34	32	0	215
	Non-member	20	51	30	+31	210
	Not working	32	43	25	+11	329

Table 6.10 *Voting in the 1983 general election by trade union membership, production sector and social class (in percentages)*

Social class	Sector	Trade union membership	Labour	Conservative	Alliance	CON lead over LAB	N
Manual workers	Public	Member	45	20	35	−25	40
		Non-member	35	35	29	0	17
		Not working	57	21	21	−36	42
	Private	Member	47	29	24	−18	55
		Non-member	37	33	30	−4	46
		Not working	43	30	27	−13	89
Non-manual classes	Public	Member	32	30	38	−2	73
		Non-member	26	53	21	+27	19
		Not working	11	54	35	+43	46
	Private	Member	12	52	36	+40	33
		Non-member	10	62	28	+52	97
		Not working	15	60	24	+45	91

alignment of people not working; Table 6.9 shows these data. Three major effects are apparent. First, current union members are less likely to vote Conservative and more disposed to vote Labour than are non-members in all social classes. Secondly, in most classes current union members show the lowest Conservative lead in their social class. However, unionized manual workers are rather *less* Labour-inclined than those not in work at all.[2] Thirdly, it is clear that manual people in work but not in trade unions are more pro-Conservative than either union members or non-working people in the same social class.

We can expand these conclusions somewhat by incorporating further controls. As we have seen, production sectors are an important influence on union membership but Dunleavy (1980b) found no additional direct effect from sectors to voting, over and above the indirect influence operating through union membership. Alt and Turner (1982) argued that a public/private split accurately captured sectoral influences in 1974. Detailed analysis of the 1983 data failed to show a difference between people in the corporate and market sectors, other than that operating through union membership. This reflects a major swing since the mid-1970s against voting Labour amongst unionized private-sector people, one that has greatly reduced the previous differences between the two private sectors (Dunleavy, 1984, p. 53). However, the public/private distinction is helpful in further illuminating what is going on, as can be seen in Table 6.10. Two effects are apparent. First, there is no Labour lead over the Conservatives among non-unionized manual workers (in both sectors) but substantial Labour leads among manual union members and those not working. This *non*-unionization effect is clearly not sectorally specific. Secondly, it is apparent that unionized non-manual people in the public sector stand out from their private sector counterparts and from non-working people

Table 6.11 *Voting in the 1983 general election by trade union membership, gender and social class (in percentages)*

Social class	Gender	Trade union membership	Labour	Conservative	Alliance	CON lead over LAB	N
Manual workers	Women	Member	52	19	29	−33	21
		Non-member	38	41	22	+3	32
		Not working	58	22	20	−36	77
	Men	Member	45	27	28	−18	74
		Non-member	32	29	40	−3	38
		Not working	42	29	29	−13	69
Non-manual workers	Women	Member	22	41	37	+19	27
		Non-member	15	46	39	+31	46
		Not working	12	62	26	+50	65
	Men	Member	33	22	44	−11	18
		Non-member	14	50	36	+36	14
Controllers, etc.[1]	Women	Member	26	42	32	+16	19
		Non-member	3	83	13	+80	30
		Not working	20	55	26	+35	55
	Men	Member	20	48	32	+28	50
		Non-member	11	64	25	+53	44
		Not working	6	69	25	+63	32

Note:
[1] 'Controllers, etc.' includes employers and the petit-bourgeoisie.

in being markedly anti-Conservative in their alignment. No similar influence can be found amongst private-sector union members. Hence this seems safely interpreted as a specific sectoral effect. The reduced Conservative lead in this group is produced by higher levels of Alliance voting as well as by increased Labour support.

Lastly on production locations, we might look for gender influences on alignment other than those operating through differential unionization. Three interesting effects are apparent in the data in Table 6.11. First, there is an increased Labour lead over the Conservatives amongst unionized manual women compared with men. Secondly, the phenomenon identified earlier of male non-manual workers being less Conservative than all other non-manual groups reappears here as an even clearer divergence from the norm, but this time restricted to unionized men in this class, who show a low Conservative vote that benefits mainly the Alliance. Finally, non-working manual women are more Labour-inclined than are comparable men, reflecting primarily the influence of housewives in boosting the Labour vote compared with mainly retired men, as Table 6.6 above showed.

6.3.1 Modelling production-side influences on alignments

We have argued so far that, in order to understand voting alignments, it helps to know whether people are working or not, in which sector, with what kinds of control over their own work tasks, what their gender is and whether they have joined a trade union. These effects are complex and more statistically sophisticated readers may wish to know how they fit together. In this section we present an overall model of production-side effects on voting using log-linear analysis (Payne, 1977; Gilbert, 1981). Readers who are prepared to accept the argument so far and want to avoid the complexities of this section may wish to go directly to Section 6.4 without losing any of the thread of our argument.

Log-linear analysis allows us to determine systematically whether each of the predictor variables that we have so far examined has a significant independent effect on voting (an additive effect) or whether the effect of particular predictors on voting varies with the level taken by other predictor variables (an interaction effect). Table 6.12 shows a sequence of logit models of the three-party vote produced by our log-linear analysis. A logit analysis is a particular type of log-linear analysis in which one variable (in our case, vote) is explicitly designated as the dependent variable and there is no interest in interactions among only the explanatory variables. The first column in Table 6.12 shows the model being tested. The second and third columns show the likelihood ratio chi-square statistic G^2 for that model and the associated degrees of freedom. The fourth column shows the overall significance for the model, expressed as a percentage figure. For a model to be seen as fitting the data well, a rough rule of thumb is that it should achieve a significance level of 50 per cent or more. The remaining columns give information not about the overall model but about the effect of adding a single new term to the model on the line above. This new term is the one italicized in the overall model description in the first column. Thus, the fifth column shows the decrease in

Table 6.12   *Logit models of production influences on voting in the 1983 general election*[1]

Model	For overall model			For new term		
	G^2	DF	Significance	Condit-ional G^2	DF	Significance
(a) *Our preferred sequence*						
1 (Vote)	192·86	94	0·1%	—	—	—
2 (Vote), (*Sector/Vote*)	184·48	92	0·1%	8·38	2	2%
3 (Vote), (Sector/Vote) (*Gender/Class/Vote*)	169·72	86	0·1%	14·76	6	2·5%
4 (Vote), (Sector/Vote), (Gender/Class/Vote), (*Class/Vote*)	76·89	80	58%	92·83	4	0·1%
5 (Vote), (Sector/Vote), (Gender/Class/Vote), (Class/Vote), (*Union membership/Vote*)	67·86	76	74%	9·03	4	7%
(b) *An empiricist sequence*						
2 (Vote), (*Class/Vote*)	95·28	88	28%	97·54	6	0·1%
3 (Vote), (Class/Vote), (*Union membership/Vote*)	82·15	84	54%	13·13	4	2%
4 (Vote), (Class/Vote), (Union membership/Vote), (*Sector/Vote*)	76·16	82	66%	5·99	2	6%
(Not included in final model)						
5 (Vote), (Class/Vote), (Union membership/Vote), (Sector/Vote), (*Gender/Class/Vote*)	67·86	76	74%	9·30	6	25%

Note:
[1] Each term or pair of terms in parentheses is an effect. The new term in each model is italicized. G^2 is the likelihood ratio statistic. DF is the degrees of freedom. The text explains the significance figures.

the likelihood ratio chi-square brought about by adding the new term to the model. The sixth column shows the degrees of freedom lost by adding the term. Finally, the last column shows the consequent significance level that can be ascribed to the term. What we are testing here is how likely it is that the effects attributed to that term are actually the product of random variations in the data. Thus, whereas we wanted a high percentage for the significance level for the overall model in the fourth column, we here want as low a percentage as possible, indicating that the term's effect is unlikely to be a chance occurrence. The choice of a significance level to serve as a cut-off point for including terms in the model must be related to the sample size, since the chi-square statistic is very sensitive to the number of respondents. With a relatively small sample of 773 respondents (those for whom we have complete data on all variables) a significance level of 7 per cent has been judged appropriate.

The sequence in which terms are added to the models has to be theoretically determined and cannot be decided merely on statistical grounds. We have tested a large number of possible models, only a few of which are described here. In our preferred model sequence, shown in Table 6.12(a), the first model is a simple vote effect, which controls for the overall party shares but otherwise assumes that the predictor variables have no influence on voting behaviour. Sector is entered second because it structures (and hence is analytically prior to) all the other variables, especially union membership but also social class. The term proves to have a significant additive effect on alignment at a better than 2 per cent level. Thirdly, we enter an interaction term for class and gender (that is, a term which supposes that how people vote varies with their class/sex combination). This placing is justified because of the interrelationship of gender and class positions discussed earlier in Section 6.2. The term also proves significant at a 2·5 per cent level. Social class is entered fourth and has an obvious and highly significant effect. Union membership is entered last because it is influenced by all the three previous variables. It proves to be significant at the 7 per cent level, which is just allowable for our model buiding, given the sample size. The additive effect for gender proved insignificant (that is, there was no general relationship between gender and voting, as we demonstrated in Section 6.2). Apart from the gender/class term already entered, no other interaction effects amongst predictor variables on voting were statistically significant. Following Goodman (1972), we measure the overall explanatory power of our model by the proportion of the no-effect model G^2 that is accounted for by our four predictor terms, which is 64·8 per cent.

Had we entered the variables in a different sequence, these results would have varied dramatically. The standard empiricist mode of proceeding would be to enter social class second (since it reduces the likelihood ratio chi-square the most), followed perhaps by union membership and then by the other additive effects, as in Table 6.12(b). On this basis union membership seems clearly significant at better than the 2 per cent level. Sector is also still significant at the 6 per cent level. Empiricists tend to drop variables with an insignificant additive effect (such as gender here) from the list of predictor variables. Even if it is included in this sequence, however, the gender/class interaction term is not significant and hence could not be included in an empiricist model. In effect, therefore, an empiricist mode of proceeding would count part of the sector and gender/class effects on voting in an artificially significant union membership effect. Finally, the proportion of the no-effect G^2 explained in the empiricist sequence is 60·5 per cent, below the level achieved by our model. The differences between these two sets of results graphically demonstrate how important it is to know why people occupy particular social locations *before* we undertake statistical analysis. Important and complex social-structural effects can easily be missed unless from the outset we have a worked-out idea of the interrelationships between predictor variables.

6.4 Consumption effects on political alignment

The political importance of housing has also been recognized by each of the approaches to voting behaviour that we reviewed in Chapter 1. Interpretations of the linkage between housing and voting obviously vary in the different approaches. In party identification accounts housing is seen as a class corollary. Some writers have argued that housing positions can *redefine* class because, for example, people can make large capital gains out of buying and selling their house, just as much as one can make money in a business (Pahl, 1975, p. 291; Saunders, 1978). Sectoral accounts differ from both these views by stressing that housing has political importance because of public/private conflicts over tax/subsidy questions (rather than because of linkages with 'class' positions or conflicts). They also emphasize that housing is not *sui generis* and that other consumption influences such as transport, education or health care can all have political importance in conditions where conflicts occur over public/private provision and financing.

It is easy enough to demonstrate that associations exist between several kinds of consumption position and political alignments. In housing different tenure groups clearly react in divergent ways to the political parties. Owner occupiers are more Conservative-inclined, council tenants more Labour-oriented, and tenants of private landlords and housing associations are intermediate between these positions, as the bottom panel of Table 6.13 shows. As the data in the body of this table demonstrate, these effects are clearly in addition to those of social class. We looked in more detail at suggestions that a much more differentiated range of 'housing-class' positions also influenced alignments but found little convincing evidence. Outright home-owners are more Conservative-inclined than those with mortgages but, as one might expect, this is chiefly because people who have paid off their mortgages are more likely to be retired. It seems clear, therefore, that this is a disguised measure of economic status, with most retired home-owners no longer having a mortgage, rather than a specific housing effect. Also in our sample were a small group of former council tenants who had bought their homes. They proved slightly more Conservative in their alignment than comparable people still in council tenure; however, the difference was not great. Finally, we asked council tenants whether or not they intended to buy, or had considered buying, their house. Again, those who wished to buy or had considered purchasing their dwelling were rather more Conservative-oriented than those who had not, but the differences were slight. Labour voting continued to predominate amongst people who had bought council houses or considered doing so.

Amongst the other consumption positions that might be associated with voting, transport obviously stands out. We examine this in Table 6.14. The divisions between households with multiple or company-subsidized car access, those with one car and those without a car are clearly linked to differences in political alignment. To some extent, this transport variable incorporates other effects such as the urban locations where people live (far fewer people have cars in inner-city areas) and household type (elderly people are less likely to own a car) as well as being influenced by people's social class. None the less, the scale of the effects within social classes is not dissimilar to those of housing tenure.

Looking at other possible areas of consumption effects (such as education or health care) becomes more difficult in survey data because far fewer

Table 6.13   *Voting in the 1983 general election by housing tenure and social class (in percentages)*

Social class	Tenure[1]	Labour	Conservative	Alliance	CON lead over LAB	N
Manual workers	Council rent	54	23	23	−31	166
	Other	46	33	21	−13	24
	Home-owner	36	33	31	−3	150
Non-manual workers	Council rent	33	49	18	+16	33
	Other	21	43	36	+22	14
	Home-owner	14	49	37	+35	152
Controllers of labour	Council	35	42	23	+7	26
	Home-owner	13	59	28	+46	149
Employers, etc.	Home-owner	9	70	21	+61	47
All classes	Council rent	50	29	21	−21	243
	Other	27	46	27	+19	55
	Home-owner	20	49	30	+29	516

Note:
[1] Where a tenure group has been omitted, the reason is that the number of cases in the group was too small for reliable percentages.

Table 6.14   *Voting in the 1983 general election by access to private transport and social class (in percentages)*

Social class	Transport category	Labour	Conservative	Alliance	CON lead over LAB	N
Manual workers	No car	54	22	24	−32	154
	One own car	40	32	28	−8	143
	Two cars[1]	34	36	30	+2	44
Non-manual workers	No car	27	22	51	+24	41
	One own car	17	41	42	+24	98
	Two cars	12	61	27	+49	59
Controllers of labour	No car	22	56	22	+34	27
	One own car	20	51	30	+31	97
	Two cars	7	69	24	+62	62
Employers, etc.	One own car	27	59	14	+32	22
	Two cars	0	78	22	+78	27
All classes	No car	45	32	23	−13	239
	One own car	28	41	31	+13	375
	Two cars	13	60	26	+47	197

Note:
[1] The two-cars category includes people in households with access to regular use of a company car (even if the household itself has only one car).

respondents fall on the minority side of the public/private divide than with housing or transport. However, we did ask three additional questions, about whether respondents had ever had an operation carried out privately in the United Kingdom, whether they had ever placed a relative in a private old people's home, and whether they had been to a fee-paying school, or sent their children to a private school, or intended to send their children to such a school. In each case around 6 per cent of respondents answered that they had and, as we expected, they proved to be a good deal more Conservative in their alignment than those who replied 'no' to each question.

To take our analysis further we need to resolve some tricky problems of interpretation. The linkages that we have so far charted could be interpreted as supporting a class-inclusive pattern of explanation in which consumption locations are seen as simply corollaries of (occupational) class. Party identification writers would see consumption effects within classes as expressing some hidden class influence, such as income – a variable notoriously hard to measure in survey research but one quite clearly linked closely with the ways in which people consume housing, transport or other services (Harrop, 1980).

The main alternative interpretation is, of course, the analysis of consumption sector cleavages put forward in the radical view. For mainstream electoral analysts the sectoral approach still remains controversial, a heresy to be alternately ignored or campaigned actively against (Franklin and Page, 1984). However, amongst authors in urban studies in particular, it has been widely accepted. The sectoral approach stresses that class-consumption linkages have been overstated in the electoral literature. People's consumption locations are not influenced solely or simply by their class positions. Rather, it is the combination of their class position and other social characteristics – such as their urban and regional environment, stage in the life cycle, household position, the time period when they entered the housing market, ability to gain access to state subsidies – all of these other factors are also involved in how people consume goods and services. The basic reality of class-structured access to consumption is not in question. Yet neither are consumption positions simply corollaries of class (Dunleavy and Husbands, 1984a, p. 16).

There is now a bifurcation, however, between the original, cumulative consumption sectors analysis, as set out briefly in Chapter 1, and a much more fragmented consumption sectors view that is best expressed by Cawson and Saunders (1983) and was first set out by Saunders (1981, pp. 219–78). Writing in a neo-Weberian tradition, they argue that consumption locations are not determined by, or related to, occupational classes in any simple way. Indeed, they claim that there is a 'necessary non-correspondence' between class and consumption sectors. Furthermore, there is no necessary linkage between patterns of consumption found in one service or issue area and patterns in other issue areas. Each fragmented consumption process produces its own pattern of interest groups, who organize and struggle in a single-issue mode rather than in any concerted or overlapping way (Cawson and Saunders, 1983, p. 24).

The key implication of the fragmented consumption sectors view is that consumption issues are characterized by a rather pluralist kind of politics, which no doubt responds to an overall context set by 'class politics' but which

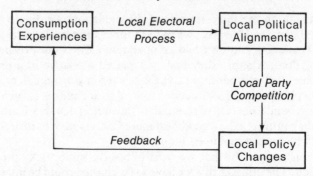

Figure 6.1   The linkages between consumption experiences, political alignments and local policy change, according to the fragmented consumption sectors model

otherwise stands outside the dominant corporatist pattern of social conflict.
Consumption issues are rarely characterized by overt conflicts between capital
and organized labour and are handled institutionally by local government,
which remains generally pluralistic in its mode of operation. Like much liberal
political theory in the 1960s and early 1970s, the fragmented sectors approach
expects there to be a fairly close and direct linkage between people's experience
in consumption processes and local politics, as depicted in Figure 6.1. Thus, the
assumption in normative theories of representative government that people's
consumption experiences directly affect their local political alignment seems to
be making a bizarre comeback amongst neo-Weberian writers and Marxist
'local state' theorists (Duncan and Goodwin, 1982; Saunders, 1984a).

    In the original statement of the sectoral approach, however, consumption
sectors are major cross-class lines of social cleavage that are essentially
cumulative in their effects (Dunleavy, 1979; 1980a, pp. 70–86). These cleavages find expression at the economic level in divergent material interests created
by consumption-specific taxes and subsidies. At the ideological level these
conflicts of interest are codified into myths about the incidence of tagged
subsidies and taxes. At the political level they trigger attempts by political
parties to differentiate their respective platforms on consumption issues as a
basis for attracting support. Considerably developing this argument, Duke and
Edgell (1984) demonstrate that classifying people by their overall involvement
in public or private consumption across several different areas of social life
(housing, transport and health care) uncovers important effects on political
alignments in the 1979 general election.

    A cumulative sectors approach offers a radically different picture of the ways
in which consumption experiences structure people's voting behaviour, and of
the mechanisms by which changes in overall alignments feed back into
consumption experiences. This model is depicted in Figure 6.2. Here there is
no reason to suppose that consumption experiences distinctively affect *local*
political alignments. On the contrary, their primary impact is on *national*
political alignments, although they are only one of many factors involved in
shaping such alignments.[3] Local voting in Britain derives largely from national

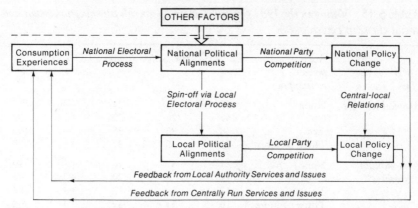

Figure 6.2   The linkages between consumption experiences, political alignments and policy changes, according to the cumulative consumption sectors model

alignments (e.g., Waller, 1980) – hence phenomena such as the Conservatives'
strength in the 1982 local elections because of the Falklands war. The pathways
between changes in alignments and local policy change are indirect. In turn, the
feedback to consumption experiences from distinctive local party strategies is
likely to be very attenuated. Local authority services and functions are
extensively regulated by non-local influences, especially central government
controls, and so the scope for major variations in council policies is limited.
Anyway, local government services form only part of people's consumption
experiences. For both these reasons (central control and non-local service
provision) we may be sceptical of the potential for building 'local socialism' in
Britain (but see Boddy and Fudge, 1984). The pathways between national
alignments and policy change in centrally run services are more direct,
however, and hence the feedback potential is more considerable. The key area
of collective consumption provision organized outside local government is, of
course, the National Health Service.

Looking from this perspective at the patterns of consumption sector
influences on alignments in 1983 shows some striking findings, as revealed in
Table 6.15. Overall consumption locations are defined in terms of the privatized
or commodified options on five consumption processes: ownership of a house,
household access to a car, family use of private medical care, family use of a
private old persons' home, and past use by respondent, or prospective family
use, of private schooling. We have grouped our respondents into those who
participated in none of these, one of them, two of them, and three or more of
them. Within the manual worker group there is a 34 percentage-point variation
in the level of Labour voting between people completely unintegrated into
private consumption of these commodities and those consuming privately in
three or more areas. The same comparison evokes a 27 percentage-point
difference in the Labour vote amongst non-manual workers and one of similar
size amongst controllers of labour. The effects upon the Conservative lead over
Labour are also large. However, amongst non-manual workers this latter index

Table 6.15 *Voting in the 1983 general election by overall consumption sector and social class (in percentages)*

Social class	Areas of private consumption	Labour	Conservative	Alliance	CON lead over LAB	N
Manual workers	None	57	21	21	−36	112
	One	47	24	29	−23	99
	Two	38	36	26	−2	100
	Three or more	23	40	37	+17	30
Non-manual workers	None	37	47	16	+10	19
	One	21	50	29	+29	38
	Two	17	48	37	+31	103
	Three or more	10	51	39	+41	39
Controllers of labour	One or none	31	44	25	+13	36
	Two	17	54	30	+37	84
	Three or more	6	70	24	+64	66
Employers, etc.	Two	16	59	25	+43	32
	Three or more	0	88	12	+88	17

mis-states the degree of variation involved, since the Alliance vote more than doubles as we move from people unintegrated into private consumption to those who are heavily involved. Quite a major difference can be uncovered here in workers' political alignments. As integration into private consumption increases amongst manual workers, so the Labour vote ebbs away in almost exactly equal proportions to the Conservatives and the Alliance. Yet amongst non-manual workers the proportion voting Conservative shows no consistent pattern of fluctuation with consumption sector. Instead, as Labour voting decreases amongst people integrated into private consumption, almost all this support shifts into voting Alliance.

Not only does a cumulative consumption sectors approach appear to throw new light on the patterning of consumption effects in 1983 but also, as we noted in Section 1.3.3, it offers a distinctive analysis of the way in which such effects have grown in importance. This account produces a distinctive set of expecta-tions about the future importance of consumption effects. Comparing the dynamic accounts given by class-inclusive, fragmented sectors and cumulative sectors approaches shows a marked divergence between them.

The implications of a class-inclusive view are quite distinctive. Changes in consumption locations are seen as fundamental, once-and-for-all shifts in the previous 'class' system (e.g., Seabrook, 1978, 1982). 'Core class' manual workers living in council housing are a dwindling group, while people who have moved into home ownership undergo a (rather mysterious) transformation of their personal relations, one that 'unlocks' their alignment to flow into a different mould. Short of some reversal of recent trends in housing tenure (or in car ownership or whatever other consumption process is under discussion), class-inclusive explanations see no prospect of earlier patterns of association between occupational class and voting being re-established. The fragmented sectors model basically agrees with this prediction, arguing that postwar social changes have brought about an irreversible shift in the influences that cause people to be mobilized into politics, away from overarching class-based movements and towards a focus on much more small-scale, micro-social interests (Saunders, 1984b).

For the cumulative consumption sectors view, however, recent trends do not suggest either a fundamental revamping of the class system or the displacement of class politics by issue-specific, micro-social mobilizations. Instead, the extent to which any single consumption process affects alignments reflects primarily two factors: the degree of fragmentation of the electorate around the line of cleavage involved (Rae and Taylor, 1970); and the importance of the issue area both in terms of its objective economic implications for people and in terms of how dominant ideological messages present the issues involved (Dunleavy, 1980a, pp. 76–86). So far in the postwar period, housing and transport have been the dominant consumption issues, absorbing a large share of people's disposable income. The growing polarization of housing tenures (weighted towards home-ownership) and the growth of car use have affected very large sections of the population, as Table 1.5 showed. Periods of rapid inter-modal or inter-sectoral shift in consumption (such as that from public transport to car use, or from private renting to home ownership or council housing, or now from council housing to home ownership) are in effect 'coerced exchanges' for many of the people involved in them (Dunleavy, 1985). In a coerced exchange people enter into a transaction not because their welfare is necessarily improved by doing so, but because their welfare will decline if they do not do so (Heath, 1976; Ellis, 1981). In such a circumstance relative tax and subsidy incidence can become extremely important in orienting people towards the political process, as can being part of a majority (growth) consumption sector rather than a minority (residualizing) one. So far in the postwar period the major effect of changes in housing and transport has been to benefit the Conservatives, who were quick to line up on the side of the growth sectors, and to harm Labour, who were committed historically and ideologically to the minority public sector forms of provision.

However, if these patterns of change in housing and transport locations have begun to stabilize, we may then expect to see a concomitant settling of their influence on alignments, especially if other consumption sector cleavages become progressively more important in economic and ideological terms. By 1986 a reasonable forecast of the impact of multiple housing trends suggests that 64 per cent of all households will be owner occupiers and under a quarter will be renting from local authorities (Forrest, 1984). Thus, the extent to which the electorate is fragmented by the housing cleavage is already beginning to decline. If there are concomitant (perhaps lagged, catch-up) reactions to this change by the major political parties and if the process of inter-sectoral change is largely exhausted at this point, then housing location and political alignment may not go on becoming more associated, as they have been in the recent past. Similarly, if increase in car use has virtually reached saturation levels and if public transport subsidies become less controversial as they sustain only a base level of provision, then transport location and alignment may not go on being associated as they are at present.

By contrast, a really potent new consumption cleavage may emerge over privatization of health care provisions. Although 94 per cent of the population currently consume health care in the public sector, there is already a powerful inter-sectoral shift in progress from public to private health care. It is being led (as with car use growth) by company-assisted medical care, so that its significance for socially and ideologically dominant patterns of health care far outweighs the numbers involved. In addition, the Conservative Party is ideologically committed to putting through a bigger change in health-care consumption patterns than is likely to occur from company-assisted medicine alone. Thus the scope for future political effects is considerable. If a 'two-tier' health care system emerges more explicitly than at present and if more people begin to confront a costly 'coerced exchange' forced on them by service deterioration in the public sector, then it is possible to foresee a period when health care issues could assume the electoral significance hitherto reserved for housing tenure questions. This time, however, the main beneficiary of such an inter-sectoral shift could be the Labour Party. Labour has historically been most associated in voters' minds with the defence of the NHS and this effect has not disappeared (Chapter 7). Moreover, however fast inter-sectoral changes in health care may develop, there will be a very lengthy period during which a large majority of people will be dependent on public health care provision.

6.5   State dependency and voting

We noted in Table 1.6 the substantial growth in the numbers of people who are dependent on supplementary benefit in order to boost their pensions, or because they are unemployed, sick or disabled. This is a particularly interesting area of social life in which to look for effects on political alignments because of the spiralling growth of unemployment in Britain from mid-1980 onwards (see Figure 3.1 above). The conventional wisdom of the 1960s that unemployment costs a government votes did not seem to be borne out on a large scale in the 1983 election, although – as we shall see in Chapter 7 – an adverse popularity effect underlying other influences on voting may still be traced.

More generally, we noted in Chapter 1 that the pattern of differences between the Conservative and Labour parties was fairly sharp, with Labour identifying itself with increases in state benefit levels generally and the Conservatives anxious to protect pensions but otherwise fairly critical of the state-dependent population. We might expect to find a pro-Labour inclination amongst the minority of state-dependent people. Any form of anti-statist populism among the working population is likely to be too generalized to reveal itself in increased levels of Conservative support but we might expect it to be more visible amongst, say, the comfortably retired who are none the less on fixed incomes. There is certainly evidence of a 'scrounger-bashing' mentality in sections of the press and this might find a particular echo amongst such groups.

It is quite difficult to form an accurate idea of state dependency amongst a

Table 6.16   *Voting in the 1983 general election by household exposure to unemployment and overall consumption sector (in percentages)*

Consumption position and exposure to unemployment	Labour	Conservative	Alliance	CON lead over LAB	N
One or no areas of private consumption ('low consumption')					
Exposed to job loss	63	18	20	−45	40
Retired	42	33	24	−9	99
Others	43	32	25	−11	186
All 'low consumption' households	46	30	24	−16	331
Two or more areas of private consumption ('high consumption')					
Exposed to job loss	21	49	30	+28	33
Retired	9	74	17	+65	90
Others	20	47	30	+27	359
All 'high consumption' households	18	52	30	+34	485

survey sample. The social stigma attached to claiming welfare state benefits in Britain and the complex judgements involved in deciding which households are state-dependent persuaded us to concentrate our analysis on two specific groups, the unemployed and the retired. Within each of these groups we have tried to distinguish between those who are heavily state-dependent because they are seriously or long-term unemployed or are living on the state pension with little or no occupational pension support, and those whose unemployment is frictional or whose retirement is relatively comfortably cushioned by an effective private pension source. We examined a number of ways of making this distinction. A control on social class that divided unemployed and retired respondents into manual workers and others did not prove useful. The most effective way of discriminating between more and less state-dependent people amongst the unemployed and pensioners seemed to be a collapsed consumption sector variable, distinguishing people involved in two or more areas of private consumption and those involved in one or no such areas. Table 6.16 shows the results of this analysis.

The pattern uncovered here needs to be interpreted a little cautiously for the unemployed, whose numbers in our sample are fairly restricted. However, when we control for consumption position, the most state-dependent people in households with one or more persons unemployed are more Labour-inclined and less prone to vote Conservative than equivalent retired or working people. This relationship is much weaker amongst households where there is a continuing high level of involvement in private consumption processes despite the incidence of unemployment. Retired people not much involved in private sector consumption processes, and hence more dependent on public services, are no more Conservative-leaning than working people in a similar consumption position. However, retired people involved in extensive private consumption, presumably funded through fairly generous occupational pensions, are fiercely Conservative and anti-Labour, much more so than working people in an equivalent consumption position. These results are encouraging for our hypothesis but they remain exploratory. We should need a larger sample and more direct information about respondents' income sources and levels to be more confident that our account of how state dependency affects people's voting is correct. However, in Chapter 7 we return to the political impact of unemployment.

7 Party Issues and Voter Attitudes, 1979 to 1983

7.1 The status of issues in electoral analysis

We argued in the previous chapter that people's social situations continue to structure their voting behaviour in important ways. Clearly, however, social-structural change in Britain cannot alone explain the undoubted political volatility and voter detachability of the past fifteen years.

Our analytic approach towards issues is very different from that of main-stream issue-oriented analysis, which invariably sees voters' attitudes as primary causal influences on their voting decision. This approach simply infers from empirical correlations between issue attitudes and voting, without inquiring in any depth *how* particular issue positions came to be held by voters. In Chapters 1 and 5 we argued that the mass media, especially the national press, have a major influence in determining political attitudes and alignments. A pattern of mass media exposure changes attitudes on certain salient subjects and over time influences voting behaviour. In addition, on certain issues voters may adopt attitudes merely to fit a voting intention produced by social influences or by views on other kinds of issue where their opinions are not subject to such adjustment. Full testing of our approach requires data collected over time on the same respondents or some extremely complex modelling of the voting decision (e.g., Page and Jones, 1979). We do not have over-time data. However, we present relationships between issue position and voting in

1983 and, drawing on other evidence about issue salience and vote change during the campaign as well as on theoretical considerations and empirical material about causal influences presented in various previous chapters, we derive the likely predominant direction of causality between issue attitudes and voting behaviour.

Many general elections can be analysed by seeing their results as successive baselines for the monitoring of the longer-term evolution of structurally determined voting behaviour. This perspective applies to the election of 1983, of course, as was shown in Chapter 6, but the special factors surrounding the 1983 campaign make it particularly appropriate for analysing the shorter-term effects of issues of policy and party leadership upon the outcome.

There is one further observation to make about our analyses. Periods encompassing general election campaigns are important because they are the times when people have to make decisions with real consequences. However, they are also atypical in other respects. Elections are usually fought at a time chosen by the party in power to maximize its own advantage, not when its relative popularity is uncertain. Increasingly, with the explicit aid of most of the national press, the Conservatives have been able to set the agenda of election campaigns, determining which issues receive prominence and which are obscured in the coverage of the campaign. The February 1974 and 1983 general elections were called by Conservative governments at times when the issues that predominated were those favouring them, even if their effects were overdetermined by other matters in the February 1974 contest. In 1979 the minority Labour government was forced from power by the failure of its devolution initiatives and by the withdrawal of the nationalist parties' support when its economic policies were particularly unpopular. Thus, during the 1970s and 1980s (with the possible but ambiguous exception of October 1974) Labour has been fighting general election campaigns on the ideological defensive. Consequently, analyses of the issue orientations predominating in the electorate around the times of such general elections reflect the ambience of these campaigns, even if they do not necessarily indicate how the electorate would respond on other occasions, when it was receiving different political stimuli.

7.2 The presentation of the issue data

There are four types of analysis in this chapter. We first explore the salience of a number of issues during the campaign. Secondly, we examine in detail three issues that are crucial in understanding the baselines of voter support at the start of the campaign and how these changed as it proceeded; the three are unemployment, defence and disarmament, and public services and the welfare state. Thirdly, we examine the state of opinion on two further issues, the effects of privatization and the European Economic Community. Finally, we use the subject of measurement error to introduce an analysis of the degree of consistency that exists between voters' responses to logically related statements.

In almost all analyses we follow a standard format of presentation. Data are presented for the total sample, for Labour, Conservative and the Alliance voters in 1983, and for subgroups of each party's voters subdivided according to how they voted in the 1979 general election.[1] People who shifted from Labour to the Alliance are, of course, of special interest in attempting to account for Labour's particular difficulties, especially as nearly one in eight of 1983 Alliance voters in the sample none the less named Labour as the party to which they generally felt closest. Equally interesting are those who shifted from the Conservatives to the Alliance between 1979 and 1983; 9 per cent of Alliance voters named the Conservative Party as the one to which they generally felt closest. Clearly, our extensive subdivision of the sample in order to look at vote switchers presents problems of small numbers of cases in a few individual subgroups. All but one subgroup (Liberals in 1979 switching to Labour in 1983) contained at least ten cases and data for these are presented in the appropriate tables; however, inferences about subgroups containing fewer than about twenty cases should be made with some caution. Finally, as with the data in Section 5.3.2, percentages given are generally of those taking the extreme position (for example, extremely important, agree strongly) on a four-point scale offered to respondents that contained extreme and moderate responses of assent and dissent on the item concerned (for example, agree strongly, tend to agree, tend to disagree, disagree strongly). These extreme responses give a better picture of genuine conviction on a subject than would the inclusion of the corresponding moderate responses.[2]

7.3   The salience of individual issues in the 1983 campaign

The assessment of how important different issues were in a campaign is a notoriously difficult task. However, the BBC/Gallup election survey conducted just before polling day does allow us to determine which issues may be regarded as 'Conservative' ones and which 'Labour' ones, as judged by the balance of opinions about the respective competences of each party (SSRC Data Archive, 1983). The BBC/Gallup survey presented its respondents with a number of issues and asked them to say which party would be best on each one. The degree of imbalance in these distributions enables us to say how unambiguously various issues were 'Conservative' or 'Labour' ones.[3]

Only two out of ten topics emerged as 'Labour' issues: 'reducing unemployment' (Labour, 38 per cent; Conservative, 30 per cent) and 'providing properly for the Health Service' (Labour, 46 per cent; Conservative, 28 per cent). Even in these cases Labour's advantage was fairly slight. On all the other issues there was a Conservative preference, often strongly so: 'ensuring that Britain is safely defended' (Conservative, 65 per cent; Labour, 16 per cent); 'standing up for Britain's interests in the EEC' (Conservative, 65 per cent; Labour, 17 per cent); 'cutting down strikes' (Conservative, 56 per cent, Labour, 24 per cent); 'reducing crime and vandalism' (Conservative, 44 per cent; Labour, 21 per cent); and 'keeping prices down' (Conservative, 47 per cent; Labour, 27 per cent).

Table 7.1 Percentages of respondents saying that various issues were extremely important to them during the election campaign, by voting path between 1979 and 1983 and by vote in the 1983 general election

	CON to LAB	LIB to LAB	Too young to LAB	LAB to LAB	All LAB voters	LAB to CON	LIB to CON	Too young to CON	CON to CON	All CON voters	CON to ALL	LAB to ALL	Too young to ALL	LIB to ALL	All ALL voters	Total sample
The level of unemployment	77	—	100	91	**88**	73	67	53	60	**60**	74	84	85	85	**80**	75
Crime rates and policing	54	—	56	60	**59**	74	50	29	71	**66**	50	56	33	57	**52**	59
Rising prices	62	—	46	62	**61**	57	42	24	48	**48**	50	64	15	56	**55**	55
Defence and nuclear weapons	54	—	27	46	**45**	46	58	59	63	**59**	57	54	15	56	**52**	52
The government's handling of the Falklands war	15	—	40	29	**30**	32	33	35	53	**49**	43	24	25	30	**31**	38
The standard of public services	23	—	55	39	**39**	23	33	12	29	**28**	21	33	31	40	**30**	32
Britain and the Common Market	39	—	18	25	**27**	41	42	44	39	**38**	33	22	17	35	**27**	31
Trade unions and industrial relations	18	—	50	33	**30**	14	27	18	28	**25**	19	23	0	35	**22**	25
Mean N:	13	4	11	187	**236**	22	12	17	261	**347**	53	72	13	54	**221**	**1007**

In our own survey we asked respondents how important a number of issues were to them personally during the campaign. Table 7.1 shows the percentages who replied that an issue was 'extremely important'. Labour's disadvantage in 1983 relative to the Conservatives is apparent. True, the issue of unemployment, upon which the Conservatives were theoretically vulnerable and which – as we shall soon see – did continue to cost them some support from their post-Falklands peak, heads the list of concerns, with three-quarters of the sample rating it as extremely important. However, below this in the order of salience were four undoubtedly 'Conservative' issues: 'crime rates and policing', 'rising prices', 'defence and nuclear weapons' and 'the Government's handling of the Falklands war'. The only other 'Labour' issue besides unemployment was 'the standard of public services', a broader version of the BBC/Gallup survey's question about the National Health Service. However, this was well down the list of public priorities, with less than a third of the sample regarding it as extremely important. 'Britain and the Common Market' was similarly low in salience; in any case, Labour's commitment to withdrawal may have had a negative rather than positive effect upon its prospects by the summer of 1983, as we shall see below. Last in our list was 'trade unions and industrial relations'. This was undoubtedly a 'Conservative' issue and so its low salience was probably a blessing for Labour. There has rarely been major support for Labour on industrial issues. Indeed, in 1979 it was largely the unpopularity of the strikes during the 'winter of discontent' that dragged Labour down. In 1983 there was little prospect of Labour's attracting support by campaigning to repeal the employment legislation passed since 1979, most of whose provisions are accepted by solid majorities of the public (e.g., *GPI*, September 1980, pp. 6–7; September 1981, pp. 9–10; September 1982, pp. 11–12). Even in more propitious circumstances Labour would have been hard-pressed to reverse the public's disposition on this subject; this was certainly not going to be achieved in the circumstances of the 1983 campaign, although the party's manifesto did in fact contain an unobtrusive promise to repeal the Conservatives' employment legislation (Labour Party, 1983, p. 9).

The major differences in terms of issue salience between voters for the different parties clearly concern their supporters' tendency to give lower salience to 'opposition' issues. While nine out of ten Labour voters rated unemployment as 'extremely important', only six out of ten Conservatives did so, placing it second in their ranking behind 'crime rates and policing'. While half of Conservatives rated ' the Government's handling of the Falklands war' as 'extremely important', fewer than a third of Labour voters did so. Similarly, Conservatives tended to rate 'defence and nuclear weapons' and the Common Market higher as issues than did Labour voters, while giving less importance to 'rising prices' and 'the standard of public services'. Amongst vote switchers between 1979 and 1983, former Conservatives voting Alliance were rather more likely to be concerned about unemployment than were Conservative loyalists and to be less concerned about 'crime rates and policing'. Labour switchers to the Alliance had no distinctive issue rankings. However, Labour switchers to the Conservatives gave higher rankings to 'crime rates and policing' and to the Common Market than did Labour loyalists. In general, in terms of issue rankings switchers tended to be between loyalists to their party of origin and voters in their new grouping.

7.4   Opinions on individual issues

7.4.1   *Unemployment*

Unemployment, like most economic issues, has been seen as almost a pure 'valence' issue (Butler and Stokes, 1974, pp. 292, 370). Such issues divide parties not in terms of purpose or ideology but of public perceptions of competence in achieving a goal that is all but universally seen as desirable. This general approach is probably appropriate in a period like the present, when unemployment is unusually high. However, there is an established literature arguing that the interests of the less well-off are best served by low unemployment (and necessarily higher inflation according to the conventional Phillips curve trade-off), whereas the better-off in fact prefer lower inflation in return for higher unemployment (Hibbs, 1977; Tufte, 1978, pp. 83–8).

The fact that high unemployment may not be universally deplored with the same strong feeling is important in explaining why the issue failed to move more votes away from the Conservatives than it did. Of course, during the 1979–83 period it did move a significant number of intended votes, as measured by the opinion polls, but rather fewer such votes than was the conventional wisdom of the early 1970s. Its role becomes clear from the results of three time-series analyses of the determinants of the Conservative government's popularity as measured by the Gallup Poll's published monthly surveys; these data were presented graphically in Figure 3.2A and the results of their analysis are reported in Table 7.2.

This analysis and several that are presented in Chapter 8 use the technique of multiple regression, which gives the relationships between a dependent variable and one or more explanatory variables. The former is measured on at least an interval scale, while the latter are either interval-scale variables or dummy variables. A dummy variable is one that conventionally takes a value of one for some cases and zero for all others. A multiple regression analysis produces a number of inferential statistics. Each explanatory variable has a metric regression coefficient and a standardized regression coefficient. The metric coefficient says how many units of the dependent variable are associated with a change of one unit in the explanatory variable, controlling on the effects of all other explanatory variables. Thus the value of the metric coefficient of a dummy variable shows how many units of the dependent variable are attributable to the net effect of whatever factor the dummy variable is coding as one. The intercept shown when metric coefficients are presented is the value of the dependent variable when all explanatory variables have values of zero. The standardized coefficients are those produced after conversion of all variables in the analysis to a common scale with the same average (in fact, a mean of zero) and the same dispersion (a variance of one); these coefficients, which are used extensively in the analyses of Chapter 8, show which explanatory variables

Table 7.2   *Ordinary least-squares regression analyses of three periods of month-by-month Conservative popularity, measured as the Gallup-Poll-reported percentage with a Conservative voting intention/inclination, 1979–83*

Period: September 1979 to April 1983
Mean of dependent variable: 36·364

	Metric regression coefficient	Student's t-value
Percentage rate of unemployment in the UK, lagged four months	−1·684	−11·733
'Falklands factor'	16·778	16·969
Intercept:	48·286	
Durbin–Watson Statistic:[1]	1·625	
Proportion of variation explained (R^2):	0·875	

Period: September 1979 to March 1982
Mean of dependent variable: 34·065

	Metric regression coefficient	Student's t-value
Percentage rate of unemployment in the UK, lagged four months	−1·760	−11·645
Intercept:	48·794	
Durbin–Watson Statistic:	1·594	
Proportion of variation explained (R^2):	0·824	

Period: May 1982 to April 1983
Mean of dependent variable: 42·708

	Metric regression coefficient	Student's t-value
Percentage rate of unemployment in the UK, lagged four months	−1·824	−2·172
Intercept:	66·920	
Durbin–Watson Statistic:	1·597	
Proportion of variation explained (R^2):	0·320	

Note:
[1] The Durbin–Watson Statistic shows the presence or otherwise of first-order serial auto-correlation; for information about how its value is to be interpreted see, for example, Kelejian and Oates (1974, pp. 200–3, 278). These three models are shown by the values of this statistic to lack such autocorrelation.

have the largest effects on the dependent variable, controlling on all other explanatory variables. The significance of individual regression coefficients may be assessed from their Student's t-value; a value of less than about −1·7 or greater than +1·7 indicates significance at more than the 5 per cent level using a one-tailed test, provided that the number of observations in the analysis exceeds thirty-five or so. A value of less than about $-2 \cdot 4$ or greater than $+2 \cdot 4$ similarly indicates significance at more than the 1 per cent level. The proportion of variation in the dependent variable that is explained by all the explanatory variables in the model is given by the statistic R^2, which may take on values between zero and one. In addition, a multiple regression analysis of time-series data conventionally tests for first-order serial autocorrelation, which should be absent from the final model (see Note 1 of Table 7.2).

The explanatory variables in the models in Table 7.2 are the rate of unemployment and the 'Falklands factor'; the latter was operationalized as a dummy variable coding all months from May 1982 to April 1983 as one and all months from September 1979 to April 1982 as zero (see Appendix C).

The analyses reported are for the whole period of the 1979–83 Conservative government, and for the pre- and post-Falklands phases (omitting April 1982 from both phases, given its status as a transition month). Despite an exhaustive series of experiments with a wide range of other possible explanatory variables[4], both economic and non-economic, only two proved persistently significant influences upon Conservative popularity: these were the rate of unemployment (lagged four months) and the 'Falklands factor'. With the rate of unemployment included all other economic relationships attenuated to statistical insignificance. Thus, this analysis disposes strongly against the view that the Thatcher government could, and can, increase unemployment with impunity and without regard to electoral effects. Despite assertions to the contrary (e.g., Butler, 1983), the electorate's reaction to high unemployment was not suspended because of the Falklands affair. The war simply gave an exogenous boost to government popularity that shifted it to a higher plane. There was inevitably going to be some decline in this support from the exceptionally high level immediately after the Falklands war (NOP recorded 51 per cent in late June 1982). In practice, however, government support ebbed away with increasing unemployment at much the same rate after the Falklands war as before it. Even the fact that Conservative support was increasing somewhat before the 'Falklands factor' was felt (e.g., Riddell, 1983, p. 50) may be interpreted as a response to a slight and temporary downturn in the rate of unemployment in the autumn of 1981. Thus, unemployment has been a politically significant issue, even if each percentage-point increase in joblessness entailed a smaller absolute loss of government support than was the case when unemployment was last a major determinant of government popularity in the early 1970s. The value of unemployment's metric regression coefficient ($-1 \cdot 684$) for the whole period from 1979 to 1983 is certainly less than half that of a corresponding one for the 1970–4 Conservative government (Husbands, 1985); however, this is not unexpected, given the greater range (9 or so percentage-points) in the rate of unemployment in the 1979–83 period. Of course, the effect of unemployment for the whole 1979–83 period appears only after control on the 'Falklands factor', which this analysis shows was worth perhaps 17 per cent to the Conservatives. Thus, but for the Falklands war, well over one in three voters supporting the Conservatives by late 1982 would not have been doing so.

However, if rising unemployment reduced the Conservatives' support

Table 7.3   *Percentages of respondents with various views on the relative priority to be given to reducing the number of unemployed people and to reducing inflation, by voting path between 1979 and 1983 and by vote in the 1983 general election*

	CON to LAB	LIB to LAB	Too young to LAB	LAB to LAB	All LAB voters
Wanting reduction of unemployment	75	—	100	91	90
Wanting reduction of inflation	25	—	0	9	10
Wanting other priority	0	—	0	0	0
Total:	100	—	100	100	100
N:	12	4	11	186	234

	LAB to CON	LIB to CON	Too young to CON	CON to CON	All CON voters
Wanting reduction of unemployment	70	64	47	61	61
Wanting reduction of inflation	30	27	47	38	37
Wanting other priority	0	9	6	2	2
Total:	100	100	100	101[1]	100
N:	23	11	17	261	345

	CON to ALL	LAB to ALL	Too young to ALL	LIB to ALL	All ALL voters
Wanting reduction of unemployment	80	94	67	89	85
Wanting reduction of inflation	18	4	25	11	13
Wanting other priority	2	1	8	0	2
Total:	100	99	100	100	100
N:	50	70	12	53	215

	Total sample
Wanting reduction of unemployment	77
Wanting reduction of inflation	22
Wanting other priority	2
Total:	101
N:	992

Note:
[1] Some of the percentage totals in this and later tables in the chapter contain rounding errors.

between 1979 and 1983, why was it not even more significant? Not for lack of salience, as we have seen. Indeed, since July 1980 the issue has consistently been perceived by Gallup's respondents as the most urgent problem facing the country (Webb and Wybrow, 1981, pp. 18, 48). Nor was it downgraded by any supposed incompatibility with another traditional goal of government, the reduction of inflation. Table 7.3 shows that almost all groups of voters saw the reduction of unemployment as a more important goal than that of reducing inflation, which – at least when viewed in the perspective of the time period from, say, early 1982 to May 1983 – was the government's central 'success story'. Only a comparatively small group of first-time voters supporting the Conservatives divided equally in the priority that they wanted to give to the reduction of unemployment and of inflation. The majority for giving priority to reducing unemployment is lowest among Conservatives (as the studies of Hibbs and Tufte cited above would have predicted) but unemployment has now reached such a level that even this group of voters is more averse to it than to inflation.

The central reasons why unemployment did not cost the Conservatives more votes were an exonerating disposition towards the responsibility of the Conservative government and the lack of plausibility of the alternative policies offered by the other parties. This is not to say, however, that the public necessarily regards reducing contemporary levels of unemployment as a totally intractable problem, but rather that voters are uncertain and dispirited about the time-span in which any significant reduction is to be expected. In November 1982 and again in May 1983 Gallup asked respondents whether they thought high unemployment was the kind of problem that no government could really solve or whether they thought it could be solved if a government really tried to apply the right measures. On both occasions about 58 per cent replied that it could be reduced by applying appropriate measures; around 35 per cent gave a fatalistic response and 7 per cent did not know (*GPI*, November 1982, p. 13; June 1983, p. 32). In January 1983 Gallup asked the public how long would be needed for a drastic reduction in unemployment: 14 per cent thought five to ten years would be needed, 17 per cent more than ten years, 22 per cent thought there would never be a drastic reduction and 19 per cent did not know (*GPI*, January 1983, p. 10). A Marplan poll on 31 May–1 June 1983 reported a similar set of findings, except for a rather higher percentage feeling that no substantial reduction would ever be achieved (*Guardian*, 3 June 1983, p. 3).[5]

Whatever may be the true degree of public fatalism about reducing unemployment, many of our respondents were willing to absolve Conservative government policies of much of the responsibility for the increase to current levels. The same Marplan poll of 31 May–1 June found that 67 per cent of respondents thought unemployment affected most industrialized countries equally. This exoneration prevailed despite the controversial publication on 24 May, during the election campaign, of a draft report from the Commons Treasury Committee (chaired by Edward du Cann) concerning international monetary arrangements, which was widely interpreted as attributing more than half the increase in unemployment since 1979 to the government's monetary policy (*Guardian*, 25 May 1983, pp. 1, 32). In our own survey we gave respondents a showcard listing a number of possible reasons for the doubling of the official unemployment rate since the beginning of 1980; the various responses had been formulated after appropriate piloting and respondents were asked their view of the most important reason and the next most important reason. Table 7.4 shows the five most frequently cited most

Table 7.4 Percentages of respondents with various views on the most important reason for the doubling of the official unemployment rate since the beginning of 1980, by voting path between 1979 and 1983 and by vote in the 1983 general election

	CON to LAB	LIB to LAB	Too young to LAB	LAB to LAB	All LAB voters	LAB to CON	LIB to CON	Too young to CON	CON to CON	All CON voters	CON to ALL	LAB to ALL	Too young to ALL	LIB to ALL	All ALL voters	Total sample
Naming:																
A worldwide recession	38	—	27	24	26	57	50	47	51	52	58	40	31	41	44	42
Conservative policies since 1979	38	—	55	50	50	19	8	0	5	6	9	39	31	31	29	24
Inability to compete because of high wages	8	—	0	4	4	5	8	18	10	10	13	3	23	9	8	8
New technology	8	—	9	10	8	0	17	18	8	8	6	7	0	11	7	9
Labour policies from 1974 to 1979	0	—	0	1	1	5	0	6	14	13	6	0	8	0	2	6
Other reasons	8	—	9	12	11	14	17	12	12	13	8	10	8	9	9	11
Total:	100	—	100	101	100	100	100	101	100	102	100	99	101	101	99	100
N:	13	4	11	178	224	21	12	17	258	343	53	67	13	54	217	977

important reasons. Almost half the sample accepted the 'worldwide recession' explanation pushed so successfully by the government. Fewer than a quarter put greatest blame upon Conservative policies since 1979. Of course, Conservative policies were blamed twice as frequently as was world recession by Labour voters, but they were almost completely discounted by Conservative voters. Even amongst Alliance voters, however, there was a far greater tendency to blame world recession than Conservative policies. Still, there is an important difference between new Alliance voters who had voted Labour or Conservative in 1979. Former Conservatives clearly exonerated their former party's policies from responsibility for the current level of unemployment, while former Labour supporters showed the greatest disposition among Alliance supporters to blame Conservative policies.

Table 7.5 allows us further insights into why the Conservatives succeeded in surviving without suffering substantial loss of support on the unemployment issue. The other parties, but Labour in particular, failed to convince the electorate of the credibility and likely effectiveness of their alternatives, although Labour certainly made much of its 'alternative economic strategy'. Table 7.5 shows the ultimate failure of Labour to convince the electorate. Only a quarter of Labour's *own* supporters felt that the party's policies on unemployment were very likely to ensure a reduction. However, this level of optimism far exceeds that amongst other voters. Only 12 per cent of Conservative and 7 per cent of Alliance voters saw their party's policies as likely to reduce unemployment. Labour's policies were still perceived by Conservative and Alliance supporters as oriented to reducing unemployment; however, only one in twenty or so believed that they were particularly plausible. Few Alliance voters could have been attracted to Labour by its alternative economic strategy.

Of course, we are not examining attitudes on this subject in a vacuum. These data were collected immediately after an election campaign in which the run of events was very unfavourable to Labour. Given this, we can expect that on almost all subjects and issues opinions about Labour will be at their most negative. Indeed, there is evidence that, although the BBC/Gallup data collected just before the election showed unemployment still to be a 'Labour' issue (even if the party's net advantage was not great), opinion on this issue moved against Labour as the campaign proceeded. Certainly, this was the message that Conservatives felt they were receiving from the findings of their private polls.

In the first week of the campaign, in a survey conducted on 11–16 May, Gallup reported that 42 per cent of respondents thought Labour had the best policies on unemployment, 28 per cent said the Conservatives, 10 per cent said the Alliance and 20 per cent did not know (*Daily Telegraph*, 19 May 1983, p. 10). This gives Labour a lead of 14 points (42 minus 28) on this issue. A poll by Marplan conducted a little later in the campaign on 23–25 May suggested even then that any advantage Labour had had on the subject was slipping. A reduced 36 per cent of respondents thought that Labour had the best policies on unemployment, 28 per cent said the Conservatives, 10 per cent said the Alliance and 26 per cent did not know (*Guardian*, 27 May 1983, p. 3). Labour's

Table 7.5 Percentages of respondents saying that each party's policies on unemployment are very likely to reduce unemployment, by voting path between 1979 and 1983 and by vote in the 1983 general election

	CON to LAB	LIB to LAB	Too young to LAB	LAB to LAB	All LAB voters	LAB to CON	LIB to CON	Too young to CON	CON to CON	All CON voters	CON to ALL	LAB to ALL	Too young to ALL	LIB to ALL	All ALL voters	Total sample
Labour Party's	23	—	45	23	25	14	0	18	4	5	6	6	25	9	8	12
Conservative Party's	8	—	9	1	1	0	17	6	14	12	4	0	0	6	2	6
SDP–Liberal Alliance's	0	—	17	6	7	0	9	0	2	2	6	9	0	0	7	5
Mean N:	12	3	9	176	221	19	12	16	240	315	51	70	12	52	214	937

lead was therefore only 8 points. The later poll by Marplan already cited, taken on 31 May–1 June, reported further declines in Labour's advantage on unemployment. The figures were now: Labour 35 per cent, the Conservatives 31 per cent and the Alliance 14 per cent, while 20 per cent did not know. Labour's lead was just 4 points. At the beginning of the final week of the campaign this advantage may even have disappeared completely according to a further Marplan poll conducted on 6 June, although the BBC/Gallup data do imply that Labour had a slightly better image on this issue at the very end of the campaign. Marplan's 6 June poll reported that both Conservative and Labour had a 32 per cent rating for superior competence to handle the unemployment problem – this in a poll that rated Labour's electoral support as low as 26 per cent (*Guardian*, 7 June 1983, pp. 1, 28). What clearly happened during the campaign was a process of dissonance reduction, as at least a minority of voters (some never Labour voters, some Labour defectors and doubtless even some persisting Labour voters) sought to bring their cognitions about Labour's competence on the central issue of unemployment into line with their other understandings about the party (Festinger, 1962, pp. 18–24, 264–5; Brown, 1965, pp. 584–604). Perceptions of the party's capability and of the viability of its policies worsened during the short campaign, as doubts about its leadership and its policies on defence and disarmament dominated large parts of the media – totally beyond the control of the party's campaign managers. One can also speculate whether, among Labour's own consistent supporters, a 'spiral of silence' phenomenon might have occurred, which meant that the party failed to hold on to its vacillating earlier supporters (Noelle-Neumann, 1977, 1979). As Labour's troubles accumulated during the campaign, its loyal supporters may well have become more secretive about their affiliation and the reasons for it, a silence producing a favourable climate for the Alliance advance in the final days of the campaign.

7.4.2 Defence and disarmament

If unemployment was the issue upon which Labour might in other circumstances have been able to gain some votes, defence and disarmament were the areas upon which it clearly lost many. We noted before that concerns about defence – although not quite the subject of the greatest salience – were clearly very important for a majority of voters.

Because of the importance of question-wording in structuring attitudinal responses, we set out in all our issue questions to give respondents a range of differently worded statements for their assessment. On defence and disarmament we used six different statements in order to tap voters' opinion; these are shown in Table 7.6.

Voters clearly supported in quite a strong way some form of direct détente with the Soviet Union. Almost half the sample agreed strongly that Britain should seek to negotiate for a reduction in each side's nuclear arms holdings; a very solid majority agreed this at strong or moderate levels of agreement. Nor were there great differences between the supporters of the different parties: 50 per cent of Labour voters, 42 per cent of Conservatives and 53 per cent of

Alliance supporters agreed strongly with this. It is important therefore to remember that many in the sample who held a range of other views about defence, including what one might call 'escalationist' ones, claimed simultaneous agreement with the principle of détente.

The second statement in Table 7.6 – in effect seeking the degree of agreement with some or all of the government's policies of introducing Cruise and Pershing missiles and developing the Trident missile – was one of three attracting the next highest amount of strong agreement from the sample, although less than a fifth agreed strongly with this: well below the question on negotiated arms reductions. On this occasion, however, the inter-party differences are more noticeable. Barely a tenth of Labour and Alliance supporters agreed strongly with this 'escalationist' question, compared with a higher 30 per cent of Conservatives – the latter still only a minority, of course. New Conservative voters recruited from Labour showed the highest level of 'escalationist' sentiment in the sample.

The third statement of Table 7.6, about basing Britain's defence on the use of conventional weapons, was intended to capture one central aspect of Labour's intended defence policy (Labour Party, 1983, p. 37). Many of the results are the obverse of those obtained for the previous item, although there is a difference. First, both attracted strong agreement from about a fifth of the sample (not the same fifth!) Both attracted a similar amount of strong agreement from the supporters of the party with which the policy was identified: 32 per cent of Labour supporters agreed strongly. Understandably, few Conservative voters, even Labour defectors, agreed strongly with Labour's policy option; however, as many as a fifth of Alliance supporters did, probably even more among former Labour voters.

The next statement in Table 7.6 corresponds to many political commentators' interpretations of the dominant mood of the public on defence – deeply worried about the escalationist implications of Cruise/Pershing/Trident, but unwilling to see Britain left 'defenceless' without any nuclear weapons.[6] Again, the statement attracted strong agreement from about a fifth of the sample, with Labour and Alliance supporters being slightly more likely to feel this way than were Conservatives.

The statement concerning American bases merely encapsulates a corollary of present and likely future government policy on nuclear weapons but it does have additional implicit anti-Americanism. Unsurprisingly, therefore, the pattern of responses tends to resemble that of the pro-Cruise/Pershing/Trident statement, except that levels of strong agreement are correspondingly reduced. The statement finds almost no strong support among Labour voters, although levels of agreement among Alliance supporters equal or even exceed those for the Cruise/Pershing/Trident item.

Finally, the full unilateralist position received least support, only 8 per cent of the sample strongly agreeing. Almost no Conservatives took this position, less than 10 per cent of Alliance voters did, and only a fifth of Labour's voters.

Just as doubts about the feasibility of Labour's policy on unemployment grew during the campaign, so is there evidence that attitudes towards the party's defence policy started poorly and worsened as the campaign proceeded.

Table 7.6 *Percentages of respondents agreeing strongly with various statements on defence and disarmament, by voting path between 1979 and 1983 and by vote in the 1983 general election*

	CON to LAB	LIB to LAB	Too young to LAB	All LAB voters	LAB to CON	LIB to CON	Too young to CON	All CON voters	CON to ALL	LAB to ALL	Too young to ALL	LIB to ALL	All ALL voters	Total sample
Britain should seek to negotiate with the Russians in order to reduce both sides' holding of nuclear weapons	54	—	64	50	35	36	41	42	56	53	58	57	53	47
Given the state of the arms race, it is necessary for Britain to introduce new types of nuclear weapons	30	—	18	12	36	25	29	30	19	11	0	7	12	19
Britain should base its defence on a strong conventional army, navy, and air force, without nuclear weapons	50	—	27	32	15	0	7	7	20	28	8	19	21	19

Britain should keep the nuclear weapons it has now, but should not introduce any new types of nuclear weapons	46	—	27	22	24	14	0	12	16	15	19	19	15	26	21	19
Britain should continue to allow its territory to be used by the United States as a base from which American nuclear weapons could be launched	15	—	10	5	6	33	18	18	24	23	18	16	0	11	14	16
Britain should get rid of its own nuclear weapons, irrespective of what other countries do	15	—	9	21	19	0	0	2	2	2	8	8	8	7	8	8
Mean N:	12	4	11	176	224	21	12	17	251	335	52	71	13	54	217	970

However, the process was more serious because it was partly poor performance on defence that triggered adverse changes on other issues. On unemployment Labour's worsening standing followed from some voters adjusting their perceptions about Labour and unemployment to the accumulating negative intelligence being received about the party on other issues. Defence and disarmament were foremost among these other issues. Labour's increasing loss of credibility here was very directly related to the adverse mass media coverage of Labour leadership differences on defence, especially over policy on Polaris. These stories broke on 24, 25 and 26 May and there was a clear movement of opinion to the Conservatives in the ensuing few days. Unsurprisingly, the party's pollster, Robert Worcester, warned the party to 'keep off defence', while Judith Hart told Foot that he had lost the nuclear issue and should drop it (Mitchell, 1983, p. 122).

Marplan's poll on 23–25 May reported a 22-point Conservative lead as the party best able to handle the issues of defence and nuclear weapons; the Conservatives were rated 45 per cent, Labour at 23 per cent (*Guardian*, 27 May 1983, p. 3). By the time of Marplan's 31 May–1 June poll, however, the Conservative net advantage had widened to 29 points, with a major net gain from previous 'don't knows'. The Conservatives' rating had risen to 52 per cent and Labour's had held steady at 23 per cent (*Guardian*, 3 June 1983, p. 3). In the final days of the campaign, with the defence issue out of the limelight, Labour's net disadvantage stabilized and may even have fallen very slightly; in Marplan's 6 June poll, three days before polling, the figure for superior Conservative competence was 50 per cent and for Labour 23 per cent, giving a Conservative lead of 27 points (*Guardian*, 7 June 1983, p. 28). The 1983 campaign, when an issue with foreign-policy implications determined more voting than did a domestic-policy issue such as unemployment, departs substantially from the experience of most postwar British general elections reviewed by Budge (1982).

Later in the chapter we return to the defence issue in our analysis of the degree to which voters have logically consistent attitudes. For the moment, however, we may note the profound unpopularity of Labour's stance on defence and disarmament, despite a less than overwhelming enthusiasm for what Conservative policy on the subject has come to mean. The key to Labour's rescuing itself, at least in the short term, from the difficulties in which it found itself on defence is as much emphasis as possible upon proposals for détente and negotiated arms reduction. This is clearly an area of deep public concern. However, there is no denying the fact that the party must have a policy on nuclear-weapons holding and there is far to go before the strong-conventional-weapons-only position, let alone overt unilateralism, will be firmly accepted. The proposals on defence that are to be presented to the 1984 Party Conference for ratification do address some of the earlier ambiguities about operationalizing a strong-conventional-weapons-only policy but they do little to grasp the nettle of presenting unilateralism to a sceptical electorate (Dunleavy and Husbands, 1984b).

7.4.3   *Public services and the welfare state*

Despite Labour's attempts to inject the National Health Service issue into the campaign, public service cut-backs did not emerge as the sort of vote-winning issue the party undoubtedly needed. Part of the reason for this failure is a measure of public ambivalence about the welfare state and related public services, over and above Labour's general difficulty about agenda-setting during the campaign. Combined with widespread purported acceptance of conventional platitudes about the achievements of the welfare state are less laudatory views, either about specific aspects of its functioning or about the expenditure that is needed to keep it viable.

We put to our respondents a variety of attitude statements about public services, as Table 7.7 shows. Nearly two-fifths of the sample did agree strongly that 'the present welfare state is one of Britain's finest postwar achievements'. Over a third of Conservative and Alliance voters and more than a half of Labour's subscribed to this view. Interestingly, however, young voters are least likely to agree with it.

The issue of efficiency in the public services – associated in the electorate's mind with overmanning, supposedly spendthrift local authorities, 'fat' and so forth – is the subject of our next item. We sought deliberately to tap a belief in the existence of extreme forms of inefficiency in the public services by using the phrase 'plenty of scope'. Yet this item – of the five with some substantive policy implications – was the one attracting the highest level of strong agreement. Nearly a third of the sample agreed that there is plenty of scope for increased efficiency without reducing the quality of service. There is very little difference between the three parties here; a third of Labour voters agreed strongly with this view. For Labour voters this might conceivably be interpreted as an indirect criticism of Conservative handling of the public sector. Alternatively, it may reflect a deficiency in the question itself; 'our public services' may be too vague a phrase for respondents who would otherwise differentiate between, say, the National Health Service and refuse collection by local authorities. Whatever the truth on this matter, agreement with this response item is inconsistent with the widely held 'élite' view that the scope for large-scale cost-cutting without loss of quality has now largely gone, if indeed it ever existed. Riddell (1983, p. 118), for example, points out the lengths to which the last Labour government went, under Joel Barnett as Chief Secretary to the Treasury, to cut back any 'surplus' public expenditure. Yet a widespread belief in the potential for cutting continues to exist – among a good majority of the electorate if one considers the additional proportion tending to agree with this statement.

Many on the left have accused the present government of wanting at heart to 'Americanize' the welfare state, to introduce a system whereby the poor would be 'ghettoized' into using less than adequately financed and staffed public services, while the better-off would use private services paid for (in the case, say, of health care) by expensive insurance policies. The next two statements in Table 7.7 relate to this possibility and, as we shall see when responses to it are jointly examined, this is a source of some ambivalence about public services. There are, however, expected differences in the results obtained on these two

Table 7.7 Percentages of respondents agreeing strongly with various statements on public services and the welfare state, by voting path between 1979 and 1983 and by vote in the 1983 general election

	CON to LAB	LIB to LAB	Too young to LAB	LAB to LAB	All LAB voters	LAB to CON	LIB to CON	Too young to CON	CON to CON	All CON voters	CON to ALL	LAB to ALL	Too young to ALL	LIB to ALL	All ALL voters	Total sample
The present welfare state is one of Britain's finest postwar achievements	62	—	27	54	51	30	45	25	37	36	30	44	18	35	34	39
There is plenty of scope for increasing the efficiency of our public services without reducing the quality of service offered	54	—	27	33	34	32	33	31	31	31	37	34	8	29	30	32
We must avoid creating a situation where the better-off use private services and public services are only for the poor	36	—	20	41	38	25	27	12	18	18	33	46	17	41	37	28
People who can afford to use private welfare services should be encouraged to use these, while public services should be concentrated more on the really needy	33	—	9	17	20	33	33	25	29	29	33	24	15	30	27	27
We must find the money to go on improving the standard of public services for all, whether or not this means higher taxes	17	—	45	39	38	23	50	18	16	18	21	33	9	31	28	27
Britain's welfare state is too expensive for our present economy to sustain	8	—	10	5	6	10	12	12	7	9	2	3	8	4	3	7
Mean N:	12	4	11	178	226	21	12	17	256	338	52	70	12	53	214	969

statements, differences that do accord with party allegiance. Almost 30 per cent of the sample (not the same 30 per cent, of course) agreed strongly with the statement opposing the 'ghettoization' of public services and with the one encouraging the better-off to use private services. However, Labour and Alliance supporters (38 and 37 per cent respectively) were most likely to oppose the view that public services should be only for the poor; only 18 per cent of Conservatives felt similarly opposed. Former Labour supporters who voted Conservative or Alliance were noticeably more likely than others who voted as they did in 1983 to oppose this 'public-services-only-for-the-poor' position, a residual effect of their earlier party allegiance. Labour voters were slightly less likely than Conservative or Alliance voters to agree strongly with encouraging the better-off to use private services. Although these findings correspond to certain types of expectation about inter-party differences – expectations based on the more rhetorical aspects of Thatcherism (Riddell, 1983, pp. 137–63) – it is important to note that there are contrary consider- ations that would lead us to expect more general support for the principle of public-service expenditure. Le Grand (1982, pp. 23–122), for example, has reviewed much evidence to argue that the subsidy effects of public expenditure are in many cases regressive, especially so in the case of the NHS, whose greatest beneficiaries have notoriously been the middle class. Of course, this was not a novel observation – it dates back almost to the foundation of the NHS – but it does imply the likelihood of considerable diffidence, even hostility, among at least some Conservative supporters towards major cut-backs in certain types of public provision.

The next statement in Table 7.7 is intended to capture what has often been argued from other data is a basic feature of attitudes towards public services, namely, a willingness to pay higher taxes in return for the improvement (or at least maintenance) of public services (e.g., Webb and Wybrow, 1981, pp. 48–9). However, a recent study found a majority (54 per cent) in favour of merely the maintenance of present tax and expenditure levels, while only 32 per cent favoured increases; even so, less than one in ten voters supported actual reductions (Bosanquet, 1984, p. 80). Twenty-seven per cent of our sample agreed strongly with the statement on finding money for improving the standard of public services; Labour supporters were rather more likely – and Conservative ones rather less likely – to do so.

The final statement in Table 7.7 is intended to measure the degree of agreement with the obverse of the previous statement, that Britain's welfare state is too expensive for the present economy to sustain. It is clearly the most 'anti-welfare state' of all the statements and attracts a very small degree of strong support (7 per cent), implying that too draconian cuts by the present government would attract opposition even from its own supporters. Only 9 per cent of Conservative voters agreed strongly with it.

7.4.4 *The effects of assessed importance and party competence/ proximity regarding the three issues: A summary analysis*

Before presenting results concerning attitudes towards privatization and the

European Economic Community, it is worth pausing briefly to summarize the overall import of our findings so far on the three major issues of unemployment, defence and the welfare state. We focus on the extent to which perceptions of their salience and reactions to the parties' policies do in fact discriminate between Labour, Conservative and Alliance supporters. For this exercise we shall need some additional data. For the subjects of defence–disarmament and public services–the welfare state, we asked respondents which major party's policy came closest to their own views, that of Labour, Conservative, the Alliance or none.

This summary analysis needs a procedure that combines into single meaningful scales each respondent's assessment of the importance of the issues concerned and attitudes on it with respect to each party. The presence of three issues and three parties means that one may construct nine individual scales of importance–competence/proximity. First, however, it should be noted that the approach to the measurement of party competence and proximity necessarily differed between unemployment, whose reduction is in general a valence issue, and defence–disarmament and public services–the welfare state, which tend to be position issues. On unemployment, as we saw, we asked respondents to assess the likely effectiveness of the different parties' policies. On the other two issues we used the questions on proximity to any party's policy. This difference has implications for the form of the nine importance–competence/proximity variables. The three scales of importance–party competence on unemployment (one for each party) range from '−6' for a respondent feeling that the issue was extremely important but that the policies of the party concerned were very unlikely to reduce current levels, to '+6' for one with the same assessment of importance but feeling that the policies were very likely to do this. The six scales of importance–proximity on the other two issues range from '0' for a respondent not feeling closest to the policies of the party concerned, through '+1' for one who did feel closest to this party but rated the issue not at all important, to '+4' for one who felt closest to this party and rated the issue as very important.[7]

Also needed, of course, is a statistical procedure that can use these variables to discriminate between the three groups of party supporters. Such a procedure is discriminant analysis (Klecka, 1980); this technique uses variables measured in interval-level form to produce 'discriminant functions'. The full number of functions that may be extracted is one less than the number of groups between which discrimination is sought, although normally one is interested only in those functions that meet a minimum criterion of statistical significance. In the case of our analysis the presence of three different groups of supporters implies two discriminant functions, both of which are significant. Each variable in the analysis receives on each function a standardized coefficient, whose absolute value indicates its importance as a discriminator. The functions are in fact analogous to the factors produced by factor analysis, with the coefficients of each variable corresponding to factor loadings. The specific groups between which are the major contrasts specified by each function can be assessed readily from the group centroids, which are the mean values of each group on each function. Finally, discriminant analysis has a goodness-of-fit

Table 7.8 *Discriminant analysis of voters for the three major parties by reported importance of issues of unemployment, defence and disarmament, and public services and the welfare state, and assessments of parties' competence or proximity on each*

	Function One	Function Two
Variables[1]		
Unemployment		
Labour's competence and issue's importance	−0·123	0·154
Conservatives' competence and issue's importance	0·318	0·084
Alliance's competence and issue's importance	−0·008	−0·244
Defence and disarmament		
Labour's proximity and issue's importance	−0·081	0·166
Conservatives' proximity and issue's importance	0·426	0·016
Alliance's proximity and issue's importance	0·067	−0·401
Public services and the welfare state		
Labour's proximity and issue's importance	−0·452	0·470
Conservatives' proximity and issue's importance	0·408	0·290
Alliance's proximity and issue's importance	−0·218	−0·383
Group centroids		
Labour voters (N=230, 88%)[2]	−1·833	0·932
Conservative voters (N=338, 87%)	1·719	0·282
Alliance voters (N=216, 70%)	−0·738	−1·434
Proportion of variation explained by each function:	0·74	0·26

Notes:
[1] Note 7 of the chapter explains at length how the nine variables were constructed.
[2] The percentages in parentheses refer to the cases in each group whose membership of that group was correctly predicted by the two functions.

component, which measures how well a set of discriminant functions classifies the original respondents, seeing how the groups (of Labour, Conservative or Alliance voters) into which the analysis predicts they should fall compare with their observed classifications.

Table 7.8 shows our results. Clearly, the first of the functions identified by the technique is the most important since this accounts for 74 per cent of the variation in the nine discriminating variables. As the values of the group centroids show, the major contrast embodied by the first function is between Labour (−1·833) and Conservative (1·719) voters. It is extremely illuminating to note the source of this contrast, as indicated by the coefficients of the variables concerned. The major discriminating variables are importance of unemployment/Conservative competence, importance of defence–disarmament/Conservative proximity, importance of public services–the welfare state/Labour proximity, and importance of public services–the welfare state/Conservative proximity. Thus voters for the two parties differed in their composite views about importance and competence concerning the Conservatives and unemployment, but they tended not to do so concerning Labour and unemployment. The same is the case on defence and disarmament. This suggests that Labour and Conservative voters felt similarly on this composite index concerning Labour and unemployment, in part because neither group had great faith in the likely effectiveness of Labour's policy proposals. They also felt similarly on defence and disarmament because a substantial number of Labour voters felt closest to the Conservatives on this issue but saw it as of lesser importance.

The second function – while less important statistically – serves to contrast Labour and Alliance voters. The noteworthy discriminating variables are importance of unemployment/Alliance competence, importance of defence–disarmament/Alliance proximity, importance of public services–the welfare state/Labour proximity, and importance of public services–the welfare state/Alliance proximity. These findings may be interpreted in the same manner as those for the Labour/Conservative contrast. Eighty-three per cent of respondents were correctly classified by the two functions, with the fit being marginally less good for Alliance supporters.

7.4.5 Privatization

Privatization has been seen as a central feature of the current Conservative ideology and involves transferring to private firms activities currently being undertaken by the public sector at both the local and national level. According to some analyses, its attractiveness lies in its ideological compatibility with *laissez-faire* Conservatism. However, writers on the left have argued that its popularity derives rather from the fact that, by diminishing the public sector, it reverses a trend of the rich having to pay for more services than they themselves needed; it also enlarges the terrain that is open to private profits at the time of a general profitability crisis brought on by the cessation of assured economic growth (Levie, 1983). At the national level there was only limited progress in selling off public corporations by June 1983. Riddell (1983, p. 49) summarized the position in saying that 'the frontiers between the public and private sectors had changed only slightly [since 1979], affecting mainly some commercial and manufacturing operations rather than the core public utilities'. Even so, from 1981 onwards the government was preparing the way for the ultimate privatization of part or all of numerous major utilities and enterprises, of which British Telecom was the best-known example in the election run-up.

The public's attitudes to privatization reveal some of the ambivalence that we noted above concerning opinions about the welfare state. Table 7.9 contains our results on this issue. Some of our response items seek to tap whether people recognize the likely objective consequences of privatization, while others test for ideologically distinctive attitudes towards it.

The suggestion that it will mean the closure of uneconomic services seems unexceptionable – certainly in the analyses of the left – and, although it attracts strong agreement from only 29 per cent of all respondents in our sample, there are no remarkable inter-party differences on the subject. Our other statements are more partisan in form and therefore show corresponding differences between the supporters of the various parties. Conservatives are by far the

Table 7.9 Percentages of respondents agreeing strongly with statements about the effects of handing parts of industries back to the private sector, by voting path between 1979 and 1983 and by vote in the 1983 general election

	CON to LAB	LIB to LAB	Too young to LAB	LAB to LAB	All LAB voters	LAB to CON	LIB to CON	Too young to CON	CON to CON	All CON voters	CON to ALL	LAB to ALL	Too young to ALL	LIB to ALL	All ALL voters	Total sample
Will mean closure of uneconomic services	18	—	22	30	30	20	27	13	32	29	25	27	17	35	27	29
Will improve efficiency	31	—	11	8	10	19	25	41	42	39	22	13	33	20	18	26
Will produce services better tuned to customers' demands	33	—	13	8	10	23	33	12	40	36	22	12	8	23	16	23
Will mean heavier job losses	0	—	11	36	31	10	17	0	6	7	18	29	0	25	23	19
Will mean selling off national assets at low prices	27	—	0	33	31	5	0	7	5	5	4	16	9	28	16	16
Mean N:	12	3	9	161	201	21	11	16	242	323	50	66	12	51	205	913

most likely to believe that privatization will improve efficiency, nearly two-fifths of them agreeing strongly with this statement. Only 18 per cent of Alliance voters believe this, as did just 10 per cent of Labour supporters. However, on this issue there are particularly noticeable effects of party of origin among those switching, whether from Conservative or from Labour in 1979.

A libertarian faith in the ability of the market to produce what customers want is a justification for privatization cited by the government (Conservative Party, 1983, pp. 15–16). Clearly, it has convinced Conservatives far more than Labour or even Alliance supporters: 36 per cent of the first group, compared with 10 and 16 per cent respectively, agreed strongly with it. Again too there are persisting effects of party of origin among those switching allegiance between 1979 and 1983. The belief that privatization will lead to heavier job losses receives strong support from nearly a third of Labour's voters and nearly a quarter of those from the Alliance; Conservatives, however, generally do not accept this view. Only 5 per cent of Conservative voters agreed strongly with the bargain-basement conception of privatization, that it means selling off national assets at low prices. However, Labour and even some groups of Alliance supporters tended to be much more sceptical.

These data show numerous differences between the supporters of the three parties concerning the principles of privatization but, even among Conservatives, there is no strong consensus about its virtues, although a majority of this group (also including those tending to agree) does accept what purport to be the positive aspects of the exercise – the improvement of efficiency and the satisfaction of consumer demand. Even so, there may well be more ambiguity in Conservatives' attitudes to this aspect of Thatcherism than is immediately apparent. In any case, privatization was a low-salience issue in the 1983 election; it undoubtedly won and lost very few votes for any party but is chiefly a case where opinions were adjusted to be consistent with prior party preference.

7.4.6 The European Economic Community

Where the Common Market is concerned, perhaps as many as a fifth of the British electorate are gutless whingers. Since Britain's entry into Europe on 1 January 1973 there have been just two periods when a solid majority of the public said that they felt positive about this country's membership. These periods happen to coincide with the two major opportunities that have been presented to the British public to consent to withdrawal. One of these was at the time of the June 1975 referendum; the other was in 1983, when Labour's manifesto committed the party to withdrawal from the EEC. Faced with Labour's clear option, the electorate changed its collective opinion to what one may call the 'handbag-shaking' approach of demanding 'our' money back. Marsh (1979, esp. pp. 278–82) has reviewed poll evidence on attitudes to the Common Market up to June 1977 and, since the date of entry, positive sentiments outnumbered negative ones only from March 1975 to July 1976 – with a peak about the time of the referendum itself. The poll evidence assembled by Gallup for the period from July 1978 until as late as November 1982 upon whether the public felt Common Market membership to be a good or bad thing presents a remarkably stable picture of overall hostility. In eleven different polls in this period the percentage of positive responses never rose above 27 or fell below 21 per cent. The percentage of negative responses ranged from 45 to 57 per cent, and responses of 'neither good nor bad' ranged from 13 to 24 per cent; there was a consistent small minority of 'don't knows'. However, by 25–30 May 1983 a remarkable turnaround had occurred; 43 per cent of Gallup's respondents were adjudging the Common Market to be a good thing, compared with 30 per cent saying it was bad and 22 per cent saying neither (*GPI*, June 1983, p. 36). To cap it all, even as soon as the end of July and beginning of August 1983, opinions were shifting back to a negative predominance. Clearly, opinions on the Common Market, usually a relatively peripheral issue upon which inconsistency with government position occasions no great dissonance, were adjusted by many voters to be consistent with the policy of the party for which they were intending to vote in June 1983. This adjustment occurred only shortly before the election and there is no evidence that the dramatic post-Falklands increase in Conservative support was accompanied by any change of opinion on the Common Market. The adjustment that we have seen is a slightly different version of what we saw happened during the campaign itself to opinions about party competences on unemployment and on defence and disarmament. The very ephemerality of the Common Market issue meant the large amount of adjustment to which the relevant opinions were subject could be undertaken without those doing it feeling that they were betraying a former commitment. As Table 7.1 showed us, a relatively small proportion of our total sample felt that the Common Market was a very important issue.

Table 7.10 contains the three statements about the EEC that were put to our respondents. Of course, none necessarily contradicts any other, certainly if different periods of time are allowed for, and all refer to widely discussed options concerning British policy towards the EEC.

The first – intended above by the sardonic reference to the handbag-shaking approach – refers to what the government sees as the central aspect of its policy, the reduction of Britain's net budget contributions and reform of the Common Agricultural Policy (Conservative Party, 1983, p. 44). A solid 55 per cent agreed strongly with this, with only one perhaps significant variation among the groups analysed separately. The purported 'political' goal of the EEC of greater West European unity attracts strong agreement from more than a third of the sample, with slight inter-party differences. Labour voters may feel this less strongly but more than half the 1979 Liberals staying with the Alliance felt this strongly. Finally, consistent with the earlier review of recent trends in public opinion about withdrawal from the EEC, only 17 per cent of the sample agreed strongly with this, with some predictable inter-party differences. Of Labour voters, 34 per cent agreed strongly with their party's manifesto commitment but a larger proportion of Alliance supporters than Conservatives felt similarly – 15 and 7 per cent respectively. On the issue of withdrawal there is some residual impact of party of origin among those switching allegiance since 1979.

Table 7.10 *Percentages of respondents agreeing strongly with various statements about the European Economic Community, by voting path between 1979 and 1983 and by vote in the 1983 general election*

	CON to LAB	LIB to LAB	Too young to LAB	LAB to LAB	All LAB voters	LAB to CON	LIB to CON	Too young to CON	CON to CON	All CON voters	CON to ALL	LAB to ALL	Too young to ALL	LIB to ALL	All ALL voters	Total sample
Britain should insist that alterations are made in the Community's agricultural policy and in the budget contributions of the various member countries, even if this makes us unpopular	50	—	38	54	53	48	50	53	51	51	53	58	46	63	55	52
Britain should be more fully committed to a more united western Europe	18	—	25	31	30	32	36	43	38	37	41	33	18	51	37	35
Britain should begin negotiations to withdraw from the Common Market over a period of years	23	—	38	35	34	14	18	0	5	7	8	23	8	9	15	17
Mean N:	11	3	8	168	207	21	11	15	246	326	51	68	11	50	207	924

7.5   Measurement error and opinion consistency

Our general findings broadly correspond, unsurprisingly, with the emphasis of Crewe's (1983) analysis of the election outcome based upon the BBC/Gallup data. The simplest inference that one could make from the data presented so far is that Labour lost the election because it had policy problems on the issues that mattered to the electorate (unemployment, defence and disarmament) and failed to establish the salience of those issues where it might have been stronger (the state of the public services and – one we have not been able to consider – schools and education). The Conservatives won for complementary reasons. Of course, to deny this simple truth would be to doubt the validity of most that has been presented in this chapter hitherto and we have no intention of, or interest in, doing that. However, without invalidating what has been argued already, it is possible, indeed necessary, to allow for some qualification to this picture, particularly since we have reason to believe from other data and (as we shall see) from our own that opinions are not as stable and firmly held as some rational-choice and issue-oriented explanations of voting behaviour would affirm. We have already seen that, under the impact of campaign events, expressed opinions on quite central political issues like unemployment and defence may shift; on more peripheral issues such as the Common Market they may move appreciably to align themselves with other political stimuli. Because a survey such as ours collects data around a single point in time, any variability in opinions that occurs over time cannot be adequately captured; recall questions are well known for their bias (Himmelweit, Biberian and Stockdale, 1978), although we are sometimes forced to use them, as in our own survey when questioning about voting behaviour in 1979. We do, however, want to ensure that inferences from a survey conducted in one time period do not give an exaggerated impression of the issue awareness and issue consistency of the electorate.

The subject of the consistency and stability of political attitudes has been approached in previous work largely using one or both of two techniques:

1   the search for stability at two or more points in time in the attitudes expressed on the same subject by the same person interviewed on each occasion;
2   the search for consistency or 'constraint' between opinions on two or more different issues, measured at the same point in time and for the same person, when the issues concerned are seen as part of some underlying syndrome (say, the left–right continuum or internationalism– isolationism).

These matters have usually been approached using various of the conventional correlational techniques across large samples. The work of Converse (1964, respectively pp. 238–45 and 227–31) contains particularly good examples of both approaches and Nie, Verba and Petrocik (1976, pp. 123–55) offer a further widely cited example of the latter. As we shall see, however, there has been some considerable dispute about how to interpret the results of these procedures, particularly the first but also the second.[8] Our own slightly different approach focuses on the degree of straightforward illogicality in responses to statements with strongly implied logical relationships.

Converse's (1964, 1970) work, especially his 1964 article, is probably the most widely known and seminal work in political science on the subject of attitude consistency. He used data collected in a panel study that interviewed the same respondents three times – in 1956, 1958 and 1960 – to show that there was a remarkable *in*stability over time in the expressed opinions held by many individuals on numerous issues, far more than could apparently be reconciled with the existence of genuine change of attitude. Converse sought to explain his results by postulating what he called a 'black-and-white' model, which saw 'a very stringent division of the population into two sharply contrasting subsets' (Converse, 1970, p. 173). The first group, a comparatively small proportion of the electorate, held genuine attitudes that remained stable between successive interviews. The second and far larger group held 'nonattitudes' and responded randomly on each occasion. Converse felt that the two groups were distinguished by their differing levels of political sophistication. Butler and Stokes (1974, pp. 276–85) have reported analogous instability in the British electorate on the issues of nationalization and nuclear disarmament, thus implying a similar division of sophistication. The concept of nonattitude and Converse's attempt to divide the American electorate into these two groups have subsequently been criticized, notably in three articles (Pierce and Rose, 1974; Achen, 1975; Erikson, 1979). The major focus of all three articles is the extent to which Converse's findings may be explained by measurement error; all claim that Converse's attitudinal data, once measurement error in them has been allowed for, exhibit a high degree of stability between successive interviews and in no way justify the division of the electorate into a minority of sophisticates and a majority without attitude on many subjects. Converse's error, so his critics argue, is to have too credulous an approach to attitude measurement. Attitudes, so they say, are not to be seen as single points on one dimension but rather as comprising a distribution of points around a true attitude position, since it is held unreasonable to expect any respondent, even when no attitude change has occurred, always to respond with precisely the same degree of objective intensity. Thus, if attitudes are conceived as located on continua, somebody who has a genuine quite strong attitude on a subject would have a distribution of repeated measured responses around this 'quite strong' position. In the case of somebody with a weak attitude position on a subject, a distribution of repeated measured attitudes might even expand across both 'agree' and 'disagree' parts of the continuum. Pierce and Rose assume that a measured attitude is the combination of a true attitude and a short-term force (constituting measurement error) that over repeated interviews would be normally distributed, independent of the attitude, have a mean zero for each respondent and have the same degree of dispersion for all respondents. Achen and Erikson do not assume equal response variability around a true attitude for all respondents and Achen has a rather more complex conception of attitude that is based on the work of Coombs (1964, pp. 106–18). Both Achen and Erikson show that individual response variation has no notable correlation with any conceptualization of, or surrogate for, political sophistication.

The revisionist outcome of this particular debate then is that stable attitudes do exist among most of the American electorate – or did exist in the 1956–60 period – on many political issues but that individual measurements of them contained high amounts of response error. This may be accurate as far as it goes but it is none the less a little difficult to reconcile with the sort of experience that Converse himself reports, and which anybody with any interviewing practice will also know, that many respondents do not appear to answer some attitude questions with either great deliberation or much awareness of any wider implications that they may contain. Rather, if stable attitudes exist, it may be because many respondents are reacting, either fairly mechanically or using ill-defined personal criteria, to a consistent set of political stimuli; in these circumstances one may wonder whether the opinions expressed can with justice be called genuine attitudes.

Schuman and Presser (1981, pp. 147–60) have in any case developed and refined Converse's notion of nonattitude, although they have done so without referring to the controversy in political science reviewed above. First of all, they confirm that perhaps 30 per cent of the American public will provide an opinion on a proposed law about which they know nothing if the question is asked without an explicit 'don't know' option. Bishop *et al.* (1980) obtained a similar result in a study in Cincinnati that inquired about a fictitious Public Affairs Act. Schuman and Presser (1981, p. 159) argue that many who offer opinions on subjects about which they know nothing do not merely respond randomly by flipping a mental coin, as the original concept of nonattitude suggested. Instead, they often use a variety of intrinsic and extrinsic cues to make a reasonable guess (though often a wrong one) about what the unknown issue being inquired about actually represents. They then offer an opinion on the basis of that guess.

This later research seems to rehabilitate the concept of nonattitude, at least in some modified form, despite the purported certainty of the conclusions of Converse's critics. Certainly, we can present some corroborating evidence which shows that on subjects where one would expect logically consistent responses, there may exist a considerable amount of ambivalence, as shown by the presence of logically inconsistent answers.

We are now almost ready to present our data on response consistency on the same subjects. As said already, these analyses differ from conventional issue-constraint approaches, which are based on the degree of correlation between attitudes on different subjects that supposedly derive from an under-lying syndrome. Instead, we focus on the degree of logical connectedness between different questions on the same subject. Of course, our own data may be subject to response error (heaven forbid!), random or otherwise, and it may be thought that this must affect the validity of the exercise being undertaken. However, this will not necessarily be the case. Individual response distri-butions for those stating strong degrees of agreement or disagreement will not usually cross the threshold into the opposing part of the scale and so our method of defining what we shall be calling strong inconsistency will not be

Table 7.11 *Percentages of respondents expressing consistent and weakly or strongly inconsistent opinions between combinations of statements on defence and disarmament and on public services and the welfare state, by vote in the 1983 general election*[1]

	Labour	Conservative	Alliance	Total sample

Defence and disarmament
Between:
1 *Given the state of the arms race, it is necessary for Britain to introduce new types of nuclear weapons,*
2 *Britain should keep the nuclear weapons it has now, but should not introduce any new types of nuclear weapons,* and
3 *Britain should get rid of its own nuclear weapons, irrespective of what other countries do*

	Labour	Conservative	Alliance	Total sample
Consistently for further nuclear weapons	18	55	29	37
Consistently for status quo	24	19	30	24
Consistently unilateralist	21	1	9	9
Weakly inconsistent	29	20	30	25
Strongly inconsistent	8	5	2	5
Total:	100	100	100	100
N:	204	317	211	920

Public services and the welfare state
Between:
1 *We must avoid creating a situation where the better-off use private services and public services are only for the poor,* and
2 *People who can afford to use private welfare services should be encouraged to use these, while public services should be concentrated more on the really needy*

	Labour	Conservative	Alliance	Total sample
Consistent	53	50	50	50
Weakly inconsistent	38	44	39	40
Strongly inconsistent	9	6	11	9
Total:	100	100	100	99
N:	222	331	209	943

Between:
1 *We must find the money to go on improving the standard of public services for all, whether or not this means higher taxes,* and
2 *Britain's welfare state is too expensive for our present economy to sustain*

	Labour	Conservative	Alliance	Total sample
Consistent	77	62	70	67
Weakly inconsistent	20	34	29	30
Strongly inconsistent	4	3	1	3
Total:	101	99	100	100
N:	219	324	206	931

Note:
[1] The derivation of the various categories of consistency and inconsistency in the case of the three statements on defence and disarmament is explained in the text.

In the two cases of pairs of statements consistency of expressed opinion has been defined as agreeing strongly/tending to agree with one statement in the respective pair and disagreeing strongly/tending to disagree with the other statement. Weak inconsistency has been defined as agreeing strongly/tending to agree with one statement and tending to agree with the other or as disagreeing strongly/tending to disagree with one statement and tending to disagree with the other. Strong inconsistency has been defined as agreeing strongly with both statements or as disagreeing strongly with both statements.

invalid on that score. In the case of the other categories, weak inconsistency and the various types of consistency, it may be said that, though some individuals may have been wrongly classified, the net effects of this should be mutually self-cancelling and the aggregate distributions are thus acceptable as a basis of inference. A more serious possibility of invalidity – one which seriously concerned Converse and which is briefly discussed by Pierce and Rose – is response-set, the well-known tendency of some respondents to agree (or disagree) seriatim with a list of statements irrespective of actual content. The possible existence of response-set must be an accompanying qualification to the inferences from these data, since we have no independent test for the existence of such a problem.

7.5.1   Defence and disarmament

We noted in Table 7.6 the basic structure of citizens' views on defence and disarmament. We remarked on the general disposition among almost all voters, whatever their other views, to favour some form of détente with the Soviet Union. However, some of the statements used implied support for different and incompatible policies and we did not at the time consider to what extent respondents were logical in their overall pattern of answers.

In the case of the other items in Table 7.11, we examine the degree of consistency between two incompatible statements, where agreement with one logically implies disagreement with the other and vice versa; classification proceeded as described in Note 1 of Table 7.11. For defence and disarmament there are more than two major policy options and the analysis of consistency is correspondingly more complicated. We may distinguish three major positions: first, an 'escalationist' one, favouring the introduction of new types of nuclear weapons (Statement 1 in Table 7.11); second, a status quo position favouring retention of currently held nuclear weapons but opposition to new ones (Statement 2); and third, a fully unilateralist position (Statement 3). There are eight combinations of agree/disagree responses among three items (2^3) and only three of these have internal consistency. In logic those consistently for escalation should agree with Statement 1 and disagree with Statements 2 and 3. Those consistently for the status quo should agree with Statement 2 and disagree with 1 and 3. Consistent unilateralists should agree with Statement 3 and disagree with 1 and 2. Respondents have been classified accordingly for the purpose of the analysis in Table 7.11, irrespective of the intensity (strong or moderate) of their agreement or disagreement. Strongly inconsistent respondents are all those with one of the five combinations of inconsistent responses, where all expressions of agreement/disagreement were of strong intensity. In contrast, weakly inconsistent respondents are those in one of these five combinations, except that their agreements and disagreements were of weak or mixed degrees of intensity.

The results in Table 7.11 belie any simple depiction of the British electorate, certainly the view that something approaching a consensus exists about the desirability of retaining nuclear weapons but that there is general hostility to the new generation of missiles. There is little real comfort for the unilateralists, since fewer than 10 per cent of the entire electorate are unambiguously for this position. Only a quarter subscribe to the status quo, or what is supposed by some to be the consensus view. The government's policy of introducing new nuclear weapons receives most support, but from fewer than two-fifths of the sample. Fully 30 per cent express inconsistent attitudes on this matter and are ambivalent in their commitment to (mostly) two different positions; nearly two-thirds of these hover between the status quo and escalation. Only a fifth of those Labour voters with a substantive opinion on all three items subscribe to what was Labour's manifesto policy, whereas 55 per cent of such Conservative supporters agreed with government plans on this subject. The bulk of Alliance voters were equally for the status quo, or for escalation, or held weakly inconsistent attitudes. The highest amount of strong inconsistency, 8 per cent, was found – unsurprisingly – among Labour's voters.

7.5.2 Public service and the welfare state

We have had occasion above (pp. 165–7) to remark on the diffidence of attitudes towards the welfare state, seen especially in the readiness to praise the principle but to engage in carping criticism of its implementation. The data in Table 7.11 allow us to explore other aspects of this, first concerning the desirability of 'ghettoizing' public services only for the poor, and secondly about the problem of financing the welfare state.

Statements 1 and 2 on the first of these subjects may be amenable to a casuistical interpretation of possible consistency – perhaps revolving around the meaning to be placed on 'encouraged' in Statement 2 – but practice implies their mutual incompatibility. Certainly, the American experience has demonstrated that publicly provided health service for the poor is usually second rate and this is the understanding behind the formulation of Statement 1. Perhaps because this is slightly esoteric, there is a high level of inconsistency between the two statements, nearly 10 per cent being strongly so and a further 40 per cent weakly so. There are no significant differences between the parties' supporters in their levels of consistency.

Statements 1 and 2 concerning the financing of public services attract less inconsistency than the previous pair, only 3 per cent of the sample being strongly so and 30 per cent weakly so. However, a significantly higher proportion of Conservative and Alliance supporters betray weak inconsistency, an indication of greater ambivalence on this subject when one moves away from Labour supporters, whose commitment to public services and the welfare state is more clear-cut and less diverted by the ideological blandishments of Thatcherism.

Conclusion

In the 1983 general election Labour lost the issue battles; first, because it was unable to establish the credibility of its own policies on the one issue, unemployment, that was central to the campaign; secondly, because it was vulnerable on a further issue, defence, that dominated the middle period of the campaign; and thirdly, because it was unable to push to prominence one issue – public services, especially the NHS and the welfare state – where it might have been able to gain votes. Even on this last, however, we have seen the large degree of public ambivalence.

Moreover, even on matters not central to the campaign, such as the EEC, opinions shifted among perhaps as many as a fifth of the electorate as the election approached so that, by polling day, there was apparently a pro-Market majority. Even on the more central questions of the campaign we have seen evidence of how expressed attitudes may shift for a minority of the electorate during the short period of an election campaign in which one party was at an increasing ideological disadvantage. Taken with the data that we have presented about levels of logical inconsistency in attitudes on the same subject, this evidence leads us to reject the supreme emphasis placed by issue-oriented approaches upon issue attitudes as determinants of voting decision.

8 The New Political Map of Britain, 1974 to 1983

This chapter presents our analyses of the constituency-level outcomes in the 1983 election. We begin by drawing attention to some caveats that need to be made in undertaking aggregate data analysis of this kind. Secondly, we look at regional variations in party support and at the effects of party position in 1979 upon vote change between 1979 and 1983. Thirdly, we analyze the extent to which spatial variations in levels of party support may be attributed to the social and economic characteristics of different constituencies. Data extracted from the 1981 Census are used to construct models of the bases of party support in 1983, as well as change in support since 1979. Fourthly, we analyse the pattern of changes in party support in the English metropolitan counties during the actual campaign – from the district council elections on 5 May 1983 to the general election only five weeks later – particularly those factors that insulated Labour to some extent from its worst vote losses. A similar analysis for Greater London compares changes between the London Borough Council elections of 6 May 1982 and the 1983 general election. Finally, we examine some factors associated with particular contests in order to ascertain whether these had any effects upon party support that were additional to those of the social and economic composition of the constituencies themselves.

8.1 The problems of constituency-level analysis

This chapter makes quite extensive use of correlation and regression analysis.

The dependent variables are the percentage levels of party support in 1983 and percentage-point changes from an earlier election. The independent or explanatory variables are what we shall call the constituency and contest characteristics. There is, however, an important difference between these two types of independent variable, one that complicates the inferences that we may draw from our analyses. Our variables measuring constituency characteristics, derived from the Census, vary within constituency; those concerning contests do not.

In order to clarify this difference, let us take an example of a contest characteristic, such as whether or not a constituency had, say, a woman candidate standing on behalf of one of the major parties. It has no variation within a constituency; either the whole of a particular constituency has such a candidate fighting for a certain party, or it does not. The only contest characteristic that we consider for which this is not quite the case is incumbency, which did sometimes vary slightly within constituency – although almost certainly inconsequentially for the analysis – because of the constituency boundary changes. Absence of within-constituency variation means that one may attribute characteristics (such as having women candidacies) to whole constituencies, thus treating the latter as genuine units of analysis and calculating the net effects of such characteristics upon parties' support levels across whole constituencies.[1]

Variables measuring social and economic characteristics are not of this sort. Typically, but not invariably, they are measured as the *percentage* of a relevant population within each constituency that has the respective characteristic. This population may sometimes be far from identical with the actual electorate of that constituency. Thus, the 'economically active' population, for example, excludes those who have retired and those who do not work and are not seeking work. It includes some who have not yet attained voting age.

An individual constituency is relatively 'high' or relatively 'low' on any given constituency-characteristic variable according to how its percentage score compares with, say, the corresponding percentage for the country as a whole. When considering geographical units as large as constituencies, it is rare to find the extreme values of 0 per cent or 100 per cent. It is true that on certain social and economic variables conventionally used in political analysis many individual constituencies have values that approach one of these extremes. For example, the constituency with the lowest percentage born in the New Commonwealth or Pakistan, Glasgow Provan, has only 0·113 per cent of its residents so classified. A further 103 constituencies in Great Britain have fewer than 0·5 per cent of their residents in this category. What is inconceivable is that there are variables for which some constituencies have a value of 0 per cent and all others one of 100 per cent. Stated in a sentence: social and economic characteristics have within-constituency variation.

This fact runs the risk of embroiling us in a debate that has now engaged social science for over thirty years. The original and seminal paper on the subject was published in 1950 (Robinson, 1950) and the subsequent literature elaborating and qualifying its central argument has been extensive (e.g., Langbein and Lichtman, 1978; Borgatta and Jackson, 1980). The debate concerns the so-called 'ecological fallacy'.[2] This refers to the legitimacy or lack of it of making inferences about the determinants of the behaviour of individuals (in our case, their voting behaviour as determined by, say, their social class) from relationships that exist between variables aggregated across larger units of which those individuals are members (say, the relationship between percentage support for Labour and the percentage of manual workers calculated across constituencies). As Langbein and Lichtman (1978) and Hammond (1979) have recently pointed out – in summarizing a plenitude of earlier work by themselves or others – there are circumstances in which it is legitimate to use the direction (positive or negative) – even if not the absolute size – of a relationship between two aggregated variables in order to make inferences about the corresponding relationship among the constituent individuals. However, there is some dispute – the details of which should not detain us – about which is the appropriate statistic to use for such inferences. There is also the unhappy fact that the conditions which should obtain for the unambiguous transfer of an inference from aggregate to individual level do not exist in many cases, although Crewe and Payne (1976) develop with some success a model of individual voting behaviour based upon aggregate data in connection with the 1970 general election. Moreover, both Hawkes (1969) and Miller (1972) have used aggregate data to estimate party-to-party vote turnover between pairs of successive general elections. Recent historical analyses of the determinants of British voting behaviour (Miller, 1977; Wald, 1983), lacking appropriate individual-level data collected by surveys, have of course used aggregate data but in at least one case (Wald, 1983, p. 79) may have been a little dismissive of the possible problems of the ecological fallacy. In our analyses we shall be as tentative as is necessary about what relationships may exist at the individual level to correspond with those found at the aggregate level.

8.2   The regional geography of party support

In recent years the 'regionalization' of British politics has become one of the better-known clichés of political discussion and commentary. The 'north–south divide', 'the affluent south–the hungry north': such expressions and their assumptions seem to have become the standby of political commentators. However, there *is* a good deal of truth in this general picture. Labour support is higher in the north and lower in the south and its percentage-point losses since October 1974 have also been lower in the north. Curtice and Steed (1980, pp. 394–5) reported that from October 1974 to May 1979 there was a 4·2 per cent two-party swing from Labour to the Conservatives in the north and a 7·7 per cent one in the south. This trend of differential loss by Labour continued between May 1979 and June 1983.[3]

Table B.1, in Appendix B p. 224, shows how the three main parties have fared in terms of regional levels of their support and of percentage-point changes in that support at the three general elections since October 1974. The regions used are the eleven standard ones of Great Britain, as defined in Note 1 of Table B.1. Because of the slightly forbidding nature of that table, its

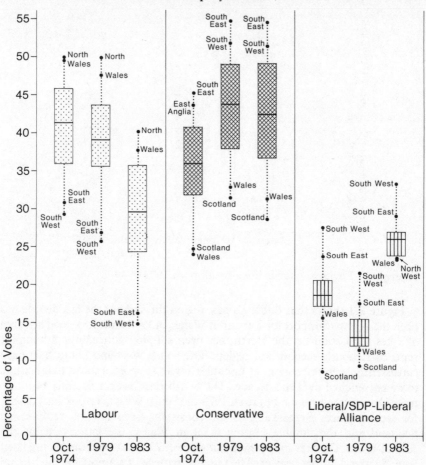

Figure 8.1 Regional party support in the October 1974, 1979 and 1983 general elections

essential features are presented diagrammatically using so-called box-and-dot plots (Erickson and Nosanchuk, 1979, pp. 56–65). Figure 8.1 represents the levels of party support for the October 1974, 1979 and 1983 general elections, while Figure 8.2 shows percentage-point changes for each party between 1979 and 1983 (net of respective mean changes). The two figures enable one to see at a glance the regions where each party has been strongest and weakest and where each did relatively well and relatively badly between 1979 and 1983.

Each box in a box-and-dot plot extends from the lower to the upper quartile of the distribution concerned, thus giving a visual image of the dispersion in the middle 50 per cent of party support from region to region. The horizontal line through each box shows the position of the mean of the distribution. Dotted lines extending from the top and bottom of each box lead to the two upper and lower extreme cases in each distribution. The length of these dotted lines indicates how atypical these extreme cases are.

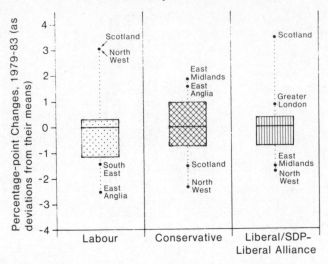

Figure 8.2   Regional change in party support, 1979 to 1983

Figure 8.1 shows that Labour's best region throughout the last decade has been the North. Support for Labour in Wales, in 1974 almost as good a source of votes for Labour as the North, has been slipping noticeably, although it remains Labour's second-best region. The South West and South East have consistently been the regions of Labour's lowest support, a status that became more entrenched over the decade. The South East has consistently been the most Conservative region but from 1979 the South West overtook East Anglia for second place. Remarkable is the consistent Conservative weakness in Scotland and the notable improvement in Wales; the latter remains the second-lowest Conservative region but since 1979 it has been distancing itself from Scotland in this respect. The regional pattern of support for the Liberal Party and, in 1983, the SDP–Liberal Alliance contains a number of interesting features. The South West in particular, but also the South East, have been the two most favourable regions throughout the three elections. In October 1974 and 1979 the Liberals performed badly in both Wales and Scotland, but very obviously so in 1974 in the latter. This was partly because the Liberals are especially susceptible to losing votes to the Nationalists but also because, in Scotland at least, many constituencies were not contested. By 1983, however, with the arrival of the SDP, the Alliance had no noticeably bad regions. Wales, with 23·3 per cent for the Alliance, was less than 3 percentage-points below the national average. The North West emerged in 1983 as the other region where the Alliance was just marginally less successful.

Figure 8.2 shows the regional distribution of relative losses and gains from 1979 to 1983. For Labour, of course, the diagram shows where its losses were smallest and where they were greatest. For the Alliance it shows where its gains were greatest and where smallest, compared with Liberal results in 1979. For the Conservatives there is a range between a gain of 0·5 percentage-points in the East Midlands to a loss of 3·7 points in the North West. Labour was most successful in shoring up its support in Scotland and the North West, where its 1983 loss was more than 3 points less than the average. Its vote losses were most precipitate in the South East and East Anglia; this reflects, particularly in the latter case, the effects of movement into these regions by traditionally non-Labour voters. The East Midlands and East Anglia were the Conservatives' bastions, their greatest losses since 1979 being in the North West, as noted, and in Scotland. The particular success story for the Alliance was Scotland and to a lesser extent Greater London, especially helped in the former case by full candidate coverage in 1983. However, even in the forty-five Scottish seats (out of seventy-two) with Liberal candidacies in 1979, the improvement in the Alliance vote exceeded the national figure, going from 14·5 to 26·9 per cent. This is an increase of 12·4 points, compared with 11·9 in the country as a whole.

Of course, regional classifications are somewhat crude and they obscure some variation of support within the various regions. We can see to what extent the parties' constituency-level support varied within, in contrast to between, regions by calculating the proportion of the variation explained by our regional classification. This may be done by regressing constituency-levels of party support against the regions, expressed as dummy variables.[4] The resulting R^2-values indicate the proportion of variation in level of support that has a regional base. The higher these values, on a scale from zero to one, the more regionally concentrated is a party's support and the less does it vary within regions. The results of this exercise are interesting. In both 1979 and 1983 there was a larger region-specific component in the distribution of Conservative support than in that of Labour support, despite the reputation that Labour has for having its votes concentrated into regional bastions. The respective R^2-values for the Conservatives are 0·402 and 0·424; for Labour they are 0·255 and 0·321. However, the regional variation in the pattern of Labour's losses between 1979 and 1983 is revealed by this notable increase in the value of R^2. Lower values of R^2 for the Liberal/SDP–Liberal Alliance show the degree of spatial spread of its support; the values are 0·139 in 1979, calculated across 594 constituencies with Liberal candidacies, and 0·172 in 1983. There is some regional pattern to percentage-point changes in Labour and Conservative voting between 1979 and 1983, but the increase achieved by the Alliance over the figures for Liberal support in 1979 has little regional specificity. R^2-values for vote change between 1979 and 1983 are for Labour, 0·140, for the Conservatives, 0·147, and for the Alliance, calculated on 594 constituencies, 0·067.

The outcome in 1983 of these various trends for and against particular parties, especially the Labour and Conservative parties, is represented in sharp focus in Figure 8.3, where the regional distribution of seats won by all parties in Great Britain is shown. Labour's parlous position in all the southern regions is immediately apparent; even in Greater London it held fewer than a third of available seats. Otherwise, with the exceptions of Bristol South, Ipswich and Thurrock, one has to travel to the Midlands to find a Labour-held seat. Furthermore, whereas in four regions of the country (the South East, the South West, East Anglia and the East Midlands) the number of seats held by

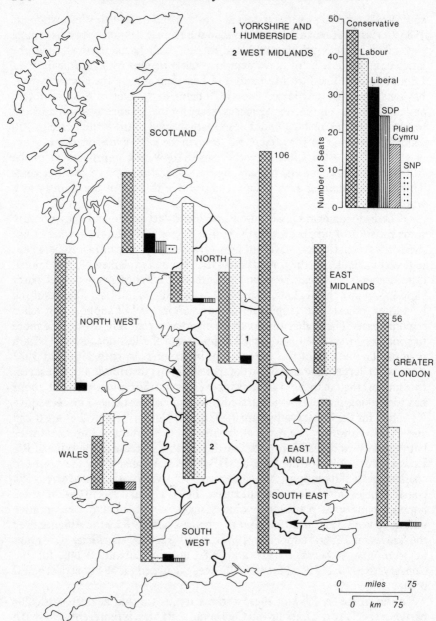

Figure 8.3   Regional distribution of parliamentary seats, 1983

Labour was almost zero or very small, the Conservatives managed a respect-
able minority of seats even in regions, such as Wales and Scotland, where they
are weaker; only the North is a slight exception to this observation. Finally, the
'peripheral' character of the Alliance's holding also deserves emphasis. Well

over half the twenty-three Liberal and SDP seats won in 1983 are from the South West, Wales and Scotland, where there are fewer than a quarter of all seats.

8.3   Party position in 1979 and vote shift from 1979 to 1983

The 1983 general election showed perhaps as much turnover of votes since 1979 as any other election this century. However, did the amount of vote switching in constituencies vary simply with the position of the parties in 1979 or with the tightness of individual contests? If so, we might expect a relationship between the 1983 results and position and vote shares in 1979, as translated on to the new boundaries (BBC/ITN, 1983). In May 1979, for example, the swing to the Conservatives was notably less in many Labour-held marginal seats (Curtice and Steed, 1980, pp. 407–10) and Thatcher did not fully benefit in terms of seats from the national pro-Conservative swing. Similarly, in the May 1981 Greater London Council elections the swings back to Labour compared with the May 1979 general election contest were much smaller in marginal seats, a pattern that contributed to the narrowness of Labour's victory (Husbands, 1981).

Of course, the new boundaries probably increased the proportion of voters who were uncertain about whether their new constituency was a marginal seat or not. After all, not every elector will have had access to *The BBC/ITN Guide to the New Parliamentary Constituencies*! Even so, it is likely that, despite the boundary revision, many voters had *some* idea about their constituency's degree of marginality.

There are two competing models of the pattern of 'swing' or 'shift' for or against a particular party,[5] depending on whether such change is seen as 'uniform' or 'proportionate' (Berrington, 1965, esp. pp. 19–20; Steed, 1965; McLean, 1973; Butler and Stokes, 1974, pp. 140–51); indeed, some authors (e.g., Rasmussen, 1965; Lawson, 1968) have attacked the very notion of analysing elections in terms of swing. However, by far the greatest amount of discussion has focused not on the utility of the concept of swing *per se* but on the uniform/proportionate issue. Uniform swing implies a percentage-point shift of similar absolute size, irrespective of the base from which the shift is occurring; such swing is across-the-board. If a party is losing support throughout the country as a whole, a decline from, say, 60 to 50 per cent in its share of the vote in one constituency implies that in another where the initial percentage was 40 per cent the support-level after switching will be 30 per cent; if the party were gaining support nationally, an increase from 30 to 40 per cent in one constituency would imply an increase to 60 per cent in another constituency where the party had won 50 per cent of the vote in the previous election. On the other hand, a model of proportionate swing asserts that the absolute percentage-point size of any switching depends upon the initial base of support (where a party is losing votes) or non-support (where it is gaining them). Imagine that a party is losing support throughout the country as a whole; if proportionate patterns of switching are operating, a decline from, say, 60 to 45 per cent in one constituency would imply a decline to only 30 per cent (not 25) in another where its initial vote was 40 per cent. If a party were gaining throughout the whole country and proportionate swing operated, an increase from, say, 60 to 70 per cent in one constituency (thus converting a quarter of those voters available for conversion) would imply an increase to 55 per cent in a constituency where the starting figure had been 40 per cent (converting a quarter of the 60 per cent available for conversion). It has usually been considered that, at least in average circumstances, uniform swing is the more appropriate model because any tendency to proportionate swing meets countervailing locality-influences (Butler and Stokes, 1974, pp. 140–50); however, Curtice and Steed (1982) have recently observed, on the basis of extensive empirical analysis, that 'since 1955 the variation in swing has been cumulatively systematic and, viewed in the long term, far from uniform'.

The full results of our analysis into patterns of vote shift are contained in Table B.2, which is in Appendix B p. 225. That table analyses vote shifts for the three major contestants from 1979 to 1983 according to both party position in 1979 and also the tightness of the 1979 result, the latter measured in terms of closeness to the nearest party in the order of results. However, because in general there was little noticeable effect of tightness, the results of Table B.2 are simplified for presentation in Table 8.1, where the focus is upon the effect of position in 1979.

Labour's average percentage-point loss differed little between constituencies where it was first in 1979, those where it was second and those where it was a close or fairly close third; the range of average loss between these three groups was a mere 1·5 points. However, in the thirty-five seats in our analysis where Labour started a poor third, its percentage-point loss was noticeably less, especially so in those twenty-four seats where it started 15 or more points behind the second-placed party. Overall, a model of uniform swing or shift accounts for most Labour results, whereas a proportionate one may apply in the latter group of constituencies. There is a point when the support even of a minority major party reaches an almost irreducible minimum. Only in the most exceptional circumstances would such a party's support be whittled away to zero, however great its overall loss throughout the country. The nearest example of total loss was the Isle of Wight, where Labour had 4·0 per cent of the 1979 vote and saw this reduced to 2·4 per cent by 1983.

Average percentage-point shifts in Conservative support from 1979 to 1983 showed no consistent pattern by position in 1979. Only the 'first' and 'second' categories contain enough constituencies for a meaningful analysis. Where the Conservatives were second in 1979, their vote fell 2 points, but they won many of these seats because of an even larger loss by Labour. Results for the Alliance, on the other hand, present a more interesting picture, since they vary systematically by Liberal position in 1979. Where the Liberals won in 1979, improvement was less than 5 points, but where they had been a poor third it averaged nearly 13. This is consistent with a model of proportionate swing and is also evidence for the widely noticed 'plateau effect' – that percentage-point gains by the Alliance were smaller the higher its starting-point.[6] Building on a reasonably high initial base implies greater difficulty in finding further con-

Table 8.1 *Percentage-point changes in support for the Labour Party, the Con-servative Party, and the Liberal Party/SDP Liberal–Alliance between the May 1979 and May 1983 general elections, by party position in 1979*[1]

Party Position	Labour	Conservative	Liberal/ SDP–Liberal Alliance
First	−9·5	−0·9	+4·6
	(222)[3]	(350)	(8)
Second	−10·2	−2·0	+7·8
	(271)	(228)	(81)
Close or fairly close third[2]	−8·7	+1·2	+10·3
	(51)	(1)	(87)
Poor third	−5·7	−0·3	+12·6
	(35)	(4)	(389)

Notes:
[1] The 1979 results used are those calculated by the BBC/ITN team and the analyses are confined to those constituencies in Great Britain where the Liberal Party had, or was deemed by the BBC/ITN team to have had, a candidacy in the May 1979 general election and where Labour, Conservative and Liberal shared the first three positions in 1979.
[2] 'Close or fairly close third' means within less than 10·0 percentage-points of the second-placed party. 'Poor third' means 10·0 or more points behind this party.
[3] The figures in parentheses are the numbers of constituencies involved in each case.

verts. Even among seats where the Liberal candidate was third in 1979, the same plateau effect is apparent. This is analogous to the behaviour of Labour's vote in seats where it was a poor third in 1979.

With the exception, then, of Labour's vote in seats where it was a poor third in 1979 and of the Alliance's vote in general, there was no consistent relation-ship between percentage-point vote shift and earlier party position or the tightness of the earlier result. We are now ready to introduce our analysis of the social and economic constituency characteristics, among which (at least for Labour and the Conservatives) we find very marked correlates of vote shift.

8.4 The correlates of party support, 1983

Table 8.2 provides a summary of the correlations between parties' percentage support in 1983 and a selection of social and economic variables. Clearly, the Census provides a plenitude of possible variables for use in an exercise of this sort; however, it would be an example of the worst sort of empiricism to seek correlations between parties' vote distributions by constituency and a host of other variables merely because these other variables are available from the Census. Instead, we have confined our choice of constituency-characteristic variables to those with some likely theoretical relevance to an understanding of voting behaviour. Thus the variables used are derived from relations of production (the nature of employment, the type of industry, and so on) and of consumption (housing and access to transport) and also include one describing the ethnic composition of each constituency.

From Table 8.2 it can be seen that, at the aggregate level, there continued to

Table 8.2 *Product-moment correlation coefficients between percentage support for the Labour Party, the Conservative Party and the SDP–Liberal Alliance in the June 1983 general election and selected social and economic variables, 633 constituencies in Great Britain*

	Labour	Conservative	SDP–Liberal Alliance
% Residents aged 16 or over in employment who are manually employed	0·670	−0·673	−0·343
% Residents aged 16 or over in employment who are non-manually employed	−0·608	0·624	0·307
% Residents aged 16 or over in employment who are in agriculture	−0·482	0·276	0·334
% Residents aged 16 or over in employment who are in manufacturing	0·425	−0·271	−0·288
% Residents aged 16 or over who are economically active and seeking work	0·743	−0·713	−0·444
% Permanent private households with residents living in council, etc., housing	0·666	−0·745	−0·308
% Permanent private households with residents living in owner-occupied housing	−0·607	0·694	0·281
% Private households with no car	0·778	−0·750	−0·431
% Residents born in the New Commonwealth or Pakistan	0·224	−0·114	−0·213

exist in 1983 the conventionally reported relationships between the constituency support for the Labour and Conservative parties and other variables, relationships that are comparable to those found by earlier studies concerning previous elections (e.g., M. J. Barnett, 1973; Rasmussen, 1973; Crewe and Payne, 1976; Miller, 1977). This is certainly the case as regards social class. Labour's vote in 1983 correlated strongly with the percentage of those economically active who are employed in manual work (that is, in the Registrar-General's socio-economic groups 7, 8, 9, 10, 11, 12, 14 and 15). The complement is true of the Conservative vote. Thus the 1983 election provides a further demonstration of the paradox that the class alignment, while alternating at the individual level (at least in comparison with the 1960s and early 1970s) persists in marked degree at the constituency level. The vote for the SDP–Liberal Alliance correlates with the class variables – as it does with almost all others – in the same direction as does the Conservative vote, although the absolute size of the coefficients is smaller. Labour's vote tends of course to be lower in areas where larger proportions of the employed population are in agriculture, which are obviously the more rural areas. There is some tendency, though not a particularly strong one, for Conservative and Alliance votes to correlate positively with this variable. The complement is true of employment in manufacturing. Labour's vote was markedly higher in areas of higher unemployment, the converse being the case for the Conservative vote and, to a lesser extent, the Alliance vote.

Labour's vote correlated strongly and positively with the proportion living in council housing and almost as negatively with the concentration of owner-occupied households. As in the case of the class variables, the Conservative and, to a lesser extent, the Alliance vote behaved conversely. The same pattern obtains for the percentage of private households lacking a car.

The final variable considered describes the ethnic composition of each constituency. The percentage of residents born in the New Commonwealth or Pakistan has been used in preference to the percentage of residents living in households whose head was born in the New Commonwealth or Pakistan. The latter is undoubtedly a better measure of the ethnic proportion of the population but it is available only for constituencies in England and Wales, whereas the former can be calculated for all 633 constituencies in Great Britain; in any case, the two correlate at 0·994 across the 561 constituencies of England and Wales. On its own the ethnic composition of a constituency tells little about its likely voting pattern, there being only a slight positive zero-order correlation with the Labour vote and slight negative ones with votes for the other two parties. As we shall see, however, the relationship between parties' vote distributions and the ethnic-presence variable improves after controlling upon social class and region.

8.4.1 Regression analyses of the vote, 1983

Our use of regression analysis for further characterizing the support for the parties in 1983 has two initial focuses: first, explanation of the constituency-level support received by each of the three major parties; secondly, explanation of differential change in support for each party by constituency between the 1979 and 1983 general elections, as before using the BBC/ITN team's estimations of the 1979 results. Later in the chapter we shall use the same technique for the analysis of changes in party support between the May 1983 district council elections/May 1982 London Borough Council elections and the June 1983 general election.

In conducting these analyses we have included two sets of independent variables:

1 Ten region dummy variables, each with a value of one or zero, corresponding to the eleven standard regions of Great Britain used in the analyses of Figures 8.1 to 8.3. As in the analysis of within-region variation, Scotland is the omitted dummy variable. These regional variables have been included in the analyses, whether or not they provided significant coefficients but, in the interest of economy and simplicity, the results have not been reported in the tables concerned.

2 Social and economic variables with significant coefficients for the dependent variable in question. The practice of showing only significant regression results was established in the time-series analyses of government popularity presented in Chapter 7. However, all variables shown in Table 8.2 were considered for inclusion in each analysis and the absence of a particular social or economic variable indicates that preliminary explorations of the data determined its lack of significance.

Table 8.3   *Ordinary least-squares regression analyses between percentage support for the Labour Party, the Conservative Party and the SDP–Liberal Alliance in the June 1983 general election and selected social and economic variables and region, 633 constituencies in Great Britain*[1]

	Standardized regression coefficient	Student's t-value
Labour		
% Residents aged 16 or over in employment who are manually employed	0·436	15·941
% Residents aged 16 or over in employment who are in agriculture	−0·375	18·840
% Permanent private households with residents living in council, etc., housing	0·224	8·802
% Private households with no car	0·122	4·417
% Residents born in the New Commonwealth or Pakistan	0·122	5·699
Proportion of variation explained (R^2):	0·863	
Proportion of variation explained excluding region dummy variables:	0·809	
Conservative		
% Residents aged 16 or over in employment who are non-manually employed	0·454	18·571
% Residents aged 16 or over in employment who are in agriculture	0·303	16·596
% Permanent private households with residents living in owner-occupied housing	0·267	10·742
% Residents born in the New Commonwealth or Pakistan	−0·084	3·827
Proportion of variation explained (R^2):	0·839	
Proportion of variation explained excluding region dummy variables:	0·671	
SDP–Liberal Alliance		
% Residents aged 16 or over in employment who are non-manually employed	0·215	4·231
% Residents aged 16 or over in employment who are in agriculture	0·262	6·526
% Residents aged 16 or over who are economically active and seeking work	−0·115	2·790
% Residents born in the New Commonwealth or Pakistan	−0·105	2·280
Proportion of variation explained (R^2):	0·337	
Proportion of variation explained excluding region dummy variables:	0·275	

Note:
[1] These analyses also *include* ten region dummy variables (excluding Scotland). The individual statistics for these have been omitted to preserve simplicity and to save space. However, the values of R^2 for the same independent variables but excluding these dummy variables are shown for comparative purposes.

Table 8.3 contains the results of the basic regression analyses of the votes for all three parties. Some of the results are unsurprising but others merit special comment.

Labour's 1983 vote was most strongly predicted by the percentage of economically active employed residents in manual occupations and by the percentage in employment who are in agriculture. The former testifies to the continuing greater appeal of Labour in more working-class constituencies and to the party's lesser appeal in more rural ones. Controlling on other relevant variables, Labour has greater appeal in constituencies with higher proportions of council tenants, of private households lacking a car and of residents born in the New Commonwealth or Pakistan. The significance of council tenancy repeats at the aggregate level the relationship for the survey data reported in Chapter 6. The correlation with non-car-ownership expresses a spatial feature of Labour voting – its special inner-city concentration. What is also interesting about Labour's support is that – despite its reputation for regional concentration – the region dummy variables make little independent contribution to explaining its between-constituency variation. Almost as good a prediction is obtained from the significant social and economic variables alone as from a model also incorporating the region variables. Thus, any future sustained recovery by Labour must transcend the social and economic, rather than the regional, characteristics of its 1983 vote.

The 1983 Conservative vote is in part a mirror-image of the Labour vote, but only in part. Conservative voting in 1983 was stronger in areas with greater non-manual employment, with a higher percentage of those employed engaged in agriculture, with higher levels of owner occupation and lower percentages born in the New Commonwealth or Pakistan. However, the regional component, over and above aggregate social and economic constituency characteristics, is far more remarkable in the Conservative vote than it was in the Labour vote. The R^2-value increases from 0.671 to 0.839 with the inclusion of the ten region dummy variables. In all regions in England the Conservative vote was higher than would have been predicted by the social and economic variables alone; in Wales and Scotland the reverse was the case.

The Alliance vote, as was true when considering the social and economic variables separately, is less well predicted than is support for both the other parties, partly because of the already noted additional effects of party position in 1979 and tightness of the 1979 contest. However, except for the rather smaller regional component, it is similar in some respects to the Conservative vote. It is higher in constituencies of greater non-manual employment and in those where the working agricultural population is higher. Unlike the Conservative vote, it tends to be significantly higher, controlling on other variables, in constituencies with lower unemployment. It is lower where there is a higher percentage of ethnic-minority population.

8.4.2 Determinants of change in party support, 1979 to 1983

As well as analysing levels of support for the three major parties in 1983, it is also instructive to examine the distribution of percentage-point changes in

Table 8.4 *Ordinary least-squares regression analyses between percentage-point changes in support for the Labour Party, the Conservative Party and the SDP– Liberal Alliance/Liberal Party between the May 1979 and June 1983 general elections, by selected social and economic variables and region, controlling on the appropriate 1979 vote*[1]

	Standardized regression coefficient	Student's t-value
Labour (N=633)		
% Labour, May 1979	−0·944	11·646
% Residents aged 16 or over in employment who are manually employed	0·327	4·576
% Residents aged 16 or over in employment who are in agriculture	−0·225	4·006
% Permanent private households with residents living in council, etc., housing	0·125	2·101
% Private households with no car	0·326	5·399
% Residents born in the New Commonwealth or Pakistan	0·240	5·086
Proportion of variation explained (R^2):	0·347	
Proportion of variation explained excluding region dummy variables:	0·220	
Conservative (N=633)		
% Conservative, May 1979	−0·460	7·501
% Residents aged 16 or over in employment who are in agriculture	0·230	5·423
% Permanent private households with residents living in owner-occupied housing	0·140	2·240
% Private households with no car	−0·389	5·813
% Residents born in the New Commonwealth or Pakistan	. −0·092	1·963
Proportion of variation explained (R^2):	0·327	
Proportion of variation explained excluding region dummy variables:	0·219	
SDP–Liberal Alliance (N=594)		
% Liberal, May 1979	−0·473	11·863
% Residents born in the New Commonwealth or Pakistan	−0·169	3·505
Proportion of variation explained (R^2):	0·224	
Proportion of variation explained excluding region dummy variables:	0·158	

Note:
[1] As in Table 8.3, these analyses also *include* ten region dummy variables (excluding Scotland). Note 1 of that table explains how these variables have been treated.

support since the general election of 1979. These analyses – conducted according to regression procedures already described – are presented in Table 8.4. In addition to the social and economic variables already used, each analysis incorporates a control on the 1979 vote of the party concerned. This is a standard procedure in any analysis of change-scores, since there is sometimes a spurious correlation between a change-score over time and initial score, a correlation attributable to the so-called 'regression effect'.[7] The solution to this is the analysis of change-scores with a statistical control on initial score (Lord, 1963). In some cases, including some of our analyses of change-scores, a relationship between change and initial score appears only in control conditions. In Table 8.4 larger percentage-point increases and smaller percentage-point decreases are associated with the variables with positive coefficients.

Labour, of course, lost nearly 10 percentage-points between 1979 and 1983 but its losses were relatively smaller, even controlling on the 1979 vote, in working-class constituencies, in those with high proportions of council tenants, in those with larger proportions of households without a car and in those with larger ethnic-minority populations. In fact, Labour's problem is that its vote maintained itself best in constituencies in which were concentrated various electoral minorities who, even together, would hardly make a viable coalition. Labour's vote fell most in constituencies with higher proportions employed in agriculture. More particularly, there was a noticeable regional pattern in Labour's losses, even controlling on other variables; corroborating the results in Figure 8.2, they tended to be lower in the North West, Wales and Scotland but disproportionately high elsewhere.

Conservative support between 1979 and 1983 held up best in agricultural constituencies, those dominated by owner-occupied housing, those with smaller proportions lacking a car and those with smaller ethnic-minority populations. As with the Labour vote, there is a marked regional basis to change, even controlling on significant other variables. Outside the North West, Wales and Scotland, the Conservative vote in 1983 was everywhere disproportionately high. Alliance change (which was usually gain, in comparison with the 1979 Liberal vote) also had some regional basis, although its only social and economic predictor was the size of the ethnic-minority population – larger populations being associated with smaller Alliance gains.

The presence of the New Commonwealth/Pakistan-born variable among the determinants of change in support for all three parties is strongly suggestive of an individual-level effect. There has been some dispute about the behaviour of the black vote, in previous elections as well as in 1983; some recent commentators have argued that the degree of past Labour support among black voters has probably been rather overestimated for a variety of reasons (Layton-Henry, 1983; Studlar, 1983). Whatever the precise truth about this matter in the past, the burden of relevant research about 1983 is that most of the black vote did stay with Labour (Crewe, 1983; Studlar, 1983; FitzGerald, 1984) and perhaps even defected less than other groups, despite its exceptionally high initial level. The results of the aggregate analysis are certainly consistent with some of the individual-level findings. Before the election there were suggestions in some sections of the media that certain ethnic-minority voters, particularly 'middle-class' Asians, might desert a traditional Labour allegiance and, unable to stomach a Conservative Party frequently revealing its racist side, would turn to the Alliance, especially the SDP. This seems to have happened, according to both individual-level and our aggregate results, only on a small scale, although Studlar (1983) implies that it may have been a more widespread phenomenon. Certainly, there were strong tactical incentives against doing this in many seats: in a seat such as Ealing North, for example, which was considered marginal on the basis of the notional 1979 results, the major effect of deserting Labour would have been to guarantee a Conservative victory, precisely what many such voters wanted to avoid. As it happened, the Conservatives did win Ealing North, but surely not because of any large-scale desertion of Labour by Asian voters.

8.4.3   Change in party support, 1982/3 local elections to 1983 general election

Thatcher called the June 1983 general election after a highly publicized analysis of the district council election results of 5 May 1983 conducted on Central Office's recently acquired computer; the analysis was supposedly pored over by her and her confidants during a 'summit' meeting at Chequers on 8 May. They were particularly interested in, and in general were reassured by, the aggregated results in certain key marginal constituencies. The general conclusion in the media, albeit without the calculation capacity of the Conservative Party,[8] was that the local elections had provided an ambiguous message about the state of the electorate (Chapter 4), although there had been published poll evidence that an important minority of voters (perhaps as many as 6 per cent) would vote Conservative in a general election but not in a local one.

Whatever the state of the electorate at the beginning of May, it is incontrovertible that during the five weeks of the campaign Labour may have lost in net terms the support of between a fifth and an eighth of those supporting it at the beginning. At the earlier time it stood at about 33 per cent in most polls but finished with scarcely 28 per cent. This haemorrhaging was larger in the last three weeks of the campaign, since there is poll evidence (Appendix A) that Labour's support rose incrementally in the first ten or so days to stand at about 36 per cent on 17–20 May.

However, Labour's losses over these five weeks were not evenly distributed. Where its losses were greatest and where least can be seen from an analysis of shifts in support between the district council elections on 5 May and the general election on 9 June. To be sure, the respective electorates are not entirely conterminous because of the lower turnout in local elections but the results are none the less a good indication of where switching during the campaign occurred on a large scale and where it did not. We confine our comments to those seats where local election ward results may be legitimately aggregated to give a constituency total.[9] Labour's largest percentage-point losses in such seats include Basildon (down 16·1 points), Bradford North (down 18·0 points because of the intervention of Ben Ford as Labour

Independent in June), and Sheffield Brightside (down 13·8 points, although from the high figure of 71·8 per cent). Elsewhere, as in Dudley West, Labour's losses were probably as high, although anomalies in candidate coverage in the local contests prevent adequate comparisons. On the other hand, there were some places where Labour's performance actually improved between May and June; Huddersfield (up 3·1 points), Keighley (up 2·5 points – doubtless reflecting in part the skilled, if unsuccessful, campaign fought by Labour's Bob Cryer), three of the six Liverpool seats, Manchester Gorton (up 3·2 points) and West Bromwich East (up 2·8 points). Correspondingly, the Alliance had some losses between the May local contests and the June general election, losses which in some of the Liverpool seats were spectacular, even discounting the split in the Alliance vote in the Broadgreen constituency.[10]

We now consider trends in party support in Greater London – using as our base the 1982 London Borough Council elections, since these are the most recent London-wide local contests in the capital. As in the comparisons with the local 1983 results, there is a range of patterns. In the 1982 London Borough Council elections the Greater-London-wide results for the three parties, unadjusted for the occasional missing candidacy in some wards, were Labour, 29·2 per cent, Conservative, 40·8 per cent, and Alliance, 23·7 per cent. In these elections Labour was protected from truly draconian losses of council seats because of the manner in which its London support is concentrated in certain boroughs; even so, it suffered badly in terms of loss in share of the total vote in boroughs such as Brent, Lambeth and Waltham Forest (Husbands, 1982b). Overall its performance slightly improved in 1983 compared with 1982, certainly in the inner London area. However, Labour was hit especially hard by the Alliance in two south-east London boroughs, Greenwich and Bexley. In the former its support fell from a half to a third between the 1979 and the 1983 general elections and by over 5 points since 1982. This was largely, though not wholly, the consequence of the success of the SDP's John Cartwright (one of Labour's defectors) against left-winger and former Labour MP for Coventry South West, Audrey Wise, in the new Woolwich seat; Labour's performance also suffered slightly in the other two constituencies in the borough. Similarly, Labour support fell in Bexley, compared even with 1982, largely but not entirely because of the near-success of James Wellbeloved, the SDP defector, in retaining the Erith and Crayford seat. The SDP's challenge also hurt Labour in the two Islington seats. Islington North was safely won by Labour only because of the intervention as an Independent Labour candidate of Michael O'Halloran, who won 11·1 per cent of the vote and doubtless reduced the support for the SDP's John Grant. Islington South and Finsbury was almost won for the SDP by George Cunningham, who was only 1 per cent behind Labour's Christopher Smith. Islington has recently become the Labour-controlled London borough that most attracts the opprobrium of the right-wing press, particularly the *Standard* and the *Daily Mail*, a role which it has perforce assumed from Lambeth. In the latter borough, spared some of the anti-left publicity that was disseminated until a year or so ago, Labour's vote improved substantially compared with 1982. The old Vauxhall seat would have been very vulnerable to the SDP on the basis of the 1982 local results, but the new seat was comfortably held by Labour's Stuart Holland, assisted to some extent by the effects of boundary revision. Brent too was the locus of a Labour recovery after a particular decline in its support in 1982, although one wonders what the outcome there would have been if the calling of the election had not aborted an incipient public row between Reg Freeson and Ken Livingstone about Labour's nomination for the Brent East seat.

We are now ready to tackle the task of understanding the overall pattern of the changes in party support between local and general elections. In order to do this we undertake a systematic analysis of the constituency-characteristic variables that explain variation in these changes. We employ the same conventional model for the analysis of change-scores already used in Section 8.4.2 of this chapter, that is, controlling on initial level of support. Our first analysis is confined to those constituencies in the six metropolitan counties whose local election results in 1983 met our criteria for inclusion and our second one covers analogous constituencies in Greater London with respect to the 1982 Borough Council results. Because of the uncertainty introduced by Independent candidacies, we have omitted Bradford North and Liverpool Broadgreen from the first analysis and Hammersmith and Islington North from the second; all these would otherwise have been eligible for inclusion on the basis of their local election results. Given their urban character, there is every reason to believe that, in general, local election results in the constituencies of our analyses are strongly related to general election outcomes (Waller, 1980); thus the pattern of what differential change there is becomes of particular interest.

Table 8.5A presents the results of the first of these analyses. Several of the results are suggestive. Let us first consider Labour's case. In the metropolitan counties Labour's vote declined least during the campaign itself in those seats where unemployment was highest, suggesting the possibility of an individual-level effect as Labour held on to the votes of the unemployed themselves. No other social or economic variables had a significant impact upon the change in Labour's fortunes during the five-week campaign. There was also some slight tendency for Labour's support to maintain itself better in Greater Manchester and South Yorkshire, controlling on Labour's initial level of support and upon unemployment level. However, these county-level effects were not great, and were complemented by greater net loss in Merseyside. After controlling upon initial Conservative vote, no social or economic constituency characteristic had any significant relationship to vote change in the six metropolitan counties. However, the general election did see a net improvement in Conservative support in Merseyside, with some slight net decrease in South Yorkshire and West Midlands. Vote change for the Alliance was the mirror image of that for Labour; whereas the overall tendency for the Alliance was an increase, this was least in constituencies with higher unemployment – strongly suggesting that the Alliance, though in general catholic in its appeal, failed to attract some support from the unemployed as its overall level of support increased late in the campaign. There is an indication too that the Alliance was particularly held back in Greater Manchester and, to a lesser extent, Merseyside. The latter occurred despite the omission from the analysis of the Liverpool Broadgreen constituency.

Table 8.5A   *Ordinary least-squares regression analyses of percentage-point changes in support for the Labour Party, the Conservative Party and the SDP–Liberal Alliance between the May 1983 metropolitan district council elections and the June 1983 general election, by selected social and economic variables and metropolitan county, controlling on the appropriate May 1983 vote*[1]

	Standardized regression coefficient	Student's t-value
Labour		
% Labour, May 1983	−1·039	7·015
% Residents aged 16 or over who are economically active and seeking work	0·964	5·962
Greater Manchester	0·149	1·325
Merseyside	−0·130	1·028
South Yorkshire	0·132	1·297
Tyne and Wear	0·064	0·632
West Midlands	−0·087	0·680
Proportion of variation explained (R^2):	0·461	
Proportion of variation explained excluding metropolitan county dummy variables:	0·406	
Conservative		
% Conservative, May 1983	−0·600	6·847
Greater Manchester	−0·002	0·000
Merseyside	0·248	2·407
South Yorkshire	−0·089	0·927
Tyne and Wear	−0·040	0·422
West Midlands	−0·122	1·112
Proportion of variation explained (R^2):	0·494	
Proportion of variation explained excluding metropolitan county dummy variables:	0·391	
SDP–Liberal Alliance		
% Alliance, May 1983	−0·677	7·093
% Residents aged 16 or over who are economically active and seeking work	−0·465	4·868
Greater Manchester	−0·196	1·861
Merseyside	−0·106	0·971
South Yorkshire	−0·026	0·279
Tyne and Wear	−0·046	0·496
West Midlands	−0·063	0·553
Proportion of variation explained (R^2):	0·539	
Proportion of variation explained excluding metropolitan county dummy variables:	0·511	

Note:
[1] These analyses cover only those seventy-eight constituencies where there were candidacies for Labour, Conservative and the Alliance in all wards in the May 1983 metropolitan district council elections and where no single 'other' candidacy in any ward won support from more than 20 per cent of those voting in that ward; they exclude the Bradford North and Liverpool Broadgreen constituencies. The metropolitan county omitted from the dummy variables is West Yorkshire.

Table 8.5B   *Ordinary least-squares regression analyses of percentage-point changes in support for the Labour Party, the Conservative Party and the SDP–Liberal Alliance between the May 1982 London Borough Council elections and the June 1983 general election, by selected social and economic variables, controlling on the appropriate May 1982 vote*[1]

	Standardized regression coefficient	Student's t-value
Labour		
% Labour, May 1982	−0·806	4·820
% Residents aged 16 or over who are economically active and seeking work	0·666	3·329
% Residents born in the New Commonwealth or Pakistan	0·669	5·635
Proportion of variation explained (R^2):	0·536	
Conservative		
% Conservative, May 1982	−1·317	7·057
% Residents aged 16 or over in employment who are non-manually employed	0·352	2·218
% Residents aged 16 or over who are economically active and seeking work	−0·556	3·337
% Residents born in the New Commonwealth or Pakistan	−0·337	2·829
Proportion of variation explained (R^2):	0·537	
SDP–Liberal Alliance		
% Alliance, May 1982	−0·251	2·029
% Residents born in the New Commonwealth or Pakistan	−0·465	3·762
Proportion of variation explained (R^2):	0·201	

Note:
[1] These analyses cover only those sixty-two constituencies where there were candidacies for Labour, Conservative and Alliance in all wards in the May 1982 London Borough Council elections and where no single 'other' candidacy in any ward won support from more than 20 per cent of those voting in that ward; they exclude the Hammersmith and Islington North constituencies.

Table 8.5B contains the results of an analogous analysis upon appropriate constituencies in Greater London. The results, particularly those for Labour, accord with the impressions made upon numerous observers when the results of the election were being declared; Labour suffered devastating losses in some outer London seats (for example, Hornchurch in the Borough of Havering) but its vote held up surprisingly well in various inner London seats with high black populations and disproportionate levels of unemployment. Both these latter variables had substantial mitigating effects upon the size of Labour's vote losses. Even so, the variation was not an inner/outer London effect *per se*, since the latter distinction (measured as ILEA/non-ILEA borough) is not significant against the variables for unemployment and ethnic-minority presence. Conservative vote change in the same constituencies was the mirror-image of Labour's, except for the additional effect of non-manual employment. Conservative gains were greatest in more middle-class constituencies. Again, there was no inner/outer London effect when the other variables were included. Alliance gains were least in seats with higher proportions of black people, consistent with earlier suggestions that, for whatever reason, black voters in London were not disproportionately attracted to the Alliance. Apparently, the general mobilization that benefited the Alliance worked less for black voters, many of them doubtless concerned that voting Alliance would merely guarantee a Conservative success.

8.5   Contests, candidates and electoral outcomes

Voting outcomes are the result of a series of causes and political scientists have differed among themselves according to whim, to the changing facts of history, and sometimes according to both, in the weight that they are willing to ascribe to various factors. We have reviewed in earlier chapters the range of long- and short-term factors (structural and ideological) that have affected, and continue to affect, election results. Most political scientists concede that these types of factors are crucial determinants. However, there has been far less research about factors specific to contests and contestants, although these will have their own impact upon outcomes. Certainly, in British political science this has not been a major preoccupation, although there is quite a body of literature on this subject in electoral geography (e.g., Taylor and Johnston, 1979, pp. 221–331). Among the few well-known and often-cited studies in political science are those of Bochel and Denver (1971, 1972), who showed that campaign activities like canvassing – frequently dismissed as merely ritualistic – could have an effect upon turnout and hence a party's (in their case, the Labour Party's) share of the vote. However, their studies focused only on local election contests and part of the observed effect clearly arose because the opposition was caught flat-footed by such unwonted electoral activity from the Labour Party! There has been a more general tendency in Britain to be dismissive about such contest characteristics as personal attributes of candidates (e.g., Kavanagh, 1970, p. 12). Pulzer (1975, p. 132) claims that ascriptive personal factors (except race) and ideological distinctiveness make no difference to electoral outcomes but he does argue that in certain circumstances incumbency can be beneficial. American political scientists have done many analyses of the specific effects of incumbency in assisting a candidate's chances for re-election. For example, Cummings (1966, pp. 56–87) has shown that incumbents may gain an advantage in particular circumstances, especially when their own party is on the defensive in a presidential contest. Stokes and Miller (1962, esp. p. 540) demonstrated that incumbents are advantaged, chiefly by being better known rather than being seen as more ideologically agreeable, since most of their respondents held an image of their Congressman that was 'barren of policy content'. The ability of incumbent Congressmen to survive a swing against their party is certainly greater than that of British MPs, for whom incumbency of a marginal seat means continual concern about the possibility of subsequent rejection.

This section now reports upon the effects of four major contest characteristics:

1 having an incumbent MP as candidate;
2 having a woman candidate, and having an incumbent woman MP as candidate;
3 having an ethnic-minority candidate;
4 having a 'carpet-bagger' candidate – an MP who took advantage of the musical chairs consequent upon boundary revision to secure nomination for a supposedly safer seat.

The models that we use to assess the importance of these factors are simply elaborations of those reported for the respective parties in Table 8.3. For each party our elaborated model includes the specific social and economic variables shown in that table as well as the ten region dummy variables, plus further dummy variables as relevant for each of the above contest characteristics. All these have been entered simultaneously into a regression analysis and the results, shown in Table 8.6, are reported in terms of the metric regression coefficients for the factors concerned. These may be interpreted as the percentage increment or decrement of support attributable to each factor after controlling on all the other variables in the elaborated models. Of course, no constituency could have more than one incumbent candidate and none had more than one ethnic-minority or 'carpet-bagger' one. However, fifteen in Great Britain had two women candidates among the three major contestants; these cases have been excluded from all analyses because of the consequent impossibility of assessing a pure woman-candidate effect.

8.5.1 Incumbent candidates

As was said earlier, British political science has been reluctant to ascribe much electoral impact to most actual or imputed characteristics of candidates, although some exceptions (such as the 1983 Bermondsey by-election) would doubtless be recognized. Butler and Stokes (1974, pp. 355–6), although without explicitly rejecting the influence of candidates, imply from the limited knowledge held about MPs by most British electors that such effects are unlikely to be large. Others have been willing to accept that incumbency is perhaps one characteristic that may have some influence upon levels of party support. Curtice and Steed (1980, pp. 407–10), for example, have argued that in 1979 some Labour MPs survived only because of incumbency effects; they also recognize the personal element in the support particularly for Liberal and minor-party candidates, as does Waller (1980, esp. p. 446). Pulzer (1975, p. 132) makes the same point and, in discussing the general effects of incumbency, he asserts that a 'familiar' MP at the height of his or her popularity may be worth an extra 1·5 to 3·5 percentage-points of swing for his or her party, figures that he takes from the work of Williams (1966–7).

Table 8.6 *Results of regression analyses, expressed in metric regression coefficients, of the effects of various candidate characteristics upon support for the Labour Party, the Conservative Party, the Liberal Party and the Social Democratic Party in the 1983 general election, controlling upon specific other factors*[1]

	Labour	Conservative	Liberal	SDP
Incumbent candidates	5·533	4·770	19·925	11·122
	(167)[2]	(263)	(9)	(17)
Women candidates	−0·352	−0·797	−1·625	−0·318
	(67)	(30)	(27)	(38)
Incumbent women candidates	−4·488	−0·709	—	—
	(8)	(6)		
Ethnic-minority candidates	−0·750	−7·238	−5·621	−3·124
	(6)	(2)	(4)	(4)
N:[3]	618	618	315	303
'Carpet-bagger' candidates	—	1·718	—	—
		(5)		
N:		157		

Notes:

[1] These other factors are in the case of each party those variables (including region dummy variables) used in the respective analyses reported in Table 8.3.

[2] The figures in parentheses are the numbers of included constituencies with the candidate characteristic in question.

[3] The N-figures are the numbers of constituencies upon which these analyses are based. They are chosen as follows:

618, all those in Great Britain where there was no or one woman candidate among those of the three major contestants;

315, all those in Great Britain where the Alliance candidate was a Liberal and where there was no or one woman candidate among those of the three major contestants;

303, all those in Great Britain where the Alliance candidate was a Social Democrat and where there was no or one woman candidate among those of the three major contestants;

157, all those in Great Britain either where there was no incumbent candidate or that were 'new seats', and where there was no or one woman candidate among those of the three major contestants; thus, of the seven constituencies with 'carpet-bagging' Conservative candidates, two (Crosby with an SDP incumbent and Keighley with a Labour one) were omitted from this analysis.

What then is the general truth on the subject? The 1983 constituencies were coded according to whether one of the candidates had been the MP for that same constituency (in the case of unchanged boundaries) or for the previous constituency that constituted the 'core' of the new one – as defined by Waller (1983a, p. 9). This is a rigorous definition of incumbency, meaning for example that Peter Shore (formerly of Stepney and Poplar) was not considered the incumbent in the new Bethnal Green and Stepney and that Ian Mikardo (formerly of Bethnal Green and Bow) was likewise not the incumbent in the new Bow and Poplar.

We examine the cases of incumbents who fought for the same party both in 1983 and when immediately previously elected, as well as those of the defectors to the SDP (all but one formerly Labour). We include all relevant constituencies in the analysis, thus averaging any differences between safe and marginal seats, although some earlier work on this subject (Williams, 1966–7) has claimed greater incumbency effects in marginal than in safe seats. Our findings with respect to incumbency differ somewhat from one party to another, but in all four cases there is some incumbency effect. Both Labour and Conservative incumbents managed a solid extra increment of support due to their status – around 5 percentage-points in each case – but the effect was even greater for both Liberal and SDP incumbents; for the nine Liberals it was worth an average of almost 20 points. Incumbency protected some Labour MPs from the worst consequences of the party's electoral decline. These findings are consistent with the already cited observations of Curtice and Steed and of Waller, especially concerning Liberal incumbents, though less with Williams's (1966–7) earlier findings that benefit from incumbency has in the past been greater for Labour than for Conservative incumbents.

The nature of the incumbency effect
It is interesting to explore precisely what the process of incumbency influence may be and the 172 constituencies with Labour incumbents and the 267 with Conservative ones provide sufficiently large samples to enable us to do this systematically.

One basic model of incumbency influence is predicated upon so-called 'network effects' among those whom a particular MP helps or who hear about his or her good offices. This seems to be what Pulzer (1975, p. 132) has in mind when he talks of MPs 'building up a personal following by conscientious constituency service'. Let us explore in more detail how such a model might work. Imagine in a simplified example that an MP can avoid actually alienating constituents and that he or she helps constant numbers of constituents in given spans of time – say, ten per week. If all in each group of ten are silent about the assistance rendered by the MP but are none the less ready to harbour private gratitude on account of it, the MP will accumulate grateful constituents at a rate of ten per week. If, however, each person helped passes on to acquaintances some news of the assistance that the MP has rendered, the diffusion of knowledge about the MP's beneficial activities occurs at a faster rate. Whether the accumulation of those directly helped or acquainted with those directly helped grows as a linear or exponential function of the passage of time depends upon other aspects of the diffusion process. If those helped tend to confine their dissemination of intelligence about it to the period shortly after the help was given and if those hearing about this from the people directly helped do not pass the news on to yet more people as a further stage of the network, the accumulation of constituents knowing of their MP's good work will be linear with time; if the network of diffusion is more complex, the accumulation will take place at an increasing rate over time. Whichever of these models is appropriate, the MP should be able to accumulate goodwill (at first or higher hand) so long as he or she continues to render assistance to constituents at a rate that outpaces the replacement of the electorate over time. Otherwise, the only limitation on this diffusion process would be its tendency to attenuate as the branching out of the network came to involve duplication. Following Williams (1966–7), Pulzer (1975, p. 132) does suggest the qualification that some very long-serving MPs might 'outstay their welcome', thus reducing the otherwise beneficial effects of incumbency. Of course, some incumbent MPs are in any case far more competent and conscientious than others and it is a little difficult (and perhaps even libellous!) explicitly to incorporate all such factors into a composite model. Even so, these complications do not seriously bias expectation that positive incumbency effects would normally increase over time till some point of attenuation was reached. In fact, our results show little such pattern.

All 172 incumbent Labour MPs and all 267 incumbent Conservative ones were classified according to the length of time of their incumbency: less than one year to six years (LAB, 42; CON, 76); seven to eleven years (LAB, 48; CON, 88); twelve to fifteen years (LAB, 30; CON, 38); sixteen to eighteen years (LAB, 12; CON, 15); and nineteen or more years (LAB, 40; CON, 50). These categories correspond to continuous incumbency since respectively the 1979 election, the two 1974 elections, the 1970 election, the 1966 election, and the 1964 election and before. By-election entrants have therefore in general been assigned to the category corresponding to the general election closest in time to their entry. After the one-woman-candidate-only rule was applied, 167 Labour incumbents and 263 Conservative ones remained for analysis. The time periods of incumbency (except the last of nineteen years or more, which was the omitted one) have been converted to dummy variables and, when the effects of length of incumbency among Labour incumbents were then assessed using the same social, economic and region variables as in the model that measured the general effect of Labour incumbency, the highest positive increment was found among the more recent incumbents, those who had entered Parliament after 1971. Among Conservative incumbents the greatest positive increment was among those who had been MPs between seven and eleven years. Even so, what effects there are were generally small. The metric regression coefficients of the relevant dummy variables in both models are:

	LAB	CON
0 to 6 years	0·589	−0·493
7 to 11 years	0·599	0·652
12 to 15 years	0·114	−0·260
16 to 18 years	−1·736	0·161

Thus, network or diffusion models of knowledge about MPs' constituency work may be inappropriate. Instead, recent Labour incumbents are most advantaged, possibly in most cases because their recent incumbency status has spurred them to be particularly assiduous in cultivating a positive reputation among their constituents. The rather longer-serving Labour incumbents, on the other hand, are on average less favoured (especially those who entered around the 1966 election), perhaps because their longer tenure has encouraged complacency and also in some cases allowed local opposition to develop against them. It is only among the very longest-serving Labour incumbents that one sees some slight return of support, suggesting that very long tenure enables a Labour MP to assume the patina of venerability merely because of his or her long tenure. The patterns among Conservatives are slightly different but neither set of findings does much to sustain either Pulzer's basic assumption about the pattern of incumbency effects or his qualification about outstayed welcomes.

8.5.2   Women candidates

Women candidates, like those from ethnic minorities, tend to be fighting the least winnable seats, although the situation for women is not quite as bad. There were seventy-seven Labour women candidates, forty Conservative ones and seventy-five Alliance ones (thirty-two Liberals and forty-three for the SDP). Despite a claim to be opening its candidacies to a range of hitherto under-represented groups, the profile of the SDP's candidates – in respect of gender, as well as of other characteristics – differed only marginally from those of the other parties (Bradley, 1983). Thirteen of the Conservative women candidates won their contests (33 per cent of the total), compared with ten of the Labour women (13 per cent of the seventy-seven); no Alliance women candidates won. Of course, one incumbent woman SDP candidate lost – Shirley Williams in Crosby.

Our results show that there is no particular disadvantage suffered by women, given that they have managed to achieve candidate status and given too the frequently barren electoral terrain upon which they are obliged to work. There is a suggestion of a slightly greater decrement suffered by Liberal women but there is no obvious reason for this. Moreover, all coefficients, though small in absolute size, *are* negative in direction. On the whole, however, women candidates were not disadvantaged. This agrees with the basic findings of Rasmussen's (1981) study of the relative performance of women candidates in British parliamentary by-elections; his article cites much of the relevant literature, even if one should be wary of the theoretical pretension encapsulated in its subtitle.

Although most women candidates do not face gender-specific electoral difficulties, there is a strong suggestion that – controlling on incumbency and their being women candidates – female Labour incumbents do fare rather worse than male ones and than Conservative women incumbents. The disadvantage among the eight Labour women incumbents fighting in contests against male candidates from the other major parties may be rather more than 4 percentage-points. However, female Conservative incumbents were, if anything, advantaged by their status.

8.5.3   Ethnic-minority candidates

In the 1983 general election there were eighteen constituencies where the candidate of one of the major parties was of Asian or Afro-Caribbean origin. There were four Conservative Asians (Helen Gardener in Newham North East, Pramila Le Hunte in Birmingham Ladywood, Paul Nischal in Birmingham Small Heath and Surendra Popat in Durham North); four Labour Asians (Rita Austin in St Albans, David Colin-Thome in Warrington South, Jim Thakoordin in Milton Keynes and Keith Vaz in Richmond and Barnes); one

Labour Afro-Caribbean (Ben Bousquet in Kensington); one Labour Afro-English candidate (Paul Boateng in Hertfordshire West); three Liberal Asians (Alex Alagappa in Feltham and Heston, Zerbanoo Gifford in Hertsmere and Maurice Nadeem in Ealing Southall); one Liberal Afro-Caribbean (Gus Williams in Birmingham Perry Barr); and four SDP Asians (Altaf Ahmed in Manchester Central, Sumal Fernando in Leicester West, Tom Mann in Brent North and Om Parmar in Birmingham Sparkbrook).

None of these was elected, of course, but there have been suggestions that even the Conservatives, sure of a sufficient proportion of the white vote for overall victory, were keen to promote their ethnic candidates. Even so, very few of them were fighting remotely winnable seats. Two of the four Conservatives were in seats where the BBC/ITN team's calculations of the May 1979 results placed them over 40 percentage-points behind the Labour winner. The closest of the four races had been in Birmingham Ladywood, where the Labour lead was 16·4 percentage-points. The six Labour candidates were not in quite such dismal situations, the average difference between the 1979 Labour vote and the winning Conservative vote on that occasion being 18 percentage-points; indeed, in Hertfordshire West (around Hemel Hempstead) the BBC/ITN team gave Labour a slight lead in 1979 of 1·1 points. Of the eight Alliance candidates, one was fighting a seat (Birmingham Sparkbrook) where there had been no Liberal in 1979 and in five of the other seven cases a Liberal candidate would have received fewer than 10 per cent of votes cast.

The results in Table 8.6 show to what extent there was backlash against ethnic-minority candidates. Labour representatives were in general not subject to this, there being only a small average decrement in their votes of slightly under 1 per cent. In fact, one case (Hertfordshire West, to be discussed below) makes this average measure for Labour candidates worse than it would otherwise have been. On the other hand, the two Conservative cases, Paul Nischal and Surendra Popat, did perform less well as Conservatives than the characteristics of their constituencies would have predicted. Two female Conservative ethnic-minority candidacies, those of Helen Gardener and Pramila Le Hunte, had to be excluded from this analysis on the one-woman-candidate-only rule; however, other evidence is that the former of these performed well, while the latter (also to be discussed below) was noticeably less successful than would have been predicted. Alliance candidates, almost invariably fighting from very low levels of initial support, were strongly handicapped *vis-à-vis* comparable white candidates – to the extent of nearly 6 percentage-points in the case of the four Liberals and over 3 points for the four Social Democrats.

These findings suggest that the Labour candidates alone were able to transcend their ethnic-minority status. The bogey for the party of the fate of David Pitt (since 1975 Baron Pitt of Hampstead) in the Wandsworth Clapham constituency in the 1970 general election – when he suffered a counter-swing of 10·2 per cent (Butler and Pinto-Duschinsky, 1971, p. 341) far more than anything in comparable south London constituencies – may have been exorcized by 1983, although one may none the less harbour misgivings that there could have been specific losses by ethnic-minority Labour candidates if many had stood in seriously winnable seats. The two Conservative cases are too few for a serious judgement but they do suggest that some normally Conservative voters can still be deterred by an ethnic-minority candidate. The Alliance – partly because it was in that form a new party – was collecting a more evanescent type of support (drawing fairly equally from the disaffected of all social groups) and some of its potential supporters were clearly deterred by a black candidate. Our findings of a probable decrement for ethnic-minority Conservative candidates do differ from those of FitzGerald (1983), who used a simpler method based on average vote shift since 1979 in order to assess these same effects.

There are two cases of very dramatic underperformance, those of Paul Boateng in Hertfordshire West and of Pramila Le Hunte in Birmingham Ladywood. These may be explained by their special circumstances, although it should in fairness be noted that they were the most marginal contests of the Labour and the Conservative candidacies. Paul Boateng never recovered from the circumstances in which he had beaten former Hemel Hempstead Labour MP, Robin Corbett, for the nomination. Even without this handicap, however, Labour had an uphill task in the constituency; in the district council elections on 5 May 1983 it had won only 31·1 per cent of votes cast, compared with 41·5 for the Conservatives and 22·4 per cent for the Alliance (who failed to contest one ward). Still, by 9 June Labour had lost a further 8·8 points, a disproportionately large decline. Pramila Le Hunte's notably poor performance may well be attributable to a negative response from her particular campaign style (FitzGerald, 1983), which sometimes involved matching the style of her clothing with the predominant ethnicity of her audience; she was also facing a woman Labour candidate, Clare Short, with a strong reputation on race- and immigration-related issues; this may well have cemented the black vote for Labour in a constituency whose electorate probably has one of the largest proportions of black and Asian voters of any in the country.

However, the reasonable performance of all Labour's ethnic-minority candidates except Boateng cannot be explained away by rates of shift away from Labour that were different for black and white voters, with the former 'shoring up' Labour's overall support by a particular commitment to Labour. True, there is evidence (FitzGerald, 1984) that there may have been almost no net shift away from Labour between 1979 and 1983 among black and Asian voters, in sharp contrast of course to the trend among white voters. However, only one black Labour candidate (Ben Bousquet in Kensington) was fighting a constituency where even as many as 10 per cent of the population were of New Commonwealth or Pakistan origin; even a special commitment to Labour among the black voters of this constituency would probably not have been sufficient to account for Bousquet's creditable performance.

8.5.4 'Carpet-bagger' candidates

Perhaps the most interesting outcome of these analyses is a counter-intuitive one. This is the finding about what are referred to as 'carpet-bagger' candidates, a term with long usage in American politics that, while still mildly pejorative, has ceased to connote the degree of opprobrium it did in Reconstruction days. By 'carpet-baggers' is meant those candidates who took advantage of the boundary revisions to secure their party's nomination for a seat that was actually or supposedly safer than the one of which their own former seat was the 'core' or formed a large part. There were of course a number of switches consequent upon boundary revision and by no means all may legitimately be termed 'carpet-bagging' (for example, Leon Brittan's switch from Cleveland and Whitby to Richmond, Yorkshire, when the former was divided between Langbaurgh and Scarborough). However, at least seven switches of seat by Conservative MPs did draw some comment about the preference of those concerned not to face what might in other circumstances have been a tough contest when they were able to graze on what they thought would be more fertile electoral pasture. These were the cases of Michael Colvin (from the old Bristol North-west to Romsey and Waterside, in Hampshire), Geoffrey Dickens (from the old Huddersfield West to Littleborough and Saddleworth), Nicholas Lyell (from the old Hemel Hempstead to Bedfordshire Mid), Iain Sproat (from the old Aberdeen South, the new version of which was won by the Tories, to Roxburgh and Berwickshire, won by the Liberal candidate), Anthony Steen (from the old Liverpool Wavertree to South Hams, in Devon), Malcolm Thornton (from the old Liverpool Garston to Crosby) and Gary Waller (from the old Brighouse and Spenborough to Keighley). Were such candidates 'punished' by their new electorates for their desertion of former seats? In fact, rather the reverse was the case, since the average advantage of the five of these included in our analysis was nearly 2 percentage-points. It may therefore be permissible to suggest that the general confusion associated with the boundary changes prevented electors from seeing these candidates as anything other than conventional Conservatives, although in one case a sitting MP whose old constituency had covered part of the area of the relevant new constituency failed to achieve the Conservative nomination. Ray Mawby had been Conservative MP for Totnes since 1955, and almost half of this was redistributed into South Hams. However, Littleborough and Saddleworth, Romsey and Waterside, and Roxburgh and Berwickshire were 'new' seats in Waller's (1983a, p. 9) usage. Bedfordshire Mid is an altered version of the old constituency of the same name but the former Conservative MP, Stephen Hastings, had announced his intending retirement before the general election.

Conclusion

The analysis of the constituency-level results has enabled us to derive further insights into the outcome of the 1983 election. One or two of our findings are perhaps to some of merely empirical interest, such as those on the relationship between vote shift from 1979 to 1983 and party position in the earlier contest, or those about the effects – or lack of them – of various contest characteristics. Other findings, however, are important for a more theoretical understanding of the evolving character of contemporary British politics. We have seen, for example, that in terms of seats Labour is very noticeably a northern-based party and that its earlier support maintained itself best in the North West and in Scotland. The Conservatives have entrenched themselves further in the East Midlands and East Anglia, the latter a region of particular loss for Labour. The breakthrough region for the Alliance was clearly Scotland, whereas its smallest growth was in the relatively more Labour-oriented North West and the more Conservative-oriented East Anglia. However, some of these apparent regional concentrations are in part artefacts of the social and economic characteristics of individual constituencies; Labour's vote in particular, while seeming to have a specific regional concentration, is in fact much more a consequence of constituency characteristics. The Alliance vote tended in any case to be both more evenly spread between regions and also to have a relatively high level of within-region variation. On the other hand, we saw that the Conservative vote has a marked regional configuration over and above the characteristics of individual constituencies.

Individual-level data are of course a better basis than are constituency results for making inferences about personal voting behaviour. Even so, it is remarkable how many of the variables identified as relevant at the individual level have their analogue in aggregate terms. The role of social class in accounting for parties' vote distribution is unsurprising, but we have also seen the aggregate affects of housing tenure, car ownership, unemployment and ethnic-minority presence. The latter two seem to have been of particular importance in accounting for shorter-term change in party support, specifically between May 1982/3 and June 1983.

In these results, as in others already presented, we see the present advantage held by the Conservatives and (even if to a lesser extent) the Alliance, and the corresponding disadvantage suffered by Labour. Conservative voting is positively predicted by a set of characteristics that are tending to increase numerically as time proceeds (non-manual workers, owner occupiers). On the other hand, Labour support is positively predicted by characteristics that are either decreasing numerically (manual workers, council tenants) or, even if not necessarily in decline, are very much minority statuses (the unemployed, ethnic-minority voters). Labour's task is therefore how to transcend this 'ghettoization' of its support in order to form a broader electoral coalition. Our conclusion and afterword address some of the issues raised for Labour by this dilemma.

9   Conclusion and Afterword

9.1   Conclusion
9.2   Afterword: events since June 1983

9.1 Conclusion

The central question that we address in this brief conclusion is how the various theoretical approaches discussed in Chapters 1 and 2 make sense of the events and the patterns of causation described in Chapters 3 to 8. We assume that all serious theoretical approaches must attempt to explain the core events and influences that are documented there, although naturally there is some room for dispute about what must be considered as central. For example, any account of the 1983 election must make some adjustment for Michael Foot's depressing Labour's performance below its baseline level. However, it is obviously difficult to arrive at a non-contentious estimate of what that baseline might be.

First, the nexus of views represented by the party identification approach and the responsible party model (Sections 1.1 and 2.1) confronts the greatest prima-facie difficulty in accommodating our major empirical findings. We found little support for the party identification account of voting behaviour. Personal contacts were mentioned by negligible numbers of respondents as influences on their voting or as important sources of political information, despite explicit prompting on our part (Section 5.1). Party loyalty was an important influence on Labour supporters and did possibly help to stem the party's otherwise adverse performance. Yet Conservative and Alliance supporters evaluated it below issues and positive attractions as an influence on their decisions. Nor was there a very high level of 'feeling close' to one or other party. Contrary to the conclusion of Särlvik and Crewe (1983, p. 295) that in 1979 only 8 per cent of people had no party identification, we found that 19 per cent of electors felt closest to none of the parties and that a further 7 per cent did not vote for the party to which they generally felt closest. Perhaps the most favourable evidence for the stress in the party identification model on the long-term stability of voting patterns is the recovery of the two major parties' vote bases from their depths of unpopularity in late 1981 to their higher levels of support in mid-1984. This suggests at the least that the 'mould' of British politics in terms of voter loyalties is harder to break than is suggested by issue voting accounts.

The responsible party model offers a partial explanation of the differential recovery of Conservative and Labour support up to June 1983, framed largely in terms of the contrast between a publicly united party of government and a patently divided and badly led opposition.

Secondly, the nexus of views represented by the issue voting approach to alignments and the adversary politics model of party competition (Sections 1.2 and 2.3) fares a good deal better in tackling the material presented here. National issues and the positive attractions of the parties were mentioned as key influences on their voting behaviour by most of our respondents, but there was also extensive evidence of negative voting to keep out a least preferred party, as the adversary politics model would expect. Voters clearly had some ability to assess party images and leadership performance and most of them held explicit views on some issue questions, such as defence and disarmament. However, we documented extensive evidence that other issue attitudes (especially those on economic policy and the Common Market) are not autonomous but rather reflect attitudinal adjustments by voters in order to reduce inconsistency between their party choice and their policy views (Sections 7.4.1 and 7.4.6). We also explored the considerable evidence of inconsistency in voters' attitudes on defence and disarmament and on the welfare state (Section 7.5). We demonstrated that, although there is a close correlation between issue attitudes and voting, there is an even stronger linkage between exposure to media influences and partisan alignment (Section 5.3).

The adversary politics model of party competition argues that the 1983 election reflects a number of factors:

1   The Conservatives were relatively advantaged in competing with Labour by their internal organization, which gave to the party leadership far more discretionary ability to settle policy, on lines suggested by Figure 2.6. The Labour leadership were uniquely hampered by the constitutional changes and activists' suspicions of the 1979–82 period from trying to tailor the party's appeal towards majority views.
2   Even so, a potential Conservative hard-line attitude was perceived by a large section of the electorate and a substantial minority of voters consciously tried to avoid a Conservative landslide.
3   Labour's disastrous performance reflected its attempt to defy public opinion on major issues, especially on defence, where fewer than one in ten voters whole-heartedly supported its policies.
4   The slump in Alliance support after the Falklands war reflected its loss of momentum as the crisis swung public support towards the government. By mid-1983 this also reflected voters' perceptions of the Alliance's inability, because of the electoral system, to achieve a breakthrough in parliamentary representation. None the less, the adversary politics view might claim that the Alliance did tap support from a mass of 'moderate', centrist voters – as witnessed by the growth of its vote during the campaign, despite the electoral threshold handicap, and by the numbers of voters in our survey who felt 'second closest' to the Alliance.

Thirdly, the radical view of voting and party competition (Sections 1.3 and 2.4) offers in our view the most complete and plausible account of our findings. We showed in Chapter 6 that its innovative account of the social bases of political alignments provides a powerful series of suggestions for analysing our survey information. We demonstrated in Section 5.3 that its stress on the power of the mass media to shape political alignments matches well the high correlation of media exposure and voting patterns that we uncovered. Chapter 7 set out our detailed objections to the issue voting model and the reasons why we see many attitudes as products of external stimuli acting on voters or as mere corollaries of voting behaviour.

In Chapters 3 and 4 we documented the critical determinants of party performance in the inter-election and campaign periods. The Conservative revival from mid-1982 owes a great deal to the creative exploitation of incumbency, most obviously in involving British armed forces in a limited war on favourable terms with accompanying 'wartime' manipulation of the mass media and public opinion. However, since 1979 a whole series of Conservative policies, especially the privatization of social services and public corporations, differential public sector incomes restraints and much of the content of macro-economic policy, are to be interpreted as attempts to restructure the distribution of voter preferences. In its own sophisticated way the Conservative government also inaugurated a distinctively monetarist political business cycle. Finally, we showed how these substantial advantages were increased by the conduct of the election campaign itself, especially the single-minded focus on Labour's poorly formulated policies on unemployment and defence and the overt stigmatizing of Labour as quasi-Communist and hence falling outside the range of legitimate party competition. Given the massive propaganda support for Conservative strategies from the Tory press and the failure of the broadcasting institutions adequately to safeguard any journalistic 'countervailing power', there were few external impediments to the Conservatives' full exploitation of the advantages of their incumbency.

Liberal democratic political arrangements are always imperfect or flawed in some respect; hence the invented political science concept of 'polyarchy' to serve as a description of a working pluralist society, retaining the concept of 'democracy' to represent the normative ideal. Yet the grounds for concern about the future of British 'polyarchy' are more substantial now than at any previous time in the postwar period. The possibly tolerable democratic flaws of an earlier period have become crucial sources of impaired legitimacy for the new Conservative government and more diffusely for a range of other state institutions controlled by government. The increasingly transparent exploitation of state power for party ends, which is implicit in the new Conservative rejection of consensus, may produce another electoral success in 1987–8. However, its longer-term importance may well be traced in the fragmentation of British political culture and an increasing resort to coercive forms of state power to enforce consent. In this deeper sense, British democracy stands at a crossroads in the mid-1980s.

9.2 Afterword: events since June 1983

A key problem with political surveys, as with family snapshots, is that people move. The snapshot becomes blurred in parts as some of the actors shift position. In our case, however, not only the voters in the foreground but also some of the background scenery of party competition have changed quite markedly. Within a weekend of losing the election, Michael Foot was on the way out as Labour leader, ungraciously urged towards the door by Clive Jenkins of the Association of Scientific, Technical and Managerial Staffs and by an eager press corps. Two days later Roy Jenkins announced his decision to stand down from the leadership of the SDP. Almost simultaneously David Steel went on an extended 'sabbatical' in Scotland for the rest of the summer, suffering from the 'exhaustion' brought on by an illness during the election campaign.

These changes in turn heralded some important new developments in each of the major parties. Foot's departure, quickly supplemented by Denis Healey's decision not to seek re-election as Labour's deputy leader, inaugurated the first full-scale use of the electoral college machinery to select a leader. With Tony Benn defeated in Bristol East and out of Parliament for a time, the leading candidates in the leadership race were Neil Kinnock and Roy Hattersley. The election of the 'dream ticket' of Kinnock as leader and Hattersley as his deputy at the 1983 Party Conference inaugurated a revival of Labour fortunes. The wide process of consultation involved also legitimized Labour's system of intra-party democracy, producing convincing majorities in all sections of the electoral college for both elected candidates. Even previously sceptical observers were moved to comment with Drucker (1984, p. 300): 'On balance it appears that the new process has much to commend it. It is arguably much superior to the process it replaced.' Labour's drive for stabilization continued following the 'unity conference' with widespread acceptance that future party debates could not be handled in the manner of the 1979–82 period. Kinnock made an impressive start in improving the party's media approach but the problems at Walworth Road were not addressed. The party recouped some of its losses in the local government elections of May 1984 but did much less well outside the conurbations and Scotland. Six weeks later, in elections to the European Parliament, Labour almost doubled its 1979 tally of MEPs but managed a vote share of only 36·4 per cent, still 5 points fewer than the Conservatives.

Meanwhile in the SDP, self-proclaimed defenders of the 'one man, one vote' principle, Jenkins was succeeded by David Owen as leader without any process of membership consultation or election. Jenkins plus the other four SDP MPs simply nominated Owen unanimously as leader and he took over as a *fait accompli*, thanks to a clause requiring nomination of leadership candidates by at least an eighth of the SDP MPs. Owen quickly assumed a dominant media role within the Alliance, which continued even after Steel's return to active politics. Strains began to surface within the Alliance as the Liberal Assembly in September 1983 voted for a unilateralist-sounding defence resolution. The sporadic post-mortem on the failure to win more seats rumbled on. Between June and November 1983 public opinion switched from seeing the Alliance as united (by 55 to 26 per cent) to seeing it as divided (by 41 to 34 per cent) (Whiteley, 1984, p. 4). While its support in the opinion polls slumped, however, the Alliance continued to do well in by-elections, greatly increasing its vote in the formerly safe seat of Penrith and the Border in a by-election to replace the ennobled William Whitelaw and in June 1984 actually winning the nominally safe Portsmouth South seat from the Conservatives with a 14 per cent swing in a dramatic last-minute surge of support. The Alliance also boosted its vote in two more Conservative seats in two of the three parliamentary by-elections fought on the same day as the local elections in May 1984. There were some Alliance successes in these local elections but they were in scattered individual seats. By mid-1984 there was some evidence of a modest Alliance recovery in both local by-elections and in the national polls. However, in the Euro-elections the size of constituencies and plurality-rule system ensured that it did not win a single seat, despite receiving 19·1 per cent of the national vote.

Lastly, the victorious Conservatives found their victory more problematic than they might have anticipated. The hostages to fortune given during the campaign on the NHS issue sparked protests at attempts within a month of polling day to implement cuts in health care personnel. The October Party Conference turned into a public relations disaster after the chairman of the party, Cecil Parkinson, was forced to resign as a Cabinet minister after a scandal about his personal life. The commitment to abolish the Greater London Council and the metropolitan counties provoked a growing volume of criticism, with public opinion in London swinging markedly in favour of the GLC and the Labour Party, chiefly because of the success of Ken Livingstone's 'balanced' public transport policies. A suddenly announced decision to abolish trade union rights at the Government Communications Headquarters in Cheltenham and the appointment of a National Coal Board chairman expected to introduce larger manpower cuts and pit closures in the coal industry both precipitated criticism, which intensified when the government became involved in a long-running miners' strike. Privatization emerged as the major continuing theme in Conservative economic policy, although its implementation continued to be fraught with difficulties.

Yet, despite all these apparently dramatic developments, the pattern of public opinion support for the Conservatives at around 40 per cent shifted relatively slowly. The main change by the summer of 1984 was a relapse of Alliance support to almost a 20 per cent baseline and the restabilization of Labour percentage support in the middle-30s range. An opinion poll taken by NOP Market Research Limited exactly one year after our own post-election survey gave Labour 37·5 per cent, the Conservatives 40·5 per cent, the SDP–Liberal Alliance 20·5 per cent, and others 1·7 per cent. There may be a slight pro-Conservative bias in these results; both Gallup (*Daily Telegraph*, 14 June 1984, p. 6) and Marplan (*Guardian*, 22 June 1984, p. 1) showed Labour fractionally ahead in June 1984, though within the limits of sampling error. Even so, NOP's figures are unlikely to be far from the truth.

First of all, let us consider the implications of these NOP figures for the

Table 9.1 *Percentage-point changes in support for the Labour Party, the Conservative Party, and the SDP–Liberal Alliance between June 1983 and June 1984 (NOP data), by three social variables*

	Labour	Conservative	SDP–Liberal Alliance
Gender			
Male	+9	+2	−11
Female	+8	−4	−2
Occupational class of head of household			
AB	−2	+7	−5
C1	+10	−5	−4
C2	+11	0	−8
DE	+12	−5	−7
Age			
18 to 24	+10	+1	−11
25 to 34	+12	−3	−10
35 to 44	0	+11	−9
45 to 54	+9	−4	−4
55 to 64	+12	−4	−7
65 or more	+10	−13	+4

distribution of seats in parliament if a general election were held. The Conservatives would still be able to form a majority administration; the situation would be similar in that respect to the outcome in October 1974, whose incoming administration did after all survive more than four years. The Conservatives would have 330 seats, Labour 283, the Alliance 15 and others 22. Even in this example Labour would remain the third-placed party in nearly a quarter of all seats in Great Britain. If the Alliance vote were to remain at 20·5 per cent, with Labour increasing to 40 per cent and a corresponding decline for the Conservatives, Labour would become the largest parliamentary party, very much as in February 1974; Labour would have 313 seats, 13 short of an overall majority, while the Conservatives would have 299. Only with 42 per cent of the total vote (an increase of almost 50 per cent on the 1983 percentage!), combined with continuing Alliance stability at 20·5 per cent and a corresponding Conservative decline, would Labour emerge as the majority party, holding 331 seats; the Conservatives would have 279. Thus, if the Alliance can hold on to its baseline vote of about a fifth of the electorate, Labour needs in excess of 42 per cent of the total vote to secure a reasonable working majority in Parliament. At the time of writing it is still some way from this figure.

Let us also examine various social groups in order to ascertain how the shifting of votes has occurred. We do this in Table 9.1, where we compare the results from our own survey shortly after the election with those of the NOP poll exactly a year later. The return to Labour is, with two exceptions, remarkably uniform, from a minimum of 8 points to a maximum of 12. The two exceptions are occupational classes AB (on the scale formulated by the

Institute of Practitioners in Advertising), professional, managerial and administrative workers, and those aged 35 to 44. Both these groups, especially the latter, show a remarkable Conservative surge since 1983. The Conservative vote among men may also have increased slightly since then and among the strategic C2 occupational class, skilled-manual workers and their wives, it has remained stable. The most noticeable Conservative decline has been among those aged 65 or more, who are apparently the one group of those considered that has increased its support for the Alliance – by 4 points. The Alliance's greatest losses have been among men and among the young.

Labour is now solidly the most popular party among the youngest age-group but support from this source is notoriously a fair-weather friend. Labour's general across-the-board recovery (with the two exceptions mentioned) does not augur well for its chances if the political going becomes rough. Support gained in this manner would be particularly likely to depart again if the party were to face unpopularity. There is therefore no evidence of any change in the residualized structural basis of the Labour vote. Although the *level* of Labour's support has improved, its *structure* is little altered. No major new policy initiatives have been made by the party in order to transcend the social factors that have so marginalized its vote.

Other considerations advise a measure of caution about Labour's prospects. Crucial issues, most obviously defence and disarmament, remain to trip the party in a tough election campaign. Labour is still committed to a unilateralism that is unambiguously endorsed by less than 10 per cent of the electorate. This sort of disjuncture may be acceptable on trivial or marginal issues; it is doubtful whether it can be sustained on an issue that will undoubtedly be among the two or three most important in any future general election (Dunleavy and Husbands, 1984b).

Appendix A *A day-by-day chronology of the major events in the campaign and the results of published opinion polls*

Major news events have been entered on the day on which they happened. This was normally the day on which they featured on the evening television news but the day *before* they were in the daily newspapers. Opinion poll findings are given for the day, or the last day, on which the fieldwork was conducted, which was usually two days before the results were published. Twenty-eight of the fifty published polls carried out during the campaign had one-day fieldwork periods; fourteen of them had two-day periods. The campaign is taken to have started on Sunday 8 May and to have lasted thirty-three days up to and including polling day, 9 June.

Date	Campaign day	Major events	Poll findings
Thursday 5 May	−3	Local election results show mixed successes and losses for all parties.	
Friday 6 May	−2	HARRIS	C 46; L 38; A 15
		MORI	C 45; L 34; A 20
		NOP	C 47; L 34; A 18

START OF CAMPAIGN

Week 1

Sunday 8 May	1	Thatcher holds Conservative 'summit' at Chequers and plays coy about election date on 'The World This Weekend'.	
Monday 9 May	2	Accouncement of polling day.	
		GALLUP	C 49; L 31·5; A 17·5
Tuesday 10 May	3	Labour force non-implementation of Finance Bill tax measures (chiefly, raising of mortgage interest tax relief threshold).	
		MORI	C 46; L 31; A 21
Wednesday 11 May	4	Labour decides to use *The New Hope for Britain* as its manifesto	
		HARRIS	C 52; L 31; A 17
		MARPLAN	C 46; L 34; A 19
		MORI	C 46; L 32; A 22
Thursday 12 May	5	Labour and Alliance press conferences start. Alliance plans to reduce unemployment by 1 million in first two years.	
		MORI	C 49; L 34; A 15
Friday 13 May	6	Parliament dissolved. Thatcher's speech to Scottish Conservatives' Conference in Perth emphasizes danger to freedom in Labour's proposals.	

Week 2

Monday 16 May	9	Labour's plan for creating jobs attacked by Conservatives and the Alliance (Owen). AUD SEL C 46; L 31; A 21 GALLUP C 46; L 33; A 19 MORI C 44; L 37; A 17
Tuesday 17 May	10	*Daily Star* leads with Tory lead down to 7 points. Thatcher finalizes summit plans; an abbreviated stay at Williamsburg, while EEC Stuttgart summit is postponed until after polling day. Prior restates 'wet' Toryism. AUD SEL C 44; L 33; A 21 NOP C 49; L 31; A 19
Wednesday 18 May	11	Conservatives launch manifesto at their first press conference: main pledges, new union law, abolition of GLC and metropolitan counties. HARRIS C 45; L 35; A 17 MORI C 47; L 30; A 21
Thursday 19 May	12	Healey launches leaked CPRS paper on dismantling the welfare state. On television Pym deprecates prospect of a landslide. MORI C 46; L 37; A 16
Friday 20 May	13	Annual inflation falls to 4 per cent. Thatcher 'humbles' Pym and Prior. HARRIS C 45; L 36; A 18 MARPLAN C 47; L 34; A 18
Sunday 22 May	15	Labour Campaign Committee discusses strategy shift to a locality emphasis. The *Observer* shows Conservative lead cut to 9 points according to Harris.

Week 3

Monday 23 May	16	Polaris confusion begins to affect Labour. AUD SEL C 45; L 32; A 20 GALLUP C 48; L 33; A 18 MORI C 51; L 33; A 15 NOP C 52; L 33; A 14
Tuesday 24 May	17	Labour fails to dispel Polaris confusion. Commons Treasury Committee draft report blames government monetary policies for half the increase in unemployment since 1979. AUD SEL C 45; L 32; A 21
Wednesday 25 May	18	Callaghan wrecks Foot's attempts at repairs to Polaris stance. Newspapers tout that Conservative lead is widening to 18 per cent. HARRIS C 48; L 33; A 18 MARPLAN C 47·5; L 32·5; A 19 MORI C 46; L 30; A 23
Thursday 26 May	19	Foot struggles again on defence. Thatcher claims Conservatives are the real 'peace party'. GALLUP C 49; L 31·5; A 18 MORI C 51; L 29; A 18

Friday 27 May	20	Thatcher calls for a landslide Conservative victory. Rumours reach the newspapers that Steel will take over as leader of the Alliance campaign.

HARRIS	C 47; L 30; A 21
MARPLAN	C 49·5; L 31; A 19

Saturday 28 May	21	Thatcher flies to Williamsburg. Powell's London speech denounces independent British nuclear deterrent as 'a delusion'.

Sunday 29 May	22	Alliance hold a 'summit' at Ettrick Bridge, with some slight further prominence to Steel and Owen its only agreed result.

Week 4

Monday 30 May	23	Foot and Jenkins attack summit 'flop' in Williamsburg. Thatcher flies home.

AUD SEL	C 41; L 30; A 24
GALLUP	C 47·5; L 28; A 23

Tuesday 31 May	24	Thatcher asserts that she would press the nuclear button if necessary. Labour hold press conference on NHS cutbacks and privatization that the Conservatives are alleged to be planning. Thatcher rebuts 'secret manifesto' charges on television.

AUD SEL	C 44; L 29; A 25
MORI	C 44; L 32; A 21

Wednesday 1 June	25	Healey accuses Thatcher of 'glorying in slaughter'. Kinnock demands inquiry into the sinking of the *General Belgrano*.

HARRIS	C 46; L 28; A 24
MARPLAN	C 47; L 30; A 22

Thursday 2 June	26	Alliance poll progress reported. Healey withdraws 'glorying in slaughter' comment on television.

GALLUP	C 45·5; L 31·5; A 22
MORI	C 43; L 32; A 23

Friday 3 June	27	Alliance poll increase definite. Rumours surface of Conservative reshuffle after the election. Unemployment figures (artificially) down to 3,049,000.

HARRIS	C 47; L 28; A 23
MARPLAN	C 44; L 27; A 27·5
MORI	C 45; L 28; A 25
NOP	C 47; L 29; A 23

Saturday 4 June	28	Enoch Powell urges a vote against the EEC.
		HARRIS C 45·5; L 28·5; A 24

Sunday 5 June	29	Newspapers predict Conservative landslide. Alliance second in *Sunday Mirror* poll. Tories hold rally with sport and showbiz stars.
		AUD SEL C 45; L 24; A 28

Final Week

Monday 6 June	30	Party leaders talk to Granada 500 audience. Kinnock makes 'guts at Goose Green' reference.

		AUD SEL	C 44; L 24; A 29
		MARPLAN	C 47; L 26; A 25

Tuesday 7 June	31	Foot and Thatcher stress a decision between the two parties. Kinnock refuses to withdraw Goose Green remark and makes his Bridgend speech.	
		AUD SEL	C 45; L 23; A 29
		MORI	C 47; L 26; A 25
		NOP	C 46; L 28; A 24

Wednesday 8 June	32	Labour and Alliance neck-and-neck in newspapers' opinion polls. Thatcher campaigns on the Isle of Wight.	
		GALLUP	C 45·5; L 26·5; A 26
		HARRIS	C 47; L 25; A 26
		MARPLAN	C 46; L 26; A 26
		MORI	C 44; L 28; A 26
		NOP	C 47; L 25; A 26

Thursday 9 June	33	Polling day.	

Appendix B *Tables*

Table B.1 *Percentage support for the Labour Party, the Conservative Party, and the Liberal Party/SDP–Liberal Alliance in three general elections from October 1974 to June 1983, by region*[1]

	Oct. 1974	May 1979	June 1983	Percentage-point gain (+) or loss (−) 1974–83	1979–83
Greater London					
Labour	43·8	39·6	29·8	−14·0	−9·8
Conservative	37·4	46·0	43·9	+6·5	−2·1
Liberal/SDP–Liberal Alliance	17·1	11·9	24·7	+7·6	+12·8
South East (excluding Greater London)					
Labour	30·7	26·8	15·8	−14·9	−11·0
Conservative	45·2	54·7	54·5	+9·3	−0·2
Liberal/SDP–Liberal Alliance	23·7	17·5	29·0	+5·3	+11·5
South West					
Labour	29·1	25·5	14·7	−14·4	−10·8
Conservative	43·1	51·7	51·3	+8·2	−0·4
Liberal/SDP–Liberal Alliance	27·4	21·4	33·2	+5·8	+11·8
East Anglia					
Labour	35·5	32·6	20·5	−14·8	−12·1
Conservative	43·8	50·8	51·0	+7·2	+0·2
Liberal/SDP–Liberal Alliance	20·6	16·0	28·2	+7·6	+12·2
East Midlands					
Labour	43·1	38·6	28·0	−15·1	−10·6
Conservative	38·2	46·7	47·2	+9·0	+0·5
Liberal/SDP–Liberal Alliance	17·2	13·7	24·1	+6·9	+10·4
West Midlands					
Labour	43·9	40·1	31·2	−12·7	−8·9
Conservative	37·5	47·1	45·0	+7·5	−2·1
Liberal/SDP–Liberal Alliance	17·8	11·6	23·4	+5·6	+11·8
Yorkshire and Humberside					
Labour	46·9	44·9	35·3	−11·6	−9·6
Conservative	31·9	39·5	38·7	+6·8	−0·8
Liberal/SDP–Liberal Alliance	20·4	14·7	25·6	+5·2	+10·9
North West					
Labour	44·6	42·5	36·0	−8·6	−6·5
Conservative	37·0	43·7	40·0	+3·0	−3·7
Liberal/SDP–Liberal Alliance	18·0	13·2	23·4	+5·4	+10·2
North					
Labour	49·9	49·8	40·2	−9·7	−9·6
Conservative	31·7	36·2	34·6	+2·9	−1·6
Liberal/SDP–Liberal Alliance	17·1	12·5	25·0	+7·9	+12·5
Wales					
Labour	49·5	47·5	37·6	−11·9	−9·9
Conservative	23·9	32·6	31·1	+7·2	−1·5
Liberal/SDP–Liberal Alliance	15·5	11·2	23·3	+7·8	+12·1
Scotland					
Labour	36·3	41·6	35·1	−1·2	−6·5
Conservative	24·7	31·3	28·4	+3·7	−2·9
Liberal/SDP–Liberal Alliance	8·3	9·1	24·5	+16·2	+15·4
Great Britain					
Labour	40·2	37·8	28·3	−11·9	−9·5
Conservative	36·7	44·9	43·5	+6·8	−1·4
Liberal/SDP–Liberal Alliance	18·8	14·1	26·0	+7·2	+11·9

Note:
[1] The individual regions are defined as follows. 1. Greater London: the thirty-two London Boroughs and the City of London; 2. South East: Bedfordshire, Berkshire, Buckinghamshire, East Sussex, Essex, Hampshire (including the Isle of Wight), Hertfordshire, Kent, Oxfordshire, Surrey and West Sussex; 3. South West: Avon, Cornwall, Devon, Dorset, Gloucestershire, Somerset and Wiltshire; 4. East Anglia: Cambridgeshire, Norfolk and Suffolk; 5. East Midlands: Derbyshire, Leicestershire, Lincolnshire, Northamptonshire and Nottinghamshire; 6. West Midlands: Hereford and Worcester, Shropshire, Staffordshire, Warwickshire and West Midlands (metropolitan county); 7. Yorkshire and Humberside: Humberside, North Yorkshire, South Yorkshire and West Yorkshire; 8. North West: Cheshire, Greater Manchester, Lancashire and Merseyside; 9. North: Cleveland, Cumbria, Durham, Northumberland and Tyne and Wear; 10. Wales: all counties; 11. Scotland: all counties.

Table B.2   *Percentage-point changes in support for the Labour Party, the Conservative Party, and the Liberal Party/SDP–Liberal Alliance between the May 1979 general election and the June 1983 general election, according both to each party's position in May 1979 and also to the percentage-point difference in that election between the first and second party or the second and third party (BBC/ITN team's estimates)*[1]

| | *Percentage-point differences between first and second/ second and third parties* | | | | |
	< 5·0	*5·0–9·9*	*10·0–14·9*	*15·0–19·9*	*> 20·0*
Labour					
First in 1979	−10·8	−8·9	−10·7	−9·9	−8·6
(differences being from second party)	(30)	(24)	(40)	(30)	(98)
Second in 1979	−9·5	−8·8	−10·6	−10·4	−10·5
(differences being from first party)	(25)	(34)	(35)	(32)	(145)
Third in 1979	−8·8	−8·5	−8·2	−5·2	−4·2
(differences being from second party)	(28)	(23)	(11)	(7)	(17)
Conservative					
First in 1979	−1·9	−1·3	−1·5	−0·7	−0·6
(differences being from second party)	(26)	(38)	(40)	(40)	(206)
Second in 1979	−0·9	−2·5	−1·6	−2·5	−2·3
(differences being from first party)	(34)	(24)	(41)	(31)	(98)
Third in 1979	+1·2	—	—	−0·1	−1·0
(differences being from second party)	(1)			(3)	(1)
Liberal/SDP–Liberal Alliance					
First in 1979	+8·0	+2·0	+3·6	+9·9	−10·5
(differences being from second party)	(4)	(1)	(1)	(1)	(1)
Second in 1979	+10·3	+3·2	+5·1	+6·7	+8·5
(differences being from first party)	(1)	(5)	(5)	(8)	(62)
Third in 1979	+9·8	+10·8	+12·2	+12·8	+12·7
(differences being from second party)	(40)	(47)	(62)	(60)	(267)

Note:
[1] These analyses have been confined to those constituencies in Great Britain where the Liberal Party had, or was deemed by the BBC/ITN team to have had, a candidacy in the May 1979 general election and where comparisons of differences in May 1979 are between Labour, Conservative and Liberal.

Appendix C *The sources of data*

The survey

The survey whose results are reported in various chapters was conducted for the authors by NOP Market Research Limited between 16 and 26 June 1983, with more than 80 per cent of the interviewing completed by 20 June 1983. The 1,023 respondents were selected using a quota sample in eighty constituencies across Great Britain. The sampling frame used was all new constituencies listed in the order of their Press Association numbers (that is, alphabetically by name) according to *The BBC/ITN Guide to the New Parliamentary Constituencies* (BBC/ITN, 1983). For reasons of interviewing practicality five constituencies in the extreme north of Scotland were excluded; these were Caithness and Sutherland, Inverness Nairn and Lochaber, Orkney and Shetland, Ross Cromarty and Skye, and the Western Isles. From the remaining 628 constituencies the final eighty were selected using a random starting-point and a constant sampling interval. These eighty constituencies were then arranged into the Registrar-General's Standard Regions and the actual number of electors in each was checked against the expected number. This revealed some minor imbalances and in two cases constituencies were deleted from a standard region and extra ones were added to another. A check was also made to ascertain that there were the correct proportions of Conservative-held and Labour-held seats; the balance was found to be satisfactory.

Each interviewer was given a quota of thirteen interviews to conduct within a single constituency. The actual quotas used are shown below.

Men working full-time	33·3%
Men not working full-time	14·4
Women working full-time or part-time	22·8
Women not working	29·4
Occupational classes ABC1, aged 18 to 34 years	13·9%
Occupational classes ABC1, aged 35 to 54 years	12·8
Occupational classes ABC1, aged 55 years or more	12·2
Occupational class C2, aged 18 to 34 years	11·7
Occupational class C2, aged 35 to 54 years	10·0
Occupational class C2, aged 55 years or more	8·9
Occupational classes DE, aged 18 to 34 years	10·6
Occupational classes DE, aged 35 to 54 years	6·7
Occupational classes DE, aged 55 years or more	13·3

These categories of occupational class are those formulated by the Institute of Practitioners in Advertising and are described by Reid (1977, pp. 46–7).

The time-series data

The month-by-month data on Conservative voting intention/inclination analysed in Chapter 7 are from Webb and Wybrow (1981, pp. 167–75; 1982, pp. 191–2) and from recent issues of the *Gallup Political Index (GPI)*.

Most of the data on the rate of unemployment were extracted from DARTS, a data-retrieval system developed by Diana Whistler at the London School of Economics. DARTS contains much of the content of the data banks of the Central Statistical Office and the Bank of England (Whistler, 1982). Recent statistics on the rate of unemployment are from the *Employment Gazette*. The data extracted from these sources are the reported rate of male and female unemployment in the United Kingdom, seasonally adjusted and including school-leavers (designated UNP in the formulae below). For the period until October 1982 it is this statistic that has been used as a measurement of the rate of unemployment in the time-series analyses of government popularity. However, two major changes in counting procedure have to be allowed for in order to ensure comparability over the entire analysis until April 1983. From November 1982 until February 1983 the rate of unemployment used in the time-series analyses has the value of the function,

$$-0\cdot086346 + 1\cdot0731 * \text{UNP}$$

and for March and April 1983 it has the value of the function,

$$-0\cdot086346 + 1\cdot0731 * (\text{UNP} + 0\cdot3)$$

The 'Falklands factor' has been coded '1' for all months from May 1982 to April 1983 and '0' otherwise, since the increased support for the Conservatives in the opinion polls began only towards the end of April 1982.

The constituency-level data

These data were assembled from a number of sources. The *BBC/ITN Guide to the New Parliamentary Constituencies* supplied estimates of the putative results in the 1979 general election. The *Daily Telegraph* (11 June 1983, pp. 17–21, plus some subsequently published corrections) was the source of the 1983 results, compared for accuracy with the corresponding listing in *The Times* on the same day (11 June 1983, Supplement, pp. I–XII). Local election data for May 1983 were collected from the relevant local newspapers. The results for the London Borough Council elections were taken from Greater London Council (1982). The 1981 Census data were extracted from the 100 per cent and the 10 per cent files for the new constituencies supplied by the ESRC Data Archive at the University of Essex. The Office of Population Censuses and Surveys has confirmed that the 10 per cent sample was unbiased and that it is appropriate to gross up all sample results by a factor of ten (OPCS, 1983).

Notes

Introduction

[1] Throughout this book we follow the convention that there are three major parties, for convenience and simplicity treating the SDP–Liberal Alliance as a single party unless it is explicitly stated to the contrary.

Chapter 1

[1] These data, and all survey results for which no specific source is given, are from a political survey conducted for the authors by NOP Market Research Limited between 16 and 26 June 1983, with more than 80 per cent of the interviewing completed by 20 June 1983. The 1,023 respondents were selected using a quota sample in eighty constituencies across Great Britain. Full details of how this survey was conducted are contained in Appendix C.

Chapter 3

[1] The data shown in Figures 3.2A and 3.2B have been derived from the following questions asked month-by-month by the Gallup Poll (Webb and Wybrow, 1981, p. 167):

Voting intention or inclination
The percentaged answers to the question: 'If there were a General Election tomorrow, which party would you support?', including the answers of the 'don't knows' to an additional question: 'Which would you be most inclined to vote for?', but excluding those who remain 'don't knows' even after the latter question.

[2] Figure 3.2B shows the 'median-smoothed' opinion poll ratings of the three major parties for the 1979–83 period. The procedure of median-smoothing replaces each month's actual score by the median of three observations: the one for that particular month, the one for the preceding month and the one for the succeeding month. This process is repeated until all scores are completely stable (that is, do not change on any further iteration). Using such a running median is particularly useful for separating fundamental turning-points in time-series data from more random variations; however, readers should ensure that they compare Figures 3.2A and 3.2B in order to note the information that smoothing has discarded. For a further description see Mosteller and Tukey (1977, pp. 52–77).

[3] The data shown in Figure 3.3 have been derived from the following questions asked month-by month by the Gallup Poll (Webb and Wybrow, 1981, p. 167):

Approval of Government Record
The percentaged 'approve' answers to the question: 'Do you approve or disapprove of the Government's record to date?'

Approval of Prime Minister
The percentaged 'satisfied' answers to the question: 'Are you satisfied or dissatisfied with . . . . as Prime Minister?'

Approval of Other Party Leaders
The percentaged 'good leader' answers to the question: 'Do you think . . . . is or is not proving a good leader of the . . . . Party?'

4 Gallup's results on public approval of the Prime Minister and of party leaders are affected to some extent by the wording of the questions asked (see Note 3 above). Other polling agencies operationalize this with rather different questions producing lower and higher aggregate results. MORI, for example, asks respondents whether they are satisfied or dissatisfied with the way that X is doing his/her job. This formulation has produced far lower positive ratings for David Steel than has Gallup's (percentages usually being in the mid-40s since May 1979 rather than around 60). It also produced a higher approval rating for Mrs Thatcher during the Falklands period than did the Gallup version; MORI's measure of satisfaction with the Prime Minister reached 59 per cent in June 1982.

Chapter 4

[1] The source of the error in Audience Research's telephone polls was not so much that poorer, more Labour-oriented people are less likely to have telephones; this fact can be more or less compensated for by weighting and adjustment procedures. The problem was that Audience Selection also weighted their results by vote in the 1979 general election (as measured by a recall question) and, because of the Alliance's emergence, there was inflated recollection of Liberal voting in 1979. See Himmelweit, Biberian and Stockdale (1978) for an analysis of this type of error in vote recall.

Chapter 5

[1] The decision to use a four-point scale to measure attitudes is defended in Note 2 of Chapter 7.
[2] The larger table containing all social class categories as controls produces very similar results but with smaller numbers of cases in individual cells.

Chapter 6

[1] The only minor exception shown in analyses more disaggregated than that shown here is among controllers of labour in private industry, where rates of unionization are for once comparable.
[2] We analysed the non-working population further in order to detect whether part of the reason for this was the inclusion in their ranks of substantial numbers of former union members. People who were previously in a trade union when at work turn out to be slightly more Labour-leaning than those who never joined but the effect is small.
[3] For similar misreadings of this aspect of the consumption sectors approach, see Harrop (1980) and Franklin and Page (1984).

Chapter 7

[1] The entries for all voters for the individual major parties include those who voted for various minor parties in 1979 or who were eligible to vote but abstained.
[2] In measuring attitudes, we also deliberately omitted a middle position from our response options. It was felt that respondents, unless lacking any knowledge of a subject (and so becoming 'don't knows'), would in general lean towards one or the

other polar alternatives, albeit with little intensity (Schuman and Presser, 1981, pp. 161–78). In any case, Schuman and Presser's research on this subject shows that, although an offered middle position leads to its choice more frequently than when it has to be volunteered, whether one is present or absent has no significant effect upon most bivariate relationships.

[3] Attached to each party name introduced in the discussion of the various issues are the percentages of all respondents with a substantive opinion of the subject who feel that the party concerned would be best on that issue.

[4] The results for the 1979–83 period, along with comprehensive models of government popularity for the 1966–70, 1970–3 and 1974–9 periods, are contained in Husbands (1985), which discusses at some length the various empirical and theoretical issues in the study of the relationship between government popularity and unemployment since the mid-1960s.

The present analysis for 1979–83 also sought possible effects from the following economic and non-economic variables: the year-on-year change in the general index of retail prices; the year-on-year change in the annual change in the general index of retail prices; the month-on-month change in the general index of retail prices; the year-on-year change in the index of average earnings of all employees; the year-on-year change in the annual change in the index of average earnings of all employees; the month-on-month change in the index of average earnings of all employees; an index of real earnings; the year-on-year change in this index of real earnings; the year-on-year change in the annual change in this index of real earnings; the month-on-month change in this index of real earnings; the month-on-month change in the percentage rate of unemployment in the United Kingdom, lagged four months; an index of money supply; the month-on-month change in this index of money supply; the seasonally adjusted visible trade balance, lagged one month; the average discount rate for treasury bills; the US dollar spot rate per £1 sterling in London; two measures for the electoral cycle, one measuring possible support depreciation in the first eighteen months of a governmental term and the other one possible support accretion in the final eighteen months of a putative full five-year term; and a measure of trend, which increased by one for each successive month.

[5] Interestingly, whether a possible Conservative or a possible Labour government was being postulated, this poll found that there was no great difference of expectation concerning the likely time-scale of a reduction.

[6] No major party in 1983 put forward a defence policy that was an unconditional continuation of the status quo. The closest to this was Alliance policy, which wanted to cancel the Trident programme but reserved its position concerning the deployment of Cruise missiles (SDP–Liberal Alliance, 1983, p. 29).

[7] The nine variables that combine respondents' assessments of party competence or proximity on the one hand and issue importance on the other have been formed as described below. In the case of unemployment responses about party competence were coded thus: '2' if a party's policies were considered very likely to reduce unemployment '1' if fairly likely, '0' if 'don't know', '−1' if fairly unlikely, and '−2' if very unlikely. Responses about the importance of the level of unemployment as an election issue were coded as '3' for extremely important, '2' for fairly important, '1' for not very important, and '0' for not at all important. The discriminant-analysis variables combining the two concepts were formed by multiplying together the constituent variables, this being repeated for each party using that party's assessed competence variable. This produced variables whose most positive scores meant that a respondent both felt the issue extremely important and also rated highly the competence on it of the party concerned, while the most negative scores meant that the issue was rated as very important but there was a low assessment of respective party competence.

In the cases of defence–disarmament and public services–the welfare state, the variables were formed separately for each party by coding a respondent '4' if he or she felt the issue extremely important and felt closest to the party concerned, '3' if fairly important and closest to the party concerned, '2' if not very important and closest to the party concerned, '1' if not at all important and closest to the party concerned, and '0' if not closest to the party concerned (among all giving a substantive response to the question concerned) – irrespective in the case of the last code of how important the respondent had seen the issue.

Clearly, all nine variables included in the discriminant analysis have distributions that are far from normal but this is not a likely source of serious error since discriminant analysis is a robust technique, giving meaningful and interpretable results even when its statistical prerequisites are not fully met.

[8] Although it is not central to the ensuing discussion, it should be noted that some of the specific findings regarding issue constraint made by Nie, Verba and Petrocik – notably their claim of an increase in this phenomenon among the American electorate between 1960 and 1964 – have been severely criticized, largely on the ground that they are artefacts of changed question-wordings (Bishop, Oldendick, Tuchfarber and Bennett, 1978; Bishop, Tuchfarber and Oldendick, 1978; Sullivan, Piereson and Marcus, 1978).

Chapter 8

[1] Of course, this does not preclude the possibility that some parts of a constituency may be more susceptible than others to the effects of candidate incumbency, women candidacies, and so forth. However, one may still obtain a figure for the *average* effects of these characteristics across all relevant constituencies.

[2] The word 'ecological' in this context has nothing to do with 'green' issues. In his original critique Robinson (1950) partly had in mind the use of aggregate data on delinquency occurrence in urban sub-areas by those working in the tradition of the Chicago School of so-called human ecology, a theoretical approach to the analysis of cities that seeks affinities between plant and animal ecology and the spatial arrangement of human urban populations.

[3] In the calculations that follow, the votes for Independent Liberals who fought against official SDP candidates for the Alliance (as in Hackney South and Shoreditch, Hammersmith, and Liverpool Broadgreen) have not been included in totals for the SDP–Liberal Alliance. Similarly, the votes for various Independent Labour candidates (as in Bradford North, Islington North and Newham North West) have not been included in the totals for Labour.

[4] In Chapter 7 we encountered the use of a so-called 'dummy variable' for measuring the 'Falklands factor' in a time-series regression equation. We shall use such variables extensively in this chapter, both to measure regional and similar effects and also to assess various contest characteristics. It will be recalled that such variables are dichotomies (having just two categories) for which the individual units in the analysis are given values of either one or zero. Dummy-variable analysis can be used in order to include in a regression analysis one or more categoric (that is, nominal-scale) variables having three or more categories (as, in this example, region, which has eleven (*sic*) categories); each category except one becomes a separate dummy variable for the purposes of analysis. Each unit receives a value of one or zero on each dummy variable so formed; thus, the constituency of Lewisham Deptford, for example, is coded '1' on the Greater London dummy variable and '0' on all the other nine dummy variables (for South East outside Greater London through to Wales). One regional category (arbitrarily chosen, but in our case Scotland) is not given its own dummy variable and is not included in

the regression equation. The regression coefficients for the other ten regional dummy variables (Greater London through to Wales) can be interpreted relative to a putative value of zero for the coefficient for this omitted region. For a straightforward discussion of dummy-variable analysis see Blalock (1972, pp. 498–502).

[5] 'Swing', which has been the most widely used measure of electoral change, is a concept focusing on net percentage-point shifts of votes *between two parties*. On the other hand, what we are calling 'shift' concerns merely percentage-point increase or decrease of support for a single party. Swing between two parties is the average of one party's percentage-point gain or loss and the other party's loss or gain, assessed of course between two elections. Most analysts of swing base their calculations on the total numbers of votes cast, producing so-called 'Butler' swing (after David Butler). Michael Steed (1965) proposed calculation upon the total numbers of votes cast for the two parties concerned, hence so-called 'Steed' swing; he claimed that this method of calculation obviated anomalies associated with certain types of third-party presence in a constituency.

Even so, use of 'Steed' swing would not capture many of the points of interest in our own analysis and so the emphasis of our interpretation is upon 'shift'. This difference is not consequential, since the arguments about whether swing is uniform or proportionate apply equally to shift.

[6] The correlation coefficient between the percentage-point change in the Liberal/SDP–Liberal Alliance vote between 1979 and 1983 and the Liberal percentage of the total vote in 1979, calculated across 594 constituencies, is −0·392.

[7] The 'regression effect' is a statistical artefact that sometimes involves very extreme values in a distribution tending to become less extreme over time. Thus, if a group as a whole undergoes no average change between two points in time, those with very high initial values will usually tend to decline and those with very low initial values will usually tend to increase. If a group is increasing on average over time, numerically larger increases will tend to be associated with lower initial scores; the opposite will be the case if a group is declining on average over time. The first of these instances, that of overall increase, is a different way of conceptualizing the plateau effect observed in connection with the Alliance vote in Section 8.3 of this chapter; the second instance encapsulates the smaller absolute losses suffered by Labour where its level of initial support was very low. For Labour, however, the *overall* regression effect in the comparison between 1979 and 1983 was in fact quite small, the correlation coefficient between change from 1979 to 1983 and Labour's 1979 percentage being a mere −0·087 across 633 constituencies. For the Conservatives the effect was even in the opposite direction, the analogous coefficient being 0·158. Of course, these results are what our analyses in Tables B.2 and 8.1 should have led us to expect. Note, however, that – as in these analyses of change from 1979 to 1983 in the Labour and Conservative votes – the significance of level of support at the earlier point of time may reveal itself in conditions of statistical control.

[8] Indeed, the BBC apparently relied for some of its data on the results derived from the Conservative Party's analysis and furnished to it by Cecil Parkinson. London Weekend Television's 'Weekend World' and Thames Television News also conducted small-scale versions of the local election analyses carried out by Conservative Central Office. Thames's analysis was confined to five marginal seats in their coverage area outside Greater London (Harlow, Hertfordshire West, Slough, Stevenage and Welwyn Hatfield) and was complicated in greater or lesser degree in all cases except Slough by problems of incomplete candidate-coverage that must have limited the usefulness of the Conservative Party's own effort.

[9] Such constituencies have been defined as those where the three major parties had candidates in each ward and where no single 'other' candidate in any ward achieved more than 20 per cent of votes cast in the local contest.

[10] There are complications in assessing Alliance performance in Liverpool because of the divisions there between the Liberal and Social Democratic parties. At one stage it looked as though independent Liberal candidates would fight official Alliance SDP nominees in several constituencies in the general election. In the event this happened only in Broadgreen, where the independent Liberal Richard Pine won 15·3 per cent of the vote, compared with only 11·2 per cent for Richard Crawshaw of the SDP. However, in the Liverpool City Council elections in May there had been six wards (none as it happens in Broadgreen) where Liberal and SDP candidates opposed each other. In all cases but one the SDP candidates were humiliated by the comparison. The six wards were, also showing respective Liberal and SDP percentages of the vote: Arundel (in Riverside constituency), 38·4% and 2·0%; Granby (in Riverside), 40·1% and 0·9%; Grassendale (in Mossley Hill), 50·7% and 2·6%; Melrose (a two-seat ward in Walton), 35·3% and 1·4%; St Mary's (in Garston), 21·2% and 3·2%; and Woolton (in Garston), 7·8% and 6·0%. These Liberal and SDP local election votes were both calculated into the relevant SDP–Liberal Alliance percentages, although, as explained in Note 3, this was not the practice followed for the general election results.

Bibliography

Achen, C. H. (1975), 'Mass political attitudes and the survey response', *American Political Science Review*, vol. 69, no. 4, pp. 1218–31.

Alt, J. E., and Turner, J. (1982), 'The case of the silk-stocking Socialists and the calculating children of the middle class', *British Journal of Political Science*, vol. 12, no. 2, pp. 239–48.

Apter, D. E. (ed.) (1964), *Ideology and Discontent* (Glencoe, Ill.: Free Press).

Barnett, A. (1982), *Iron Britannia* (London: Allison & Busby).

Barnett, M. J. (1973), 'Aggregate models of British voting behaviour', *Political Studies*, vol. 21, no. 2, pp. 121–34.

Barry, B. (1978), *Sociologists, Economists and Democracy* (Chicago, Ill.: University of Chicago) [first published in 1970].

Baumol, W. J. (1971), 'Macroeconomics of unbalanced growth; the anatomy of urban crisis', in Heilbroner and Ford (1971), pp. 108–16.

BBC/ITN (1983), *The BBC/ITN Guide to the New Parliamentary Constituencies* (Chichester: Parliamentary Research Services). [In the text the authors/compilers of this publication are referred to as 'the BBC/ITN team'.]

Berrington, H. B. (1965), 'The general election of 1964', *Journal of the Royal Statistical Society*, Series A (General), vol. 128, pt 1, pp. 17–51.

Bishop, G. F., Oldendick, R. W., Tuchfarber, A. J., and Bennett, S. E. (1978), 'The changing structure of mass belief systems: fact or artifact?', *Journal of Politics*, vol. 40, no. 3, pp. 781–7.

Bishop, G. F., Oldendick, R. W., Tuchfarber, A. J., and Bennett, S. E. (1980), 'Pseudo-opinions on public affairs', *Public Opinion Quarterly*, vol. 44, no. 2, pp. 198–209.

Bishop, G. F., Tuchfarber, A. J., and Oldendick, R. W. (1978), 'Change in the structure of American political attitudes: the nagging question of question wording', *American Journal of Political Science*, vol. 22, no. 2, pp. 250–69.

Blalock, H. M., jun. (1972), *Social Statistics*, 2nd edn (Tokyo: McGraw-Hill Kogakusha).

Blondel, J. (1981), *Voters, Parties, and Leaders: The Social Fabric of British Politics* (Harmondsworth: Penguin) [first published in 1963].

Blowers, A. (1982), *Finance and Planning in Land and Property Development*: Unit 20 in Course D202 'Urban Change and Conflict' (Milton Keynes: Open University).

Bochel, J. M., and Denver, D. T. (1971), 'Canvassing, turnout and party support: an experiment', *British Journal of Political Science*, vol. 1, no. 3, pp. 257–69.

Bochel, J. M., and Denver, D. T. (1972), 'The impact of the campaign on the results of local government elections', *British Journal of Political Science*, vol. 2, no. 2, pp. 239–60.

Boddy, M., and Fudge, C. (eds) (1984), *Local Socialism?: Labour Councils and New Left Alternatives* (London: Macmillan).

Borgatta, E. F., and Jackson, D. J. (eds) (1980), *Aggregate Data: Analysis and Interpretation* (Beverly Hills, Calif. and London: Sage).

Bosanquet, N. (1984), 'Social policy and the welfare state', in Jowell and Airey (1984), pp. 75–104.

Bradley, I. (1981), *Breaking the Mould?: The Birth and Prospects of the Social Democratic Party* (Oxford: Martin Robertson).

Bradley, I. (1983), 'The SDP mould', *New Society*, 27 January, pp. 129–30.

Brittan, S. (1977), *The Economic Consequences of Democracy* (London: Temple Smith).

Brown, R. (1965), *Social Psychology* (New York: Free Press).

Budge, I. (1982), 'Electoral volatility: issue effects and basic change in 23 post-war democracies', *Electoral Studies*, vol. 1, no. 2, pp. 147–68.

Budge, I., Crewe, I., and Farlie, D. (eds) (1976), *Party Identification and Beyond: Representations of Voting and Party Competition* (London: Wiley).

Butler, D. (1983), 'Winning in spite of themselves', *The Times*, 9 December, p. 14.

Butler, D., and Halsey, A. H. (eds) (1978), *Policy and Politics: Essays in Honour of Norman Chester, Warden of Nuffield College 1954–1978* (London: Macmillan).

Butler, D., and Kavanagh, D. (1975), *The British General Election of October 1974* (London: Macmillan).

Butler, D., and Kavanagh, D. (1980), *The British General Election of 1979* (London: Macmillan).

Butler, D., and Pinto-Duschinsky, M. (1971), *The British General Election of 1970* (London: Macmillan).

Butler, D., and Stokes, D. (1969), *Political Change in Britain: Forces Shaping Electoral Choice* (London: Macmillan).

Butler, D., and Stokes, D. (1974), *Political Change in Britain: The Evolution of Electoral Choice*, 2nd edn (London: Macmillan).

Byrne, P., and Lovenduski, J. (1983), 'Two new protest groups: the Peace and Women's Movements', in Drucker *et al.* (1983), pp. 222–37.

Carchedi, G. (1977), *On the Economic Identification of Social Classes* (London: Routledge & Kegan Paul).

Cawson, A., and Saunders, P. (1983), 'Corporatism, competitive politics and class struggle', in R. King (1983), pp. 8–27.

Central Statistical Office (1972), *Annual Abstract of Statistics*, no. 109 (London: HMSO).

Central Statistical Office (1976), *Economic Trends*, February, no. 268 (London: HMSO).

Central Statistical Office (1977), *Annual Abstract of Statistics*, no. 114 (London: HMSO).

Central Statistical Office (1979), *Social Trends, 1980*, no. 10 (London: HMSO).

Central Statistical Office (1983), *Economic Trends*, February, no. 352 (London: HMSO).

Central Statistical Office (1984a), *Annual Abstract of Statistics*, no. 120 (London: HMSO).

Central Statistical Office (1984b), *Regional Trends*, no. 19 (London: HMSO).

Charlot, M. (1975), 'The ideological distance between the two major parties in Britain', *European Journal of Political Research*, vol. 3, no. 2, pp. 173–80.

Coates, D. (1975), *The Labour Party and the Struggle for Socialism* (Cambridge: Cambridge University).

Community Development Project (1976), *Whatever Happened to Council Housing?* (London: National Community Development Project).

Conservative Party (1983), *The Conservative Manifesto 1983* (London: Conservative Central Office).

Converse, P. E. (1964), 'The nature of belief systems in mass publics', in Apter (1964), pp. 206–61.

Converse, P. E. (1970), 'Attitudes and non-attitudes: continuation of a dialogue', in Tufte (1970), pp. 168–89.

Coombs, C. H. (1964), *A Theory of Data* (New York: Wiley).

Crewe, I. (1973), 'The politics of "affluent" and "traditional" workers in Britain: an aggregate data analysis', *British Journal of Political Science*, vol. 3, no. 1, pp. 29–52.

Crewe, I. (1974), 'Do Butler and Stokes really explain political change in Britain?', *European Journal of Political Research*, vol. 2, no. 1, pp. 47–92.

Crewe, I. (1976), 'Party identification theory and political change in Britain', in Budge, Crewe and Farlie (1976), pp. 33–61.

Crewe, I. (1982a), 'Is Britain's two-party system really about to crumble?: the Social Democratic–Liberal Alliance and the prospects for realignment', *Electoral Studies*, vol. 1, no. 3, pp. 275–313.

Crewe, I. (1982b), 'The Labour Party and the electorate', in Kavanagh (1982), pp. 9–49.

Crewe, I. (1983), 'The disturbing truth behind Labour's rout', *Guardian*, 13 June, p.6; 'How Labour was trounced all round', *Guardian*, 14 June, p. 20.

Crewe, I., and Payne, C. (1976), 'Another game with nature: an ecological regression model of the British two-party vote ratio in 1970', *British Journal of Political Science*, vol. 6, no. 1, pp. 43–81.

Crewe, I., Särlvik, B., and Alt, J. E. (1977), 'Partisan dealignment in Britain 1964–1974', *British Journal of Political Science*, vol. 7, no. 2, pp. 129–90.

Cummings, M. C., jun. (1966), *Congressmen and the Electorate: Elections for the U.S. House and the President, 1920–1964* (New York: Free Press).

Curtice, J., Payne, C., and Waller, R. (1983), 'The Alliance's first nationwide test: lessons of the 1982 English local elections', *Electoral Studies*, vol. 2, no. 1, pp. 3–22.

Curtice, J., and Steed, M. (1980), 'Appendix 2: An Analysis of the Voting', in Butler and Kavanagh (1980), pp. 390–431.

Curtice, J., and Steed, M. (1982), 'Electoral choice and the production of government: the changing operation of the electoral system in the United Kingdom since 1955', *British Journal of Political Science*, vol. 12, no. 3, pp. 249–98.

Curtice, J., and Steed, M. (1983), 'Turning dreams into reality: the division of constituencies between the Liberals and the Social Democrats', *Parliamentary Affairs*, vol. 36, no. 2, pp. 166–82.

Dahl, R. A. (1961), *Who Governs?: Democracy and Power in an American City* (New Haven, Conn.: Yale University).

Downs, A. (1957), *An Economic Theory of Democracy* (New York: Harper & Brothers).

Dowse, R. E., and Hughes, J. A. (1977), 'Sporadic interventionists', *Political Studies*, vol. 25, no. 1, pp. 84–92.

Drucker, H. (1984), 'Intra-party democracy in action: the election of leader and deputy leader by the Labour Party in 1983', *Parliamentary Affairs*, vol. 37, no. 3, pp. 283–300.

Drucker, H., Dunleavy, P., Gamble, A., and Peele, G. (eds) (1983), *Developments in British Politics* (London: Macmillan).

Drucker, H., Dunleavy, P., Gamble, A., and Peele, G. (eds) (1984), *Developments in British Politics*, revised edn (London: Macmillan).

Duke, V., and Edgell, S. (1984), 'Public expenditure cuts in Britain and consumption sectoral cleavages', *International Journal of Urban and Regional Research*, vol. 8, no. 2, pp. 177–201.

Duncan, S. S., and Goodwin, M. (1982), 'The local state and restructuring social relations: theory and practice', *International Journal of Urban and Regional Research*, vol. 6, no. 2, pp. 157–86.

Dunleavy, P. (1979), 'The urban basis of political alignment: social class, domestic property ownership and state intervention in consumption processes', *British Journal of Political Science*, vol. 9, no. 4, pp. 409–43.

Dunleavy, P. (1980), *Urban Political Analysis: The Politics of Collective Consumption* (London: Macmillan).

Dunleavy, P. (1980b), 'The political implications of sectoral cleavages and the growth of state employment: Part 1, The analysis of production cleavages; and Part 2, Cleavage structures and political alignment', *Political Studies*, vol. 28, no. 3, pp. 364–83, and no. 4, pp. 527–49.

Dunleavy, P. (1982), 'How to decide that voters decide', *Politics*, vol. 2, no. 2, pp. 24–9.

Dunleavy, P. (1983), 'Voting and the electorate', in Drucker *et al.* (1983), pp. 30–58.

Dunleavy, P. (1984), 'Voting and the electorate', in Drucker *et al.* (1984), pp. 30–58.

Dunleavy, P. (1985), 'Socialized consumption and economic development', *International Journal of Urban and Regional Research*, vol. 9, forthcoming.

Dunleavy, P., and Husbands, C. T. (1984a), 'The social basis of British political alignments in 1983', Paper presented to the 1984 Conference of the Political Studies Association, University of Southampton, 4 April.

Dunleavy, P., and Husbands, C. T. (1984b), 'One last chance: the case for a nuclear referendum', *New Socialist*, September, pp. 7–12.

Dunleavy, P., and Ward, H. (1981), 'Exogenous voter preferences and parties with state power: some internal problems of economic theories of party competition', *British Journal of Political Science*, vol. 11, no. 3, pp. 351–80.

Edelman, M. (1964), *The Symbolic Uses of Politics* (Urbana, Ill.: University of Illinois).

Edgell, S., and Duke, V. (1983), 'Gender and social policy: the impact of the public expenditure cuts and reactions to them', *Journal of Social Policy*, vol. 12, no. 3, pp. 357–78.

Ellis, A. (1981), 'The paradox of affluence: positional competition or coerced exchange?', *Politics*, vol. 1, no. 1, pp. 9–12.

Erickson, B. H., and Nosanchuk, T. A. (1979), *Understanding Data* (Milton Keynes: Open University).

Erikson, R. S. (1979), 'The SRC panel data and mass political attitudes', *British Journal of Political Science*, vol. 9, no. 1, pp. 89–114.

Festinger, L. (1962), *A Theory of Cognitive Dissonance* (London: Tavistock) [first published in 1957].

Finer, S. E. (ed.) (1975), *Adversary Politics and Electoral Reform* (London: Wigram).

Finer, S. E. (1980), *The Changing British Party System 1945–1979* (Washington, DC: American Enterprise Institute for Public Policy Research).

FitzGerald, M. (1983), 'Are blacks an electoral liability?', *New Society*, 8 December, pp. 394–5.

FitzGerald, M. (1984), 'The parties and "the black vote"', Paper presented to a Conference on 'Political Communications: the Media, the Parties and the Polls in the 1983 General Election', University of Essex, 13–15 January.

Forrest, R. (1984), 'Privatization, council housing and the restructuring of the welfare state', Paper presented to a Conference on 'The Housing Question', Australian Studies Centre, University of London, 16 March.

Franklin, M. N. (1984), 'How the decline of class voting opened the way to radical change in British politics', *British Journal of Political Science*, vol. 14, no. 4, pp. 483–508.

Franklin, M. N., and Mughan, A. (1978), 'The decline of class voting in Britain: problems of analysis and interpretation', *American Political Science Review*, vol. 72, no. 2, pp. 523–34.

Franklin, M. N., and Page, E. C. (1984), 'A critique of the consumption cleavage approach in British voting studies', *Political Studies*, vol. 32, no. 4, pp. 521–36.

Frey, B. S. (1978), *Modern Political Economy* (New York: Wiley).

Friedman, M. (1953), 'The methodology of positive economics', in his *Essays in Positive Economics* (Chicago, Ill.: University of Chicago), pp. 3–43.

Galbraith, J. K. (1972), *The New Industrial State*, 2nd edn (Harmondsworth: Penguin).

Gamble, A. (1979), 'The free economy and the strong state', in Miliband and Saville (1979), pp. 1–25.

Gamble, A. (1983), 'Thatcherism and Conservative politics', in Hall and Jacques (1983), pp. 109–31.

Gilbert, G. N. (1981), *Modelling Society: An Introduction to Loglinear Analysis for Social Researchers* (London: Allen & Unwin).

Glasgow University Media Group (1976), *Bad News* (London: Routledge & Kegan Paul).

Glasgow University Media Group (1980), *More Bad News* (London: Routledge & Kegan Paul).

Goldthorpe, J. H., Llewellyn, C., and Payne, C. (1980), *Social Mobility and Class Structure in Modern Britain* (Oxford: Clarendon).

Goldthorpe, J. H., Lockwood, D., Bechhofer, F., and Platt, J. (1968), *The Affluent Worker: Political Attitudes and Behaviour* (Cambridge: Cambridge University).

Goodman, L. A. (1972), 'A modified multiple regression approach to the analysis of dichotomous variables', *American Sociological Review*, vol. 37, no. 1, pp. 28–46.

GPI (Gallup Political Index), various issues.

Grant, J. (1977), *The Politics of Urban Transport Planning* (London: Earth Resources Research).

Greater London Council (1982), *London Borough Council Elections, 6 May 1982* (London: Greater London Council).

Griffith, J. A. G. (ed.) (1983), *Socialism in a Cold Climate* (London: Allen & Unwin).

Gwyn, W. B. (1980), 'Jeremiahs and pragmatists: perceptions of British decline', in Gwyn and Rose (1980), pp. 1–25.

Gwyn, W. B., and Rose, R. (eds) (1980), *Britain: Progress and Decline* (London: Macmillan).

Hall, S. (1982), 'The empire strikes back', *New Socialist*, July/August, pp. 5–7.

Hall, S., and Jacques, M. (eds) (1983), *The Politics of Thatcherism* (London: Lawrence & Wishart).

Halsey, A. H. (ed.) (1972), *Trends in British Society since 1900: A Guide to the Changing Social Structure of Britain* (London: Macmillan).

Hammond, J. L. (1979), 'New approaches to aggregate electoral data', *Journal of Interdisciplinary History*, vol. 9, no. 3, pp. 473–92.

Harris, C. W. (ed.) (1963), *Problems in Measuring Change* (Madison, Wis.: University of Wisconsin).

Harris, R. (1983), *Gotcha!: the Media, the Government and the Falklands Crisis* (London: Faber).

Harrop, M. (1980), 'The urban basis of political alignment: a comment', *British Journal of Political Science*, vol. 10, no. 3, pp. 388–98.

Harrop, M. (1984), 'Press coverage of post-war British elections: changes and consequences', Paper presented to a Conference on 'Political Communications: the Media, the Parties and the Polls in the 1983 General Election', University of Essex, 13–15 January.

Hawkes, A. G. (1969), 'An approach to the analysis of electoral swing', *Journal of the Royal Statistical Society*, Series A (General), vol. 132, pt 1, pp. 68–79.

Heath, A. (1976), *Rational Choice and Social Exchange: A Critique of Exchange Theory* (Cambridge: Cambridge University).

Heilbroner, R. L., and Ford, A. M. (eds) (1971), *Is Economics Relevant?: A Reader in Political Economics* (Pacific Palisades, Calif.: Goodyear).

Hibbs, D. A., jun. (1977), 'Political parties and macroeconomic policy', *American Political Science Review*, vol. 71, no. 4, pp. 1467–87.

Hillman, M. (1973), *Personal Mobility and Transport Policy* (London: Political and Economic Planning).

Himmelweit, H. T., Biberian, M. J., and Stockdale, J. (1978), 'Memory for past vote: implications of a study of bias in recall', *British Journal of Political Science*, vol. 8, no. 3, pp. 365–75.

Himmelweit, H. T., Humphreys, P., Jaeger, M., and Katz, M. (1981), *How Voters Decide: A Longitudinal Study of Political Attitudes and Voting Extending Over Fifteen Years* (London: Academic).

Hindess, B. (1971), *The Decline of Working-Class Politics* (London: MacGibbon & Kee).

Hobsbawm, E. (1983), 'Falklands fallout', in Hall and Jacques (1983), pp. 257–70.

Hopkin, B. (1983), 'Recovery's here, but can 364 economists all be wrong?', *Guardian*, 16 November, p. 20.

Husbands, C. T. (1981), 'Scarlet or blue?', *Marxism Today*, June, pp. 3–5.

Husbands, C. T. (1982a), 'The politics of confusion', *Marxism Today*, February, pp. 6–12.

Husbands, C. T. (1982b), 'The London Borough Council elections of 6 May 1982: results and analysis', *London Journal*, vol. 8, no. 2, pp. 177–90.

Husbands, C. T. (1983), 'Race and immigration', in Griffith (1983), pp. 161–83.

Husbands, C. T. (1985), 'Government popularity and the unemployment issue, 1966–1983', *Sociology*, vol. 19, no. 1, pp. 1–17.

Irvine, J., Miles, I., and Evans, J. (eds) (1979), *Demystifying Social Statistics* (London: Pluto).

Jenkins, R. (1982), 'Home thoughts from abroad: the 1979 Dimbleby lecture', in Kennet (1982), pp. 9–29.

Jessop, B. (1974), *Traditionalism, Conservatism and British Political Culture* (London: Allen & Unwin).

Johnson, R. W. (1973), 'The British political elite, 1955–1972', *European Journal of Sociology*, vol. 14, no. 1, pp. 35–77.

Jowell, R., and Airey, C. (eds) (1984), *British Social Attitudes: The 1984 Report* (Aldershot: Gower).

Kavanagh, D. (1970), *Constituency Electioneering in Britain* (London: Longman).

Kavanagh, D. (ed.) (1982), *The Politics of the Labour Party* (London: Allen & Unwin).

Kelejian, H. H., and Oates, W. E. (1974), *Introduction to Econometrics: Principles and Applications* (New York: Harper & Row).

Kennet, W. (ed.) (1982), *The Rebirth of Britain* (London: Weidenfeld & Nicolson).

King, A. (1975), 'Overload: problems of governing in the 1970s', *Political Studies*, vol. 23, nos 2–3, pp. 284–96.

King, R. (ed.) (1983), *Capital and Politics* (London: Routledge & Kegan Paul).

Klecka, W. R. (1980), *Discriminant Analysis* (Beverly Hills, Calif. and London: Sage).

Labour Party (1983), *The New Hope for Britain: Labour's Manifesto 1983* (London: Labour Party).

Lambert, J., Paris, C., and Blackaby, B. (1978), *Housing Policy and the State: Allocation, Access and Control* (London: Macmillan).

Langbein, L. I., and Lichtman, A. J. (1978), *Ecological Inference* (Beverly Hills, Calif. and London: Sage).

Lawson, N. (1968), 'A new theory of by-elections', *Spectator*, 8 November, pp. 650–2.

Layton-Henry, Z. (1983), 'Immigration and race relations: political aspects – No. 9', *New Community*, vol. 9, nos 1/2, pp. 109–16.

Le Grand, J. (1982), *The Strategy of Equality: Redistribution and the Social Services* (London: Allen & Unwin).

Levie, H. (1983), 'Britain goes to the sales', *Marxism Today*, April, pp. 28–32.

Lindblom, C. E. (1977), *Politics and Markets: The World's Political-Economic Systems* (New York: Basic).

Linton, M. (1983), 'Disaster snatched from the jaws of defeat', *Guardian*, 30 June, p. 17.

Lockwood, D. (1966), 'Sources of variation in working class images of society', *Sociological Review*, new series, vol. 14, no. 3, pp. 249–67.

Lord, F. M. (1963), 'Elementary models for measuring change', in C. W. Harris (1963), pp. 21–38.

Lukes, S. (1975), 'Political ritual and social integration', *Sociology*, vol. 9, no. 2, pp. 289–308.

McKenzie, R. T. (1955), *British Political Parties: The Distribution of Power within the Conservative and Labour Parties* (London: Heinemann) [2nd edn published in 1963].

McKenzie, R. T., and Silver, A. (1968), *Angels in Marble: Working Class Conservatives in Urban England* (London: Heinemann).

McLean, I. (1973), 'The problem of proportionate swing', *Political Studies*, vol. 21, no. 1, pp. 57–63.

Marsh, C. (1979), 'Opinion polls – social science or political manoeuvre?', in Irvine, Miles and Evans (1979), pp. 268–88.

Michels, R. (1962), *Political Parties: A Sociological Study of the Oligarchical Tendencies of Modern Democracy* (New York: Free Press) [first published in 1915].

Miliband, R. (1973), *Parliamentary Socialism: A Study in the Politics of Labour*, 2nd edn (London: Merlin).

Miliband, R. (1982), *Capitalist Democracy in Britain* (Oxford: Oxford University).

Miliband, R., and Saville, J. (eds) (1979), *The Socialist Register 1979* (London: Merlin).

Miller, W. L. (1972), 'Measures of electoral change using aggregate data', *Journal of the Royal Statistical Society*, Series A (General), vol. 135, pt 1, pp. 122–42.

Miller, W. L. (1977), *Electoral Dynamics in Britain since 1918* (London: Macmillan).

Miller, W. L. (1978), 'Social class and party choice in England: a new analysis', *British Journal of Political Science*, vol. 8, no. 3, pp. 257–84.

Miller, W. L., Brand, J., and Jordan, M. (1982), 'On the power or vulnerability of the British press: a dynamic analysis', *British Journal of Political Science*, vol. 12, no. 3, pp. 357–73.

Miller, W. L., and Mackie, M. (1973), 'The electoral cycle and the asymmetry of government and opposition popularity: an alternative model of the relationship between economic conditions and political popularity', *Political Studies*, vol. 21, no. 3, pp. 263–79.

Minkin, L. (1980), *The Labour Party Conference: A Study in the Politics of Intra-Party Democracy* (Manchester: Manchester University).

Mitchell, A. (1983), *Four Years in the Death of the Labour Party* (London: Methuen).

Mosley, P. (1984), *The Making of Economic Policy: Theory and Evidence from Britain and the United States since 1945* (Brighton: Wheatsheaf).

Mosteller, F., and Tukey, J. W. (1977), *Data Analysis and Regression: A Second Course in Statistics* (Reading, Mass.: Addison-Wesley).

Mueller, D. C. (1979), *Public Choice* (Cambridge: Cambridge University).

Nairn, T. (1983), 'Britain's living legacy', in Hall and Jacques (1983), pp. 281–8.

Nie, N. H., Verba, S., and Petrocik, J. R. (1976), *The Changing American Voter* (Cambridge, Mass.: Harvard University).

Noelle-Neumann, E. (1977), 'Turbulences in the climate of opinion: methodological applications of the spiral of silence theory', *Public Opinion Quarterly*, vol. 41, no. 2, pp. 143–58.

Noelle-Neumann, E. (1979), 'Public opinion and the classical tradition: a re-evaluation', *Public Opinion Quarterly*, vol. 43, no. 2, pp. 143–56.

O'Connor, J. (1973), *The Fiscal Crisis of the State* (New York: St Martin's Press).

O'Muircheartaigh, C. A., and Payne, C. (eds) (1977), *The Analysis of Survey Data: Volume II: Model Fitting* (London: Wiley).

OPCS (Office of Population Censuses and Surveys) (1983), 'Evaluation of the 1981 Census; the 10 per cent sample', *OPCS Monitor*, CEN 83/6.

Ostrogorski, M. (1964), *Democracy and the Organization of Political Parties* (Chicago, Ill.: Quadrangle) [first published in English in 1902].

Page, B. I. (1978), *Choices and Echoes in Presidential Elections: Rational Man and*

Electoral Strategy (Chicago, Ill.: University of Chicago).

Page, B. I., and Jones, C. C. (1979), 'Reciprocal effects of policy preferences, party loyalties and the vote', *American Political Science Review*, vol. 73, no. 4, pp. 1071–89.

Pahl, R. E. (1975), *Whose City?: And Further Essays on Urban Society* (Harmondsworth: Penguin) [first published in 1970].

Parkin, F. (1971), *Class Inequality and Political Order: Social Stratification in Capitalist and Communist Societies* (London: MacGibbon & Kee).

Payne, C. (1977), 'The log-linear model for contingency tables', in O'Muircheartaigh and Payne (1977), pp. 105–44.

Philo, G., Hewitt, J., Beharrell, P., and Davis, H. (1982), *Really Bad News* (London: Writers and Readers).

Pierce, J. C., and Rose, D. D. (1974), 'Nonattitudes and American public opinion: the examination of a thesis', *American Political Science Review*, vol. 68, no. 2, pp. 626–49.

Pinto-Duschinsky, M. (1981), *British Political Finance, 1830–1980* (Washington, DC: American Enterprise Institute for Public Policy Research).

Price, R., and Bain, G. S. (1976), 'Union growth revisited: 1948–1974 in perspective', *British Journal of Industrial Relations*, vol. 14, no. 3, pp. 339–55.

Pulzer, P. G. J. (1975), *Political Representation and Elections in Britain*, 3rd edn (London: Allen & Unwin).

Rae, D. W., and Taylor, M. (1970), *The Analysis of Political Cleavages* (New Haven, Conn.: Yale University).

Rasmussen, J. S. (1965), 'The disutility of the swing concept in British psephology', *Parliamentary Affairs*, vol. 18, no. 4, pp. 442–54.

Rasmussen, J. S. (1973), 'The impact of constituency structural characteristics upon political preferences in Britain', *Comparative Politics*, vol. 6, no. 1, pp. 123–46.

Rasmussen, J. S. (1981), 'Women candidates in British by-elections: a rational choice interpretation of electoral behaviour', *Political Studies*, vol. 29, no. 2, pp. 265–71.

Reid, I. (1977), *Social Class Differences in Britain: A Sourcebook* (London: Open Books).

Rex, J., and Moore, R., with the assistance of Shuttleworth, A., and Williams, J. (1967), *Race, Community, and Conflict: A Study of Sparkbrook* (London: Oxford University).

Riddell, P. (1983), *The Thatcher Government* (Oxford: Martin Robertson).

Robertson, D. (1976), *A Theory of Party Competition* (London: Wiley).

Robinson, W. S. (1950), 'Ecological correlations and the behavior of individuals', *American Sociological Review*, vol. 15, no. 3, pp. 351–7.

Roger Tym and Partners (1983), *Monitoring Enterprise Zones: Year Two Report* (London: Department of the Environment and Department of the Environment for Northern Ireland).

Rose, R. (1974), 'Britain: simple abstractions and complex realities', in Rose (ed.), *Electoral Behavior: A Comparative Handbook* (New York: Free Press), pp. 481–541.

Rose, R. (1976), *The Problem of Party Government* (Harmondsworth: Penguin) [first published in 1974].

Ross, J. (1983), *Thatcher and Friends: The Anatomy of the Tory Party* (London: Pluto).

Särlvik, B., and Crewe, I. (1983), *Decade of Dealignment: The Conservative Victory of 1979 and Electoral Trends in the 1970s* (Cambridge: Cambridge University).

Saunders, P. (1974), *Who Runs Croydon?: Power and Politics in a London Borough*, Unpublished PhD Thesis, Chelsea College, University of London.

Saunders, P. (1978), 'Domestic property and social class', *International Journal of Urban and Regional Research*, vol. 2, no. 2, pp. 233–51.

Saunders, P. (1981), *Social Theory and the Urban Question* (London: Hutchinson).

Saunders, P. (1984a), 'Rethinking local politics', in Boddy and Fudge (1984), pp. 22–48.

Saunders, P. (1984b), 'Beyond housing classes: the sociological significance of private property rights in means of consumption', *International Journal of Urban and Regional Research*, vol. 8, no. 2, pp. 202–27.

Scarman, Lord (1982), *The Scarman Report; The Brixton Disorders, 10–12 April 1981: Report of an Inquiry by the Right Honourable Lord Scarman, OBE, Presented to Parliament by the Secretary of State for the Home Department by Command of Her Majesty, November 1981* (Harmondsworth: Penguin).

Schuman, H., and Presser, S. (1981), *Questions and Answers in Attitude Surveys: Experiments on Question Form, Wording, and Context* (New York: Academic).

SDP–Liberal Alliance (1983), *Working Together for Britain: Programme for Government* (London: SDP–Liberal Alliance).

Seabrook, J. (1978), *What Went Wrong?: Working People and the Ideals of the Labour Movement* (London: Victor Gollancz).

Seabrook, J. (1982), *Unemployment* (London: Quartet).

Seymour-Ure, C. (1974), *The Political Impact of Mass Media* (London: Constable).

Sharpe, L. J. (1978), '"Reforming" the grass roots: an alternative analysis', in Butler and Halsey (1978), pp. 82–110.

SSRC Data Archive (1983), *SN 1852: BBC 1983 Election Survey* (Colchester: SSRC Data Archive).

Steed, M. (1965), Comment on Berrington (1965), *Journal of the Royal Statistical Society*, Series A (General), vol. 128, pt 1, pp. 57–60.

Stephenson, H. (1982), *Claret and Chips: The Rise of the SDP* (London: Michael Joseph).

Stokes, D. E., and Miller, W. E. (1962), 'Party government and the saliency of Congress', *Public Opinion Quarterly*, vol. 26, no. 4, pp. 531–46.

Studlar, D. T. (1983), 'The ethnic vote, 1983: problems of analysis and interpretation', *New Community*, vol. 9, nos 1/2, pp. 92–100.

Sullivan, J. L., Piereson, J. E., and Marcus, G. E. (1978), 'Ideological constraint in the mass public: a methodological critique and some new findings', *American Journal of Political Science*, vol. 22, no. 2, pp. 233–49.

Tatchell, P. (1983), *The Battle for Bermondsey* (London: Heretic).

Taylor, P. J., and Johnston, R. J. (1979), *Geography of Elections* (Harmondsworth: Penguin).

Tufte, E. R. (ed.) (1970), *The Quantitative Analysis of Social Problems* (Reading, Mass.: Addison-Wesley).

Tufte, E. R. (1978), *Political Control of the Economy* (Princeton, NJ: Princeton University).

Wald, K. D. (1983), *Crosses on the Ballot: Patterns of British Voter Alignment since 1885* (Princeton, NJ: Princeton University).

Waller, R. (1980), 'The 1979 local and general elections in England and Wales: is there a local/national differential?', *Political Studies*, vol. 28, no. 3, pp. 443–50.

Waller, R. (1983a), *The Almanac of British Politics* (London: Croom Helm).

Waller, R. (1983b), 'The 1983 Boundary Commission: policies and effects', *Electoral Studies*, vol. 2, no. 3, pp. 195–206.

Webb, N. L., and Wybrow, R. J. (eds) (1981), *The Gallup Report* (London: Sphere).

Webb, N. L., and Wybrow, R. J. (1982), *The Gallup Report: Your Opinions in 1981* (London: Sphere).

Whistler, D. (1982), *User Manual for DARTS: Data Retrieval System* (London: London School of Economics Computer Unit).

Whiteley, P. (1983), *The Labour Party in Crisis* (London: Methuen).

Whiteley, P. (1984), 'Can the Alliance replace Labour as the main party of opposition?', *Politics*, vol. 4, no. 1, pp. 3–7.

Williams, P. M. (1966–7), 'Two notes on the British electoral system', *Parliamentary Affairs*, vol. 20, no. 1, pp. 13–30.

Worcester, R., and Jenkins, S. (1982), 'Britain rallies 'round the Prime Minister', *Public Opinion*, June/July, pp. 53–5.

Wright, E. O. (1978), *Class, Crisis and the State* (London: New Left Books).

Wright, E. O. (1979), *Class Structure and Income Determination* (New York: Academic).

Index

A 'c' in parentheses next to the name of a place or places indicates that it refers to either an 'old' (pre-1983) or a 'new' parliamentary constituency.